TROJAN HORSES
of
ISLAMIC SUPREMACY

"Stomping Across American"

"Understanding Jihad"

> **The Muslim Brotherhood**
> **CAIR**
> **al-Qaeda**
> **ISIS**
> **Hamas**
> **Hezbollah**

William W. Urban, Ph.D.

Published by William W. Urban, Ph.D.

www.inthewarroom.us

To subscribe to News Alert
send us email at trojan.horses.supremacy@gmail.com
and

https://www.facebook.com/Trojan-Horses-of-Islamic-Supremacy-296467187552586/

First Edition

"My people are destroyed for lack of knowledge,
Because you have rejected knowledge …
Hosea 4:6 (ESV)

"But if they do not listen,
They perish by the sword and die without knowledge …
Job 36:12 (ESV)

"… if My people who are called by My name will humble
themselves, and pray and seek My face,
and turn from their wicked ways,
I will hear from heaven,
and will forgive their sin and heal their land."
2 Chronicles 7:14 (NKJ)

If any of you lacks wisdom, let him ask of God,
who gives to all liberally and without reproach,
and it will be given.
James 1:5 (NKJ)

In 1776, Ben Franklin & Mrs. Powell had a conversation:

"Well, Doctor, what have we got …
a Republic or a Monarchy?"
"A Republic, if you can keep it."
Mrs. Powell & Dr. Franklin, Philadelphia

TROJAN HORSES
of
ISLAMIC SUPREMACY

Foreword

Major General (ret) William Klein
Brigadier General C. William Fox Jr., MD

For centuries Western Civilization has been fighting against the jihadi attacks from Islamic Supremacists and their threats of "World Domination." Muslim leaders and their followers, who believe in the strict interpretation of all tenants set forth in the Koran and who accept only absolute adherence to these principles, have patiently plotted to control the world. Their approaches have included: violent conquest; religious intimidation; hostage taking; bribery; smuggling; drug dealing; and political subversion.

European nations were the first to fall prey to Islamic Supremacists. During the First Caliphate (630 - 1185 AD), Islamists forced their beliefs and their system of governmental totalitarianism and religious dominance, on the peoples of the Iberian Peninsula and southeastern Europe. These Muslims were driven out during the Crusades, back into northern Africa and the Middle East.

During the Second Caliphate (1375 – 1920 AD), Islamic Supremacists expanded their control deeper into southeastern Europe, but for the most part ignored Spain and Portugal. By the 16th century, these two countries were major political powers with dominant navies. Spain and Portugal, along with Great Britain and France, were exploring the "New World", establishing colonies and seizing new riches. Their ships might have been fair targets but, by this time, their homelands were fortified sanctuaries.

The nations of the Barbary Coast of North Africa (Morocco, Tunisia, Algeria and Libya) were safe havens for Islamic pirates, who seized merchant vessels of other nations. These ships, their crews and their cargoes were held for ransom. In many situations, the crews were sold into slavery. These same pirates offered "protection" for the vessels of nations, which paid an annual tribute (tax).

"The practice of state-supported piracy and ransoming of captives was not unusual for this time. Many European nations commissioned privateers to attack others' merchant vessels and to also participated in the transatlantic slave trade. Two major European powers, Great Britain and France, found it expedient to encourage these Barbary States' policy and to pay tribute to them, as it allowed their merchant shipping an increased share of the Mediterranean trade. The Barbary leaders also preferred not to challenge the superior British or French navies." [1]

"Prior to independence, American colonists had enjoyed the protection of the British Navy. However, once the American Colonies declared their independence, British diplomats were quick to inform the Barbary States that the American ships were open for attack. In 1785, Dey Muhammad of Algiers declared war on the 'States of America' and captured several American ships. The financially troubled Confederation government was unable to raise a navy or to pay the tribute that would protect the American ships." [2]

Thomas Jefferson, along with John Adams and Benjamin Franklin, serving as foreign emissaries to Europeans nations, worked to resolve issues with the Muslim nations in North Africa, which were seizing our ships and holding the crews for ransom. During one of the meetings, Jefferson asked the Ambassador of Tunisia, "Why they were attacking our ships, when we have done nothing to harm your nation or people?" The answer given by the Ambassador was, "that their actions were founded in the laws of their prophet Muhammad and were written in their Quran." He added, "that all nations who do not acknowledge their authority were infidels and that it was their right and their duty to make war upon them wherever they could be found; that they were called to make slaves of all that they took as prisoners; and that every Muslim who died in battle was sure to go to paradise." [3]

---

[1] Office of the Historian, Bureau of Public Affairs, US Department of State, Washington, DC.

[2] ibid #1

[3] Letter by Thomas Jefferson, written 1796 while he served as Secretary of State in Washington Administration

The 1st war against the Barbary Pirates (1801-1805), began during the administration of John Adams, our 2nd president, and marked the establishment of the Marines. The victory in the 2nd war (1815-1819) occurred during the administration of James Monroe, our 5th president, and ended with the signing of an agreement to cease attacks against US ships.

Muslim Supremacists have continued to pressure the European nations throughout the 19th, 20th, and 21st centuries, with violent jihad and through civilization jihad. [4] (see Chapters I, II, and III).

"Dr. Urban's book is a must read for every American. The threat is real; and he lays it out in a clear, concise and understandable manner."

Major General (ret) William Klein
former Vice Director of Plans and Policy for the Joint Chiefs of Staff
first Director of Operations, U.S. Special Operations Command

---

"*Trojan Horses* is a must read for those who want to understand the clear and present danger to America; to our way of life; and to our future. It is an accurate assessment of the Islamic Supremacist threat. It should be used as a reference book in all schools for social studies."

Brigadier General C. William Fox, Jr., MD
former Commanding General, Brooke Army Medical Center
former Commanding General, Great Plains Medical Command
former Chief Operating Officer & Executive Vice President, Project Hope

---

[4] ibid #1

TROJAN HORSES
of
ISLAMIC SUPREMACY

PURPOSE

To bring awareness ... to the true nature of Islamic Supremacy and the serious, world-wide threat which Islamic Supremacy poses to America and to our way of life.

APPROACH

To expose ... the strategic plans of **The Muslim Brotherhood** and to reveal their objectives and their timetables for achieving ... **World Domination.**

To identify ... operational capabilities which give **Islamic Supremacists** specific advantages over domestic and military enemies in different theaters.

To present ... written documents from Islamic authors and recorded statements from Islamic political/religious leaders, which confirm the intent of their pronouncements ... **World Domination.**

RESULT

Reader(s) of the book will be able to inform others (family and friends, neighbors, church members, government officials, and business associates) of the dangers of Islamic Supremacy.

Some readers may ponder why it was necessary to include the historical, detailed information in Chapter II (The History of Islam) & Chapter III (WWI & WWII: Germany and The Islamic Supremacists).

It is important that all readers understand how long **Islamic Supremacists** have been working towards their goal of **"World Domination"** under Sharia Law. In addition, Islamic Supremacists show no tolerance for other religious beliefs or other cultural mores.

Every reader must be encouraged to listen to the facts; To appreciate the patience which Islamic Supremacists have demonstrated, as they have pursued their specific political and cultural goals, in more than 150 countries around the world for well over one hundred years.

About the Author

Dr. Urban served as an advisor to The US Arms Control & Disarmament Agency, at the US State Department, and to the US Defense Department. His political awareness into situations in the former Soviet Union, Central Asia and the Middle East was used to anticipate opportunities; to develop strategies for campaigns; and to resolve confrontations. His business experience was used to transfer military technologies to commercial market opportunities.

In the corporate world, Dr. Urban served as Vice President of Finance of the Bunker Ramo Corporation (Fortune 500 Company) and later as President of the Brown-Miller Division, Beatrice Foods Company (Fortune 50 Company).

Dr. Urban started his own consulting firm (Urban & Associates) in Houston and later move the offices to Washington, DC.

Dr. Urban has taught economics in the MBA at the Graduate School of Business and in the Ph.D. program in the Department of Economics at The University of South Florida.

DEDICATION

To my wife for the hours she allowed me to spend as I researched the topics and put words to paper. To her discernment and prayerful support, as she and I encountered so many challenges.

ACKNOWLEDGEMENTS

I owe my gratitude to many more people than I can mention here. I want to acknowledge their encouragement and their active support as they walked with me during the development of this book.

Their combined insight convinced me: 1) that there is a need to know about this complex problem, by the public in general, and by Americans in particular; and 2) that I could tackle the subject matter in such a way that others will be able to understand the gravity of the threat.

To my accountability partners, Ed Jackson, Dick Palke, Colonel (ret) Tom McDonald and Bob Buhlmann, for their diligent reading and reviewing of the text, and for their contributions in editing the final product, so that the book is readable by people of many different backgrounds.

To Dragan Nikolic for his knowledge in preparing text material for publication and for his insight into formulating the final product to attract readers and to meet their expectations.

To the many prayer warriors who stood in the fire and provided protection and encouragement for my wife and myself as we came under spiritual attack. Yes, there were times when we felt the cost could be too much and we should cancel the whole project.

GLOSSARY OF TERMS

See **Appendix A, page 151** for definitions of terms which may be unfamiliar.

Introduction

Islam is a *"Challenge."* As such, it is both an *"Opportunity"* and a *"Threat."*

Islam is more than just a "religion." It is a "religious code of conduct," controlling every aspect of Muslim life: government & institutions; finance & banking; culture & family life; education & entertainment; crime & punishments; and trade & foreign relations.

As with any cult-religion, Islam has its **"Believers"** and **"Pretenders."**

THE OPPORTUNITY

Islam disguises itself as a "religion." Contrary to Christian beliefs, Islam denies the deity of Christ and claims Jesus is a prophet as is Muhammad; it doesn't recognize the existence of The Holy Spirit; and it claims Allah, it's god, is one in the same as the God of The Bible.

As such, Islam offers an opportunity for Christians to witness to Muslims, many of whom don't know the truth about Islam and Muhammad nor understand the truth of Christianity and the "mission" of Jesus.

Muslims do not understand their need for a Savior. They view the religion of Islam as ritualistic and not a relationship with a "loving God." Allah, their god, is to be *"feared"* and not to be *"loved"*; nor *"trusted"*; nor *"held in awe."* The concept of *"faith"* in God is foreign to them.

The difficulty of ministering to members of other religions is understanding the spiritual component of their belief system and the role which the "religion" has in their culture. This is particularly true of Islam, with its paternalistic family structure and its all-encompassing cultural mores. If a member of a Muslim family accepts Christ as their Savior, they will be ostracized from the family and the community. Possibly, they could be killed (honor killing) by the father or older brother of maturity, because they have dishonored the family.

Domestic/international efforts which bring the Gospel of Jesus Christ to Muslims, can be successful on the level of individual-to-individual witnessing or as a ministry of the church or a not-for-profit foundation.

These evangelical programs have a better chance of bringing the entire family to Christ if they bring the father first. If the father is not one of the first to accept Christ, then a place of safety must be available to the new convert(s).

THE THREAT

Islamic Supremacists, defined as those believing in all the tenants of "Sharia Law" as set forth in the Koran, govern approximately 60% of the Muslim world. Islamic Supremacists agree that it is the goal and the duty of Islam "to dominate all other societies."

Islamic Supremacists tolerate "only temporary integration" by Muslims into other societies, for fear of weakening their own beliefs. Islamic Supremacists must dominant all other cultures, never truly assimilating into any other civil structures.

Specifically, the paramount objectives of Islamic Supremacists for America include:

> 1) implementing Sharia Law to replace the US Constitution; the Bill of Rights; and all federal, state & local laws in all American courts;
> 2) dominating public education in America;
> 3) gaining control of the American media; and
> 4) implementing Zakat in all banking transactions.

Unregulated and uncontrolled migration of legal immigrants and/or illegal immigrants, who *"choose not to assimilate"* into the society of the host country, will be an *"invasion"* of the host country and will bring about the *"destruction"* of the society; the culture; and the institutions of the host country.

Chapter I

Totalitarian Regimes -- 20th Century Communism; Stalinism; Fascism; Nazism; Maoism; and Islam

The Twentieth Century saw the defeat of *Leninism, Stalinism, Fascism, Nazism, Maoism* and other Totalitarian Regimes. People have been liberated from the tyrannical control by these dictators of the past. However, now there is a new global totalitarian threat: ***Islamic Supremacy.*** [1]

The Ideologies of Islamic Supremacists, Nazism, and Communism

"A close examination of Islamic Supremacists terror reveals significant similarities to its counterparts of the twentieth century: Nazism and Communism. While the methods may have been different --- the Nazis had their concentration camps and the Communists had their gulags --- the ideology remains the same. Islamic Supremacy, Nazism, Fascism and Russian & Chinese Communism all have in common, the lust for other people's lives and property and the desire to exercise complete control of their subjects' lives. All three have been justified by a self-reverential system of thought and belief that: 1) perverts the meaning of words; 2) stunts our sense of moral clarity; and 3) destroys souls." [2]

In a 1979 speech, Yusuf al-Qaradawi stated,

"To you [Americans & Europeans], the killers of the people in the Far East countries, Vietnam, Korea and Japan ... the killers of the people in the Southern America and the Middle America ... the killers of the people in the Middle East, the people all over the Islamic countries are with the Iranians."

---

[1] *Islamic Supremacy*; Robert Spencer, American Freedom Center; 2017
[2] *The Next Nightmare;* Peter Feaman; 2012; p 54

"The people [Islamic Supremacists] in the Arabian Peninsula are sharing with the rest of the Muslim peoples, their will in establishing **THE ISLAMIC GOVERNMENT OF THE WHOLE UNIVERSE ...**" {emphasis theirs} [3]

"Islamic supremacists believe in the power of the state to sponsor and impose the Islamic religious code, known as "Sharia Law", on all of its citizens. Such a government is a "church-state" that contemplates no separation of church and state; and tolerates no freedom of thought, no freedom of press, nor freedom of religion." [4]

THE VOID CAUSED BY THE DECLINE OF RUSSIAN COMMUNISM

With the decline of the Soviet Union (USSR) in the late 1970's and early 1980's, there emerged a void in political power in Central Asia and a shift in the control of drug trafficking in the region.

From the end of World War II, the USSR had supported and financed the advancement of Communism through their own treasury and through moneys obtained controlling the source of drug production in Central Asia.

For many years the USSR had designs on a warm-water, southern port on the Indian Ocean for their navy. To achieve this goal, their plan was to invade Afghanistan and then to conquer southern Pakistan.

When the invasion of Afghanistan failed, Russia withdrew in humiliation, never to regain its prestige in the region.

(Author's Opinion) If the USSR had initiated the takeover of Afghanistan and Pakistan in the late 1940's, when they successfully annexed Eastern Europe, the United Nations and the Western Allies would probably have acquiesced to their desires. They would have gained the southern port on the Indian Ocean, they later coveted.

---

[3] Speech at The Organization of the Islamic Revolution in the Arabian Peninsula
   Yusuf al-Qaradawi; 1979

[4] ibid #2

With the USSR withdrawing to their southern borders of Tajikistan, Uzbekistan, and Turkmenistan, the Islamic Supremacists quickly moved to re-establish their culture in the region and to re-gain political control over the region. They also established control over drug trafficking and its immense source of revenues.

Now Islamic Supremacists could advance their totalitarian form of government [the Islamic church-state and a "religious code of conduct"] with moneys from: 1) their treasuries; 2) the production and sale of crude oil; 3) and drug trafficking.

Chapter II

The History of Islam

Documented secular history and "written" Islamic records are inconsistent and frequently contradict each other.

> "Islamic chronicles and literary sources starting in the 8th century present a vast collection of anecdotal material which pious religionist authors have drawn from, in order to forge a storyline for early Islam." [1]   "Written Records of Islam"

Islamic documents claim that Muhammed, the spiritual founder of Islam, was born circa 570AD; that he moved to Mecca in approximately 620AD; and died in Medina 632AD. [2] Compared with recorded secular history, the earliest mention of the city of Mecca is the mid-eighth century. Before this time the region of Mecca was controlled by Jewish settlers. Secular history records (with maps) identify the existence of the city of Medina in approximately 600AD. [3]

> "The task of recovery of verifiable historical events has been made difficult by a general unwillingness of the Islamic theological community to subject its accounts to historical methodology and scrutiny. In response to the examination of its cultural roots by non-traditionalistic scholars, Muslim polemicists have in many cases adopted an adversarial position aimed at discrediting and refuting any and all research that challenges traditional Islamic narration." [4]

> "Secular scholars pinpoint the actual beginnings of the classical Islamic identity to the 9th century, thus the formative stage of Islam was not within the lifetime of Mohammed but evolved over a period of two to three centuries." [5]

---

[1] *New Advent Catholic Encyclopedia "Mohammed and Mohammedanism*

[2] *The Muslim Issue.* wordpress.com/2013/0719

[3] ibid #2

[4] *The Need for Qar'inc Criticism*; Ibn Warraq

[5] *Islamic History; A Framework for Enquiry*; Stephen Humphreys; Princeton

"In recent years, Saudi Arabia and other Islamic countries (for example, Brunei) have established chairs of Islamic Studies in Western universities, which are encouraged to present a favorable image of Islam. Scientific research, leading to objective truth, no longer seems to be the goal. Critical examination of the sources or the Qur'an is discouraged. Scholars such as Daniel Easterman have even lost their posts for not teaching about Islam in the way approved by Saudi Arabia."[6]

"The earliest surviving Muslim sources are comparatively late, and so reflect less what happened, than what later Muslims wanted to remember as having happened. This is a point which has been a staple of at least Western scholarship since Ignia Goldzihcr's pioneering study of Hadith (i.e., the "traditions" which purport to record the deeds and words of Mohammad and his companions), in which he demonstrated that many Hadith accounts were later fabrications, although the degree of the materials unreliability has always been a matter of some debate." ... "Much of that narrative is a product of traditions, which serves to explain Koranic verses which, to later Muslim audiences, seemed opaque. In other words, the Koran and the exegetical problems it poses in some sense generated the stories that were used to explain them." [7]

THE 1ST JIHAD AND THE 1ST CALIPHATE (622- 1175AD)

Legacy of "The Religion of Peace?"

Five hundred years of "Islamic Jihad" took tens of thousands of lives and spread great terror. Early Muslims systematically killed huge numbers of their non-Islamic neighbors. Their Jihadi warriors pushed far to the north, in an attempt to convert or eradicate southern Europe.

---

[6] ibid #4

[7] *Formation of Islam: Religion and Society in the Near East, 600-1800*; Jonathan Porter Berkey; Cambridge University Press; 2003; p59

Jihad was then, as it is now, primarily a product of Islamic theology -- not a reaction against American policies, Western decadence, or anything else. The West may have its share of vices and shortcomings, but it was centuries of "Islamic Jihad" that provoked the violent defensive thrust from Europe, referred to as the Crusades.

A Caliphate is an area governed by an Islamic steward known as a Caliph, the leader of the entire Islamic community and a person considered to be a religious successor to the Islamic Prophet Muhammad.

The History of Islamic Jihads and Subsequent Caliphates, which led to the Crusades, is briefly summarized.

The Rashidun Caliphs directly succeeded Muhammad as leaders of the Muslim community, from 632 - 661AD. [8]

The standard Arabian practice at the time was for the prominent men of a kinship group, or tribe, to gather after a leader's death and elect a leader from amongst themselves. There was no specified procedure for this Shura or consultation. Candidates were usually, but not necessarily, from the same lineage as the deceased leader. Capable men, who would lead well, were preferred over an ineffectual heir. [9]

When Muhammad died in 632AD, Abu Bakr claimed to be the legitimate Caliph to lead the Muslims. He demonstrated his authority by attacking Syria. This first Arab Conquest gave them significant riches, which propelled further expansion.

Abu Bakr, the first successor of Muhammad, nominated Umar as his successor on his deathbed in 634AD. Umar, the second Caliph, was killed by a Persian named Piruz Nahavandi. His successor, Uthman, was elected by a council of electors (majlis). Uthman was killed by members of a disaffected group.

Ali then took control; but he was not universally accepted as Caliph by the governors of Egypt, and later by some of his own guard. He faced two major rebellions and was assassinated by Abd-al-Rahman ibn Muljam, a Khawarij.

---

[8] ibid #7
[9] ibid #7

Ali's tumultuous rule lasted only five years. This period is known as the Fitna, or the first Islamic civil war. The followers of Ali later became the Shi'a ("shiaat Ali", partisans of Ali) minority sect of Islam. They rejected the legitimacy of the first 3 caliphs. The followers of the Rashidun Caliphs (Abu Bakr, Umar, and Uthman) became the majority Sunni sect.

Sunni Muslims believe that Abu Bakr was chosen by the community and argued that a Caliph should ideally be chosen by election or community consensus. The Shia Muslims believe that Ali, the son-in-law and cousin of Muhammad, was chosen by Muhammad to be his spiritual and temporal successor, as the Mawla (the Imam and the Caliph) of all Muslims in the event of Ghadir Khumm. [10]

The Umayyad Caliphate (661-750AD) directly succeeded the Rashidun Caliphate, taking the 1st Caliphate to its largest land area. The Caliphate grew rapidly to India on the east; to the Caucasus on the north; to Morocco and the Iberian Peninsula on the west; and along to southern shores of the Mediterranean Sea and the entire Arabian Peninsula. [11]

In the decades following 750AD, the 1st Caliphate began to collapse, as new Islamic leaders (some illegitimate successors to Muhammad) seized control.

In 1095, Pope Urban II, issued a papal cyclical to the kings and religious leaders of Western Europe, to attack the Islamists and to drive them out of Europe, back to the Middle East. The crusaders responded by liberating the Iberian Peninsula and eventually marching all the way to what is "modern day Turkey."

---

[10]   ibid #7

[11]   ibid #7

The 1st Caliphate (circa 10th century)

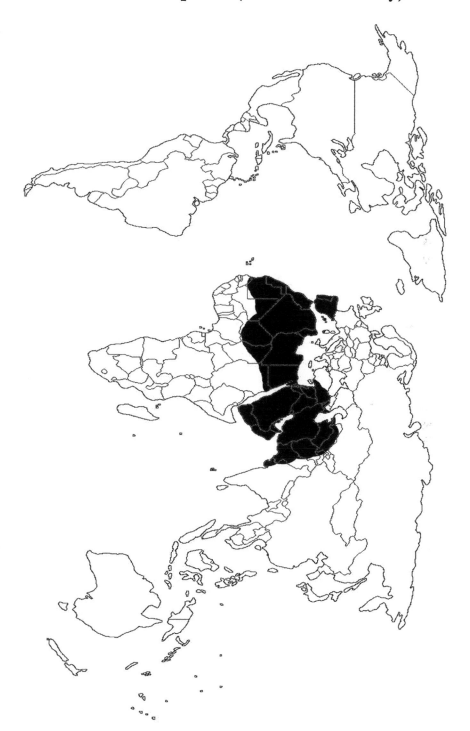

THE 2ND JIHAD AND THE 2ND CALIPHATE (1290 ~ 1918AD)

"Against Arab, European, African & Asian Interests"

The Ottoman Empire was founded in the latter part of the 13th century, in northwestern Anatolia, in the vicinity of Bilecik and Sogut by the Oghuz Turkish tribal leader, Osman. By 1354, with the fall of Constantinople, the Ottomans had crossed into Europe. With the conquest of the Balkans, the Ottoman Beylick Empire became a transcontinental empire. [12]

During the 16th and 17th centuries, at the height of its power under the reign of Suleiman the Magnificent, the Ottoman Empire (the 2nd Caliphate) was a multinational, multilingual empire controlling much of Southeast Europe, parts of Central Europe, Western Asia, the Caucasus, North Africa, and the Horn of Africa. At the beginning of the 17th century the Empire contained 32 provinces and numerous vassal states. Some of these vassal states were later absorbed into the Ottoman Empire, while others were granted various types of autonomy, over the centuries. [13]

---

[12] ibid #7

[13] *The Early Islam Conquests*, Fred Donner, 1981

The 2nd Caliphate (circa 17th century)
The Ottoman Empire

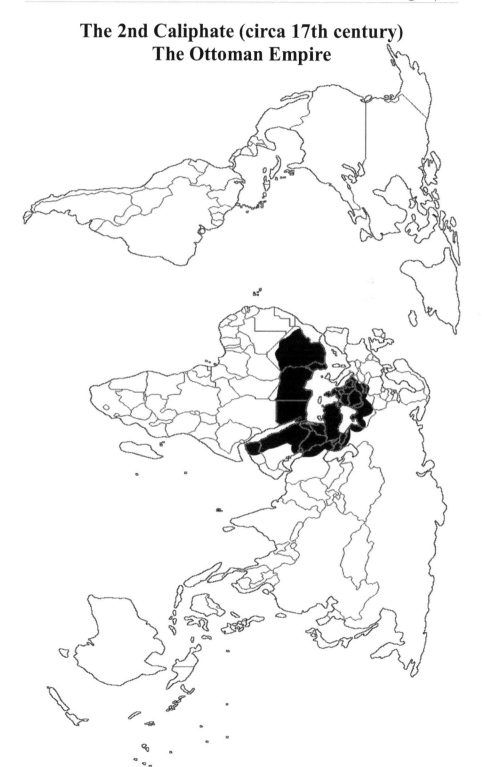

With Constantinople as its new capital, the Ottoman Empire was at the center of interactions between the Eastern and Western worlds for six centuries. The maintenance of good roads allowed East-West trade to flourish. While the Empire was once thought to have entered a period of decline following the death of Suleiman the Magnificent, this view is no longer supported by the majority of academic historians. Only the roads in lands of the nation-states, serving as a buffer to southeast Europe, were allowed to fall into disrepair. [14]

The Ottoman Empire continued to maintain a flexible and strong economy, society, and military throughout the 17th and much of the 18th century. However, during a long period of peace from 1740 to 1768, the Ottoman military system fell behind that of their European rivals, the Habsburg Empire and Russian Empire. The Ottomans consequently suffered severe military defeats in the late 18th and early 19th centuries, which prompted them to initiate comprehensive reforms in command and control, and to modernization of their military weaponry.

Over the course of the 19th century, the Ottoman state became vastly more powerful and better organized. Despite suffering further territorial losses, especially in the Balkans, where a number of new states emerged. [15]

The Empire aligned with Germany in the late 19th century and early 20th century, hoping to escape from the diplomatic isolation, which had contributed to its recent territorial losses. Subsequently, they joined World War I on the side of the Central Powers.

While the Empire was able to hold its own during the conflict, it was struggling with internal dissent, especially with the Arab Revolt in its Assyrian holdings. Starting before World War I and growing increasingly more common, major atrocities were committed by the Ottoman government against the Armenians, the Assyrians and the Pontic Greeks.

---

[14] ibid #13

[15] ibid #13

ROOTS OF GENOCIDE AGAINST ARMENIAN CHRISTIANS: THE OTTOMAN EMPIRE

While Armenia has been a separate nation since the 4th century, it has found itself under the control and domination of one empire after another for most of its existence. Armenia was the first nation in the world to declare Christianity as its official religion.

Armenia was absorbed by the Ottoman Empire in the 15th century. The Ottoman rulers were Muslim, like most of their subjects. While these rulers permitted other religious minorities (like the Armenian Christians) to maintain some autonomy, they subjected the Armenians, whom they viewed as "infidels," to unequal and unjust treatment. Christians had to pay higher taxes than the Muslims citizens and had very few political or legal rights.

Between 1894 and 1896, in response to large scale protests by the Armenians, the Turkish military, officers and soldiers, along with ordinary men raided Armenian cities and villages, and massacred hundreds of thousands of citizens.

In 1908, reformers established a new Muslim government in Turkey, the neighboring country in the Ottoman Empire to the south of Armenia. However, nothing changed; and the reformers intensified the efforts to rid the Ottoman Empire of "Infidels."

In 1915, the government of the Ottoman Empire set in motion a plan to expel and murder the last remaining Armenian Christians, who lived anywhere in the Ottoman Empire. While the Islamic Turkish government, which succeeded the Ottoman Empire after the conclusion of the WWI, has denied that this genocide occurred, historians have confirmed that more than 1.5 million Armenian Christians were slaughtered. [16] Today in Turkey, it is still against the law to discuss in public the genocide of Armenian Christians.

The defeat of the Ottoman Empire and the occupation of part of its territory by the Allied Powers in the aftermath of World War I, resulted in the Empire being partitioned and the loss of all their Middle Eastern territories. New countries were established, with alliances beneficial to the United Kingdom and France.
(see Sykes-Picot Treaty; page 34)

---

[16] ibid #13

The successful Turkish War of Independence against the occupying Allies led to the emergence of the Republic of Turkey in the Anatolian heartland and the abolition of the Ottoman monarchy and the desolation of the 2nd Caliphate. [17]

---

[17] ibid #2

Chapter III

World Wars I & II
Germany & The Islamic Supremacists

"In 1835, the Prussian (German) Captain Helmuth von Moltke traveled to Turkey (Ottoman Empire), assigned as a military instructor to the Ottoman army. Over the next several decades, leading up to WWI, other officers and military personnel followed, charged with promoting Europeanization of the Ottoman Empire." [1]

At the beginning of WWI, the Central Powers consisted of the German Empire and the Austro-Hungarian Empire. The Ottoman Empire joined the Central Powers later in 1914. The Kingdom of Bulgaria joined the alliance in 1915. The name "Central Powers" was derived from the location of these countries; all four were located between the Russian Empire in the east and France and the United Kingdom in the west. "During the early stages of WWI, a German expeditionary force of more than 20,000 soldiers was sent to support their Turkish allies in the Middle East." [2]

ECONOMIC ALLIANCES

Since the early 1870's Germany had understood the economic potential of establishing a railway connection to the Persian Gulf. A rail network from Berlin through Vienna on to Constantinople and Bagdad, finally reaching the Persian Gulf, would provide much improved delivery of supplies to the German colonies in eastern Africa and greatly improved access to petroleum from the Middle East at much reduced costs. This economic vision would also solidify Germany's political influence in the region. [3]

---

[1] *German Soldiers in the Ottoman Empire, 1835-1918*; Oliver Janz, Freie Universitat Berlin.

[2] ibid #1

[3] A Century of War: Anglo-American Oil Politics and the New World Order;

The Ottoman Empire also recognized that it would derive significant economic benefits from connections with Germany through the Berlin-to-Baghdad railway project and to the subsequent construction of other rail lines through Turkey, all down to the Persian Gulf.

In 1872 German railway engineer, Wilhelm von Pressel was retained by the Ottoman government to develop railways in Turkey. Private enterprise could not build the railroads without subsidies, thus the revenue strapped Ottoman government turned to the Deutsche Bank for financing and thus gave Germany additional control over the new rail system. [4] Construction of the Constantinople to Bagdad line began in 1888. [5]

Against this historical backdrop, the Orient Express had been operating since 1883, providing regularly scheduled passenger service from Paris through Munich to Vienna to Constantinople and return. [6]

With the outbreak of WWI, these other projects proved to be too far into the future and were cancelled and rescheduled for much later dates. [7] [8] [9]

WAR JUSTIFICATIONS

In early July 1914, in the aftermath of the assassination of Austro-Hungarian Archduke Franz Ferdinand and the immediate likelihood of war between Austria-Hungary and Serbia, Kaiser Wilhelm II and the German government informed the Austro-Hungarian government that Germany would uphold its alliance with Austria-Hungary and defend it from possible Russian intervention, if a war between Austria-Hungary and Serbia took place. [10]

---

[4]   Turkey, The Great Powers and the Bagdad Railway; Edward Meade Earle: Russell and Russell; 1923 (reprint 1966)

[5]   Origins of WWI: Wilhelm von Pressel, the Constantinople-Baghdad-Bahn Railway," www.revisionist.net/hysteria/baghdad-bahn,html.

[6]   *A History of the Orient Express;* Mark Smith, 2013.

[7]   ibid #1

[8]   ibid #3

[9]   ibid #5

[10] *Eagles on the Crescent: Germany, Austria, and the Diplomacy of the Turkish Alliance 1914-1918;* Frank G. Weber, Cornell Press, 1970.

When Russia enacted a general mobilization, Germany viewed the act as provocative. The Russian government promised Germany that its general mobilization did not mean preparation for war with Germany but was a reaction to the events between Austria-Hungary and Serbia. The German government regarded the Russian promise of "no war" with Germany to be nonsense, in light of its general mobilization. Germany, in turn, mobilized for war. [11] [12] [13] [14]

On 1 August 1914, Germany sent an ultimatum to Russia stating that since both Germany and Russia were in a state of military mobilization; an effective state of war existed between the two countries. Later that day, France, an ally of Russia, declared a state of general mobilization in expectation of war. [15] [16] [17] [18]

On 2 August, Germany waged war on Russia. The German government justified that military action against Russia was necessary. Russian aggression had been demonstrated through the mobilization of the Russian army. This in turn had resulted in Germany mobilizing it army. On 3 August, Germany responded to this action by declaring war on France, the Russian ally. [19] [20] [21] [22]

The Ottoman Empire made a formal military alliance with Germany, signed on 2 August 1914. The alliance treaty expected that the Ottoman Empire would become involved in the conflict in a short amount of time. However, for the first several months of the war the Ottoman Empire maintained neutrality, though it allowed a German

---

[11] ibid #10

[12] *The Treaty of Alliance Between Germany and Turkey*; Yale University.

[13] *The First World War: Volume I: To Arms;* Hew Strachan; (2003) pp 644-693

[14] *The Berlin-Baghdad Express: The Ottoman Empire and Germany Bids for World Power, 1898-1918* Sean McMeeKin, Guardian Books, 2010

[15] ibid #10

[16] ibid #12

[17] ibid #13

[18] ibid #14

[19] ibid #10

[20] ibid #12

[21] ibid #13

[22] ibid #14

naval squadron to enter and stay near the Strait of Bosporus. [23] Officials of the Ottoman Empire informed the German government that the country needed time to prepare for conflict. Germany was providing financial aid and weapons shipments to the Ottoman Empire. [24] [25]

After pressure escalated from the German government, demanding that the Ottoman Empire fulfill its treaty obligations, or else Germany would expel the country from the alliance and terminate economic and military assistance, the Ottoman government entered the war. With the recently acquired cruisers from Germany, the Yavuz Sultan Selim (formerly SMS Goeben) and the Midilli (formerly SMS Breslau), the Ottoman government launched a naval raid on the Russian port of Odessa, thus engaging in a military action in accordance with its alliance obligations with Germany. The Triple Entente (Russia, France & Britain) declared war on the Ottoman Empire. [26] [27] [28] [29]

THE SYKES-PICOT AGREEMENT 1916

"The Middle East was reshaped by the British and the French in a secret agreement, which created the countries of Syria, Lebanon, Iraq and Jordan. The British received territory, divided into Palestine and Transjordan, from which Iraq and later Israel emerged in 1947. France got Greater Syria and the coastal state lands that include modern-day Lebanon and Syria." [30] [31]

"The state of Iraq included: non-Arab Sunni Kurds in the north; Sunni Arab Muslims in the western and central portions; and Shi'ite Muslim Arabs to the south.

---

[23]   ibid #4
[24]   ibid #10
[25]   ibid #14
[26]   ibid #10
[27]   ibid #12
[28]   ibid #13
[29]   ibid #14
[30]   *The Sykes-Picot Agreement*, Wikipedia
[31]   *A Peace to End all Peace: The Fall of the Ottoman Empire and the Creation of the Modern Middle East*, David Fromkin, Owl Publishers, New York. 1989

The British also created the modern state of Jordan out of the Transjordan region and promised the Jews and the Palestinians homelands of their own under the Balfour Declaration." [32] [33]

"In Lebanon, the French gave the Christian Maronites (political) status and carved out borders (districts) that gave the Christians a majority (control) over both Sunni and Shi'ite Muslims. Syria was similarly divided, giving the Alawites and Druze (Christians) their own areas of the country. The Sunni Muslims were given Damascus and Aleppo." [34] [35]

WORLD WAR II: GERMANY AND TURKEY

Muslim extremists were strong supporters of Hitler. On the eastern front Soviet Muslims had abandoned the Soviet army to fight with Hitler. The Nazis and these Muslim extremists had common ideologies and common enemies. They both hated the Jews; they both were staunchly against Communism; and they both wanted the British out of "Palestine." [36]

In January 1931, the Second International Islamic Conference of Motamar Al-Alam Al-Islami, was held at Bautil Maqdis, Jerusalem. Muslim leaders affirmed their respect and allegiance for Hitler and the Nazis. [37]

The Grand Mufti of Jerusalem was a very influential Muslim leader at that time, almost equivalent to the Pope in the Roman Catholic church. The Grand Mufti was one of Hitler's strongest allies. He recruited Arabs and Muslims for service in the German military and SS police. [38]

---

[32] ibid #29

[33] ibid #30

[34] ibid #29

[35] ibid #30

[36] *Relations Between Nazi Germany and the Arab World, 1933-1945,* Wikipedia.

[37] *Proceeding from the Second International Islamic Conference,* Bautil Maqdas, Jersulem, January 1931

[38] ibid #36

Support for Nazism was not limited to the Grand Mufti. Other Arab leaders at the council meeting, praised Hitler and the Nazi movement. [39]

"We admired the Nazis. We were immersed in reading Nazi literature and books ... We were the first who thought of an Arab translation of *Mein Kampf*. Anyone who lived in Damascus at that time was a witness to the Arab inclination towards Nazism," recalled Sami al-Joundi, one of the founders of the Syrian Ba-ath Party. [40]

Indeed, a popular World War II song heard in the Middle east featured the words: ***"Bisamma Allah - orio olord Hitler"*** - "In heaven Allah; on earth Hitler." [41]

Posters were put up in Arab markets and elsewhere proclaiming, "In heaven Allah is thy ruler; on earth Adolph Hitler." [42]

"The only religion I respect is Islam. The only prophet I admire is the Prophet Muhammad" (testimonial by Adolph Hitler). [43]

"In October 1933, the pro-Axis, Young Egypt Party was founded. Styling itself after its German ideal, the new party built a storm-trooper unit, marching with torches under the slogan, 'One folk, One party, One Leader.' Among the members was a young Gamal Abdel Nassar. Nasser's brother, Nassiri, was the translator of *Mein Kampf* into Arabic, describing the Fascist despot in glowing terms." [44] [45]

The reasons for the recruitment, in particular of Serbian Muslims (from the Independent States of Croatia), by the SS were many-fold. First, Himmler was fascinated by the Islamic faith, and thought Muslims to be fearless soldiers willing to kill for their religion. Second, the Germans were hoping to rally the World's 350 million Muslims to their side, in a struggle against the British Empire.

---

[39] ibid #36

[40] ibid #36

[41] ibid #36

[42] ibid #36

[43] *The Political Testament of Adolf Hitler*, 7th February 1945

[44] *The Young Egypt Party and Egyptian Nationalism, 1933-1945*, James Paul Jankowski, University Microfilms, 1982.

[45] *The Young Egypt Party*, Wikipedia

And third, the creation of a Muslim division, albeit European Muslim, was considered a stepping stone to this greater end. [46]

Adolf Hitler approved of Himmler's idea and the division was created on March 5, 1943. The divisional strength reached the required 26,000 men in 1943. The new division was named the 13th SS Hanjar (Sword) Division, which fought against Yugoslav partisans led by General Tito, and carried out police and security details in fascist Hungary. Hajj Amin al-Husseini, The Grand Mufti of Jerusalem made a substantial contribution to the Axis war effort by organizing "in record time" recruitment to Muslim SS units in Croatia, that would be involved in some of the worst atrocities of the Second World War. [47]

From 1941 until 1945, the Nazi-installed regime of Ante Pavelic in Croatia carried out some of the most horrific crimes of the Holocaust (known as the Porajmos by the Roma), killing over 800,000 Yugoslav citizens; 750,000 Serbs; 60,000 Jews; and 26,000 Roma (gypsies). [48]

In these crimes, they were helped by Muslim fundamentalists in Bosnia and Kosovo, who were openly supported by the Palestinian Grand Mufti of Jerusalem, Hajj Amin al-Husseini. [49]

A notorious anti-Semite, he encouraged Muslims to join Nazi units which would be later implicated in genocide and crimes against humanity - the infamous Hanjar (or Handschar) 13th Waffen SS division. One of these notorious crimes was the massacre at Koritska Jama Gorge, in Bosnia during 1941. Many more victims were murdered at Jasenovac, the third largest death camp, where over 200,000 people - mainly Orthodox Serbs - met their deaths. [50]

The Nazi's recruited two other SS divisions from Yugoslavia's Muslim population: the infamous Bosnian 13th Waffen Hanjar (Handschar) SS division, and the Albanian Skanderbeg 21st Waffen SS division.

---

[46] *Nazis, with the Help of an Arab Cleric, Used Muslim Extremists as a Tool,* Louis Anslow,
[47] ibid #45
[48] ibid #45
[49] ibid #45
[50] ibid #45

SS conscription in Yugoslavia during the war, produced 42,000 Waffen SS and police troops. [51]

"Towards the end of World War II, another future Egyptian president, Anwar El Sadat wrote to the Fuhrer, 'My dear Hitler, I congratulate you from the bottom of my heart. Even if you appear to have been defeated, in realty you are the victor. You succeeded in creating dissentions between Churchill, the old man, and the Allies, sons of Satan. Germany will win because her existence is necessary to maintain world balance. Germany will be reborn, in spite of Western and eastern powers. There will be no peace unless Germany becomes what she once was'." [52] [53] [54]

Earlier, Anwar Sadat had met with Hussein al-Banni, founder and leader of The Muslim Brotherhood, an ardent supporter of Nazi Germany. The meeting put Sadat in contact with Abd al-Munni Adb al-Rauf, who went on to become a leading member of the Free Officers and a chief propagandist and protagonist of the Brotherhood. [55] [56] [57]

Sadat also met with Dr. Ibrahim Hasan, the Second Deputy of Ikhwan. The two men agreed that "salvation of the country could be assured only by a coup at the hands of military, because of the Kings support of the Allies." [58] [59] [60]

On February 24, 1945, Ahmed Maher Pasha, the Prime Ministry of Egypt, was assassinated by a member of the National Party, and also

---

[51] ibid #45

[52] *The Legacy of Islamic Anti-Semitism: From Sacred Text to Solemn History*, Andrew G. Bostom.

[53] *Witness to History,* Mike Walsh, 2017.

[54] *The Genealogy of Evil: Anti-Semitism from Nazism to Islamic Jihad*, David Patterson, 2010.

[55] ibid #51

[56] ibid #52

[57] ibid #53

[58] ibid #51

[59] ibid #52

[60] ibid #53

an operative of the Muslim Brotherhood, as he was reading "the declaration of war" against Germany. [61]

EUROPE: POST WORLD WARS

In Europe, two devastating wars eliminated much of two generations from the population. Infrastructure and production assets were destroyed and had been rebuilt only to be destroyed and rebuilt again.

In the second half of last century, the confluence of three events created a situation, particularly favorable for "Islamic Supremacists": 1) a decline in birth rates in all European countries, well below the 2.1 per couple needed to maintain population stability; 2) an enormous Muslim immigration to assist in the reconstruction of war torn Europe; and 3) the use of "Civilization Jihad" to infiltrate all aspects of life in these European societies.

Guest Worker Programs

World Wars I & II decimated the working age population both through combat and in the high number of civilian deaths caused by the lack of precise weapons of attack, such as carpet bombing.

Each time the war was over, the countries of central Europe were faced with the daunting challenge of cleaning up and rebuilding. The quantity of construction materials and the expense in hard currency was monumental. Even more challenging was the lack of skilled, able-bodied workers, whose numbers were greatly reduced by war casualties.

To meet the required number of workers, most countries (in particularly Germany, France and Italy) established "guest worker programs," through which they invited skilled and semi-skilled workers to come to the host country and work in the rebuilding: from Turkey (to Germany); from Libya & Tunisia (to Italy); and from Algeria (to France). These programs were not well monitored and became open-end in terms of allowing many of the guest workers to stay permanently.

---

[61] *The Dual Nature of Islamic Fundamentalism*, Johannes J. G. Jansen, !997.

The societal impact on the host countries probably was never considered. But today, it has become very evident that the societies in each host country has been radically changed to more closely match the culture of the "sending country" (ie the Muslim cultures of Turkey, Libya, Tunisia, Algeria, and others). The result has been the gradual, and permanent, transformation of the society in each host country.

Demographic Transformation of Europe in the 21st Century

Baseline demographic studies of the 21st century suggested that: by the year 2040, the Muslim population of France would be greater than 50%; and by 2050, the Muslim populations of Germany and Belgium would each be greater than 50%.

However, these timelines have been greatly accelerated by the mass migration of Muslim refugees in 2015-2017; from Syria and other Middle East countries into Eastern/Central/Northern Europe, and from Libya and other North African countries into Italy and France.

It is difficult to understand why Angela Merkel, the Prime Minister of Germany, welcomed so many undocumented Muslim refugees from Syria. However, her decision seems to follow a pattern of relationships between Germany and the Muslim dominated Middle East, dating back to the 1870's

New studies suggest that: Belgium will have a Muslim majority by 2030; France will have a Muslim majority by 2035; Germany will have a Muslim majority by 2040; and Sweden and Norway will have Muslim majorities by 2050.

To make things worse, France has modified their welfare programs to allow multiple wives for Muslim men (up to 4 wives and 8 children), while maintaining the traditional limit of one wife and two children for other families.

In addition, Germany passed federal laws allowing local school districts to choose their own teaching curriculum to meet the needs of the "majority" race/culture/religion. Thus, Muslims have relocated to dominate selected neighbors and therefore, be able to select an Islamic curriculum for the elementary schools. They have even gone so far as to reserve all school entrances on the east side of the building, "for Muslims Only." Members of other religions must use entrances on other sides of the building.

While England did not resort to guest worker programs to rebuild after WWII, in recent years they have welcomed refugees to the point that Muslims now dominate the electorate in "Londonistan." Thus, London now has their first Muslim mayor, Sadiq Khan. There are now more than 100 Sharia courts, "officially" recognized by local authorities.[62]

Since 2001, 500 churches in the London metropolitan area have closed, while 423 new mosques have opened. It is estimated by 2020 that the number of Muslims attending prayer weekly will reach 683,000 and the number of Christians attending services will decline to 679,000.[63]

Poland and Portugal are the only countries of Europe which will probably not succumb to the "purposeful Muslim population explosion." Portugal does not openly welcome any immigrants, Muslim nor other ethnic/religious groups. Instead they select Portuguese speaking immigrants from Brazil.

Poland has chosen to resist European Union directives to receive Muslim refugees from any country. Their strong Roman Catholic beliefs will also serve as a deterrent to cultural and/or religious changes.

---

[62] *Londonistan: 423 New Mosques; 500 Closed Churches*, Giulio Meotti, www.gatestoneinstitute.org, April 2, 2017.
[63] ibid #61

Chapter IV

Continuing Genocide of Christians by Islamic Supremacists

Christians are being persecuted in 139 nations around the world. It is estimated that up to four out of five acts of religious discrimination worldwide are directed against Christians. Countries that were previously moderate, or avowedly secular, have stepped up their hostility towards Christians. [1] Against this backdrop, and quite possibly driving this persecution forward, the genocide of Christians by Islamic Supremacists has steadily increased throughout the 20th and 21st centuries.

The Koran specifically calls for the genocide of "infidels" in many verses:

Koran (2:191): "Kill the unbelievers wherever you find them;"

Koran (8:12): "Terrorize and behead those who believe in other than the Koran;"

Koran (9:5): "When the opportunity arises, kill the infidels wherever you catch them;"

Koran (9:30): "The Jews and the Christians are perverts; fight them;" and

Koran (9:123): "Make war on the infidels living in your neighborhood."

(other verses are listed in **Appendix B**)

---

[1] Why Don't We Hear About Persecuted Christians? www.abc,net.au/news, August 1, 2014

Examples of how The Muslim Brotherhood and its surrogates have gained control of many countries.

According to Palmer Williams, American Center for Law and Justice, just as the Palestinians intend to wipe the Jewish people off the face of the planet and to destroy the state of Israel, ISIS seeks to eradicate Christians from all areas it has taken control of in the Middle East, Africa and Asia. [2] In Iraq and Syria, 1.0 to 1.8 million Christians have been slaughtered or displaced. Six hundred thousand have been displaced in Syria alone over the past 4 years. Iraq's Christian population is nearing complete annihilation, as the numbers have plummeted from 1.4 million to a mere 270,000. [3]

Iraq: At the beginning of the 21st century, more than 300,000 Christians lived in the region of Iraq and Syria, surrounding Mosul and Raqqa. For the first time in perhaps 1,600 years, no Christian services have been held in Mosul in recent weeks. [4]

Syria: A century ago, more than one million Christians lived there.

In 2014, ISIS gained control of this region and claimed Raqqa as their new capital. In July 2015, ISIS announced the establishment the 3rd Caliphate. [5] [6]

Today fewer than 1,000 Christians reside there. The region is run by Sharia Law. The Christian places of worship have been destroyed and their former congregations have been slaughtered. [7]

Turkey: Over the last century, the Christian presence has dwindled from 32% of the population to a tiny minority of 0.15%. [8] [9]

---

[2] Genocide is Happening Now - Not a Thing of the Past
www. aclj.org/persecuted church.

[3] ibid #2

[4] ibid #2

[5] ibid #1

[6] ibid #2

[7] ibid #2

[8] ibid #1

[9] ibid #2

Lebanon: In 1960, Lebanon was a Christian-majority nation.

Over the past 50 years, hundreds of thousands of Christians have been massacred, displaced or exiled, due to the so called "civil war."[10] [11]

Egypt: A century ago, there were more than one million Christians living there. Now there are less than 50,000 Christians in Egypt. [12] [13]

The Sudan: Since the Islamic takeover of the Sudan in 1989 and the separation of the former country into two independent nations (The Sudan & Southern Sudan), more than one million Christians have been killed in **Southern Sudan** because of their faith. Even refugees, in UN refugee camps, have been slaughtered, when raiding Muslim militias from **The Sudan** could not find any Christians living in the villages. [14]

Indonesia: More than half-million Christians have been displaced. [15]

---

[10] ibid #1

[11] ibid #2

[12] ibid #1

[13] ibid #2

[14] ibid #2

[15] ibid #1

Chapter V

The Muslim Brotherhood & Islamic Supremacy in the 21st Century

The Muslim Brotherhood was founded in 1928 by Hassan Al-Banna, an Islamic preacher, with twin strategies:

1) Political organization with charity outreach; and

2) World Domination.

This influential, powerful group has played, and will continue to play, a dominate role in leading and uniting Muslims around the world. [1]

Under the one banner and the one goal of establishing a "World-wide Islamic Caliphate", The Muslim Brotherhood's sole purpose is to subjugate and to govern all peoples of the world under the requirements of "Sharia Law," as set forth in the Koran. [2]

"It is the nature of Islam to dominate, not to be dominated; to impose its laws on all nations; and to extend its power to the entire planet." Hassan Al-Banna (1928) and Ayattollah Rahollah Khomeini (2005). [3]

The Muslim Brotherhood has three separate geographic strategies for spreading Islam and for establishing the 3rd Caliphate: 1) the Middle East & Africa; 2) Europe; and 3) the United States & the Western Hemisphere. [4]

---

[1] *The Muslim Brotherhood, Fountain of Islamic Violence,* by Cynthia Farahat, Middle East Quarterly: Spring 2017 - Volume XXIV: Number 2, page 3.

[2] The Zawahiri letter and the Strategy of Al-Qaeda; *Current Trends in Islamist Ideology*, vol. 3, February 16, 2006 by Shmuel Bar and Yair Minzilil, Hudson Institute.

[3] Speech by Ayatollah Ruhollah Khomeini (quoting Hassan Al-Banna, founder of The Muslim Brotherhood 1928), Associated Press, September 9, 2016.

[4] Speech by Iran President Mahmoud Ahadinejad, Tehran Conference Oct. 17, 2005.

MIDDLE EAST & AFRICA

The Muslim Brotherhood does not view the Middle East and the countries of Africa as being individual nations, with unique boundaries and identities. They believe that these countries are opportunities to liberate the people from foreign occupation and to unite them under "Sharia Law."

They endorse the use of violence only against Western "occupations of Islamic lands," such as Afghanistan, Iraq and Israel, which the Brotherhood views as Western-style outposts built on Muslim territory.

EUROPE

The Muslim Brotherhood has been extremely successful in utilizing "Civilization Jihad" in Europe and the United States.

In 1998 Yusuf al-Qaradawi wrote, "Islam will return to Europe as a conqueror and victor, after having been expelled from it twice … The conquest this time will not be by the sword but by preaching and ideology."

Speaking on Al Jazeera TV (January 1999), al-Qaradawi further declared; "The friends of the Prophet heard that two cities, Romiyya [Rome] and 'Hirqil [Constantinople/Istanbul], would be conquered by Islam. The Prophet said that Constantinople would be <u>first</u> and Rome would fulfill the prophecy." [5]

In Europe, The Muslim Brotherhood seeks to utilize multiculturalism to ultimately turn Islam into the governing political force on the continent.

They will continue to utilize population expansion through increased birth rates of Muslim families (husbands with multiple wives). They will force governments to adopt domestic policies favorable to minorities and immigrants and to accept cultural and ideological differences. (Recall Chapter III; pages 39-41)

---

[5] Speech by Yusuf al-Qaradawi on Al Jazeera TV, January 1999.

THE UNITED STATES

In America, The Muslim Brotherhood has quietly founded hundreds of Muslim organizations and networks, mostly funded by Persian Gulf countries. Many of these groups are aligned with various international Islamic Supremacist groups and/or anti-America groups.

These Islamic Supremacist groups have been successful in lobbying members of Congress, for the purpose of influencing legislation. They also infiltrated the Clinton, Bush and Obama administrations. The objective has been: 1) to establish domestic policies consistent with "Shari'a Law;" and 2) **to control foreign policies, which would be friendly to unlimited immigration from poor countries, including Muslim majority countries.**

Their intention is to transform America by overwhelming the current cultural, through changing the demographics of the existing population, so as to create a permanent under-class, easily controlled by "Shari'a Law."

"THE RESPONSE FROM FREEDOM"

In the 5th century BC, Chinese General Sun Tzu wrote in *The Art of War* :

> "It is said that if you know your enemies and know yourself, you will not be imperiled in a hundred battles; If you do not know your enemies but do know yourself, you will win one and lose one; If you do not know your enemies nor yourself, you will be imperiled in every single battle." [6]

On May 6, 1941, speaking to Parliament, Winston Churchill declared:

> "Our policy ... 'is to wage war, by sea, by land and by air, with all our might and with all the strength that God can give us: to wage war against a monstrous tyranny, never surpassed in the dark lamentable catalogue of human crime. That is our policy.'

---

[6] *The Art of War,* General Sun Tzu, China, circa 500 BC.

You ask, 'what is our aim?   I can answer with one word: **VICTORY** -- victory at all costs; victory, in spite of all terror; victory, however long and hard the road may be; for without victory, there is no survival'." [7]

"POLITICAL CORRECTNESS WILL DESTROY AMERICA"

In 2006, speaking at the *Intelligence Summit* in Washington, DC, Bridgette Gabriel warned:

"The most important element of intelligence has to be understanding the mindset and intention of the enemy. The West has been wallowing in a state of ignorance and denial for thirty years, as Muslim extremists perpetrated evil against innocent victims in the name of Allah … America cannot effectively defend itself in this war unless, and until, the American people understand the nature of the enemy that we face."

"We are fighting a powerful ideology that is capable of altering basic instincts. An ideology that can turn a mother into a launching pad of death. A perfect example is a recent Hamas official, and mother, in the Palestinian territories who raves in heavenly joy about sending her three sons, homicide bombers, to death, and offering the ones who are still alive, at home, for the cause." [8]

---

[7] Speech by Prime Minister Winston Churchill, House of Commons, May 13, 1940.

[8] Speech by Bridgette Gabriel, "Intelligence Summit", Washington, DC, 2006.

Chapter VI

"In Their Own Words"

The Muslim Brotherhood
"A Fountain of Islamic Violence"
(see **Appendices C & D**)

CREED OF THE MUSLIM BROTHERHOOD

"Allah is our Objective;
The Prophet is our Leader;
The Qur'an is our Law, Jihad is our Way;
Dying in the Way of Allah is our highest Hope." [1]

PHILOSOPHY AND AUTHORITY

"It is the nature of Islam to dominate, not to be dominated; to impose its laws on all nations; and extend its power to entire planet."

"Killing the infidels is our religion; Slaughtering them is our religion; Until they convert to Islam or pay us tribute." [2]

In 2005, al-Qaida in Iraq warned Pope Benedict XVI that its war against Christianity and the West will go on until Islam takes over the world. Iran's supreme leader called for more protests over the pontiff's remarks on Islam. ... **"You and the West are doomed."** [3]

---

[1] *The Muslim Brotherhood's Conquest of Europe;* Middle East Quarterly, Winter 2005

[2] *Fear The Muslim Brotherhood;* National Review, Andrew C. McCarthy, Jan. 31, 2011.

[3] *The Muslim Brotherhood in Egypt: Historical Evolution and Future Prospective;* K. Helaby; 2006.

At the October 26, 2005 Tehran Conference, Iran president Mahmoud Ahmadinejad spoke. Ahmadinejad said Iran has developed a strategic "War Preparation Plan" that it calls the **"Destruction of Anglo-Saxon Civilization."** [4]

"You infidels and despots, we will continue our jihad and never stop until Allah avails us to chop your necks and raise the fluttering banner of monotheism; when Allah's rule is established, governing all people and nations." [5]

"When one studies a little or pays little attention to the roles of Islamic government, Islamic politics, Islamic society, and Islamic economy, he will realize that Islam is a 'very political religion.' Anyone who will say that religion is separate from politics is a fool; he does not know Islam nor politics." [6]

THE MUSLIM BROTHERHOOD: A CHRONOLOGICAL HISTORY [7]

1928 **The Muslim Brotherhood** was founded by Hassan Al-Banna, Islamic preacher, with twin strategies:

1) Political organization with charity outreach; and

2) World Domination.

"It is the nature of Islam to dominate, not to be dominated; to impose its laws on all nations; and to extend its power to the entire planet."   (proclamation by Hassan Al-Banna 1928)

1938 Al-Banna called for creation of Islamic State in Egypt

1943 **The Muslim Brotherhood** created a "secret apparatus" in Egypt to achieve its goals through violent means

---

[4] Speech by Iran President Mahmoud Ahadinejad, Tehran Conference, WorldNetDaily, Oct. 17, 2006.
[5] *Jihad Groups in Iraq take an Oath of Allegiance,* Statement released by the Mujahideen Shura Councill;, reported MEMRI, Oct. 2006.
[6] *The Muslim Brotherhood, Fountain of Islamic Violence,* by Cynthia Farahat, Middle East Quarterly: Spring 2017 - Volume XXIV: Number 2, page 3.
[7] ibid #6

1945 **The Muslim Brotherhood** established offices in Jerusalem.

1948 Abd al-Majid Ajmad Hasan, member of **The Muslim Brotherhood,** assassinated Egyptian Prime Minister, Mohamoud al-Nuqrashi.

1949 Egyptian government assassinated Hassan Al-Banna.

1950's **The Muslim Brotherhood** members fled Egypt to Saudi Arabia, Middle East, Central Asia, Europe, North America, & Argentina.

1963 **The Muslim Brotherhood** founded **The Muslim Student Association** at University of Illinois, Champaign-Urbana. Now there are hundreds of chapters at universities across America.

1973 **North American Islamic Trust**, founded by the **Muslim Student Association**, a financial holding company which owns mosques, Islamic centers and other properties in America worth billions of dollars. (Headquarters in Oak Brook, IL)

1974 ***"The Phased Plan"*** issued by **The Muslim Brotherhood.**

1978 **The Muslim Brotherhood** established al-Qaeda.

1981 **The Muslim Student Association** created **Islamic Society of North America**, which receives moneys from Islamic Supremacists (governments and individuals around the world): supporting Muslim communities; developing educational, social and outreach programs; and fostering good relations with other civic & service organizations in the United States. (Headquarters in Plainfield, IN)

1981 **The Muslim Brotherhood** assassinated Egyptian President, Anwar Sadat.

1981 **The Muslim Brotherhood** established the Islamic Palestine Association.

1982 ***"The Project"*** issued by **The Muslim Brotherhood**.

1983 **SAAR Foundation** established by **The Muslim Brotherhood** as umbrella organization (a cluster of 100 "charities" & "think tanks").

1988   **International Institute of Islamic Thought (IIIT)** Think tank committed to the "Islamization of Knowledge," founded by **The Muslim Brotherhood.**

1991   **Al Taqwa Bank** (Lugana, Switzerland with branches in Italy, Liechtenstein and the Bahamas) founded by leaders of **The Muslim Brotherhood.**

1991   **"Explanation Memorandum on the General Strategic Goals of the Group"** issued by **The Muslim Brotherhood.**

1994   **The Muslim Brotherhood,** through the Islamic Palestinian Authority, established the **Council on American Islamic Relations (CAIR),** as public relations firm to represent the interests of the Muslim Brotherhood.

1995   **Osama Bin Laden** declared war on the United States.

2002   The **"Memorandum"** by the King of Saudi Arabia to spread Islam through-out the United States; to implement Sharia Law in America. [8]

2005   **"The Twenty Year Strategic Plan for World Dominance:" 2001 – 2020.** [9]

---

[8]   *A Strategic Plan to Spread 'Sharia Law' Worldwide,* Memorandum by Saudi King Fahd bin Abdul Aziz, Reaud, Saudi Arabia, 2002
[9]   "The Zawahiri Letter and the Strategy of Al-Qaeda"; July 9, 2005, from Ayman al-Zawahari to Abu Musah, outlining the stages of action, leading to the establishment of "The Third Caliphate" & "The Ultimate Victory of Islam over Western Civilization;" *Current Trends in Islamist Ideology*, vol. 3, February 16, 2006 by Shmuel Bar and Yair Minzilil, Hudson Institute.

"THE PHASED PLAN:
STEALTH CIVILIZATION JIHAD" [10]

Phase One: Discrete and Secret Establishment of Leadership in governmental agencies (federal, state, and local); in financial institutions; in the media; and in education (both secondary and post-secondary).

Phase Two: Gradual Appearance on the Public Scene. The Muslim Brotherhood established important goals: 1) to gain influence in various sectors of federal, state and local government; 2) to infiltrate religious institutions; 3) to create schools of Middle Eastern Studies at America Universities; 4) to gain public support and sympathy; and 5) to establish a shadow government (secret) within the government, "Stealth Jihad Organizations."

Phase Three: Escalation prior to Conflict and Confrontation with the rulers, through utilizing mass media.

(The Muslim Brotherhood has successfully implemented Phases One, Two & Three in the United States).

Phase Four: Open Public Confrontation of US Government through exercising the public opinion approach. It is aggressively implementing the above-mentioned approach. Training on the use of weapons domestically and overseas with the anticipation of zero-hour.

(The Muslim Brotherhood and CAIR have established noticeable activities in the United States in this regard).

Phase Five: Seizing power to establish the new Islamic Nation in America, under which all parties and Islamic groups are united.

(The Muslim Brotherhood and CAIR have planned their strategy and are ready to implement this final phase).

---

[10] 1974 - *Phases of the World Underground Movement Plan,* paper specifying Five Phases of The Muslim Brotherhood Movement in North America, obtained in raid on Elbarassee home (Virginia),

"EXPLANATION MEMORANDUM ON THE GENERAL STRATEGIC GOALS OF THE GROUP"

"A STRATEGIC PLAN FOR AMERICA"
(written by Mohammad Akron; May 22, 1991)

Purpose of Memorandum:

1) to destroy the Western Civilization in America from within and by our [The Muslim Brotherhood] own means.

2) to establish a Global Caliphate for Allah.

"The Muslim Brotherhood has, as a matter of undeniable fact, established, built, and maintained control over most of the prominent Muslim organizations in America."

"They have clearly stated their goal of one day seeing a Muslim president at the helm of what once was 'Old Glory'."

"Yes, whether you believe it or not, The Muslim Brotherhood has laid out a 'Phased Plan' to transform the USA into a Caliphate ruled by Islamic Law (Sharia Law)."

"Impossible? The Muslim Brotherhood not only believes it possible, but certain to happen." [11]

"...[W]e will stand against the whole world and will not cease until the annihilation of all [infidels]" ... "Either we shake one another's hands in joy at the victory of Islam in the world, or all of us will turn to eternal life and martyrdom." [12]

---

[11] Islam in the American Government: The Plan, Maoz Report, January 2015.

[12] Speech by Ayatollah Ruhollah Khomeini, Iran

Chapter VII

2002 Memorandum
"A Strategic Plan to Spread 'Sharia Law' Worldwide"
by Saudi King Fahd bin Abdul Aziz

Just months after nineteen Islamic terrorists flew four airplanes into US targets on September 11, 2001, King Fahd of Saudi Arabia issued a written memorandum, establishing a six-step strategic plan:

> 1) to instruct Muslims residing in non-Muslim countries around the World, to form their own segregated communities and not to assimilate with non-Muslims; and
>
> 2) to accelerate the implementation of Sharia Law in non-Muslim countries.

The memorandum set forth an entire management system, using the Institute of Muslim Minority Affairs [IMMA] as a vehicle to achieve specific goals. In the United States, IMMA will work through the Islamic Society of North America [ISNA], the Muslim Student Association [MSA], Council on American Islamic Relations [CAIR], and the North American Islamic Trust [NAIT] to **"Plan, Oversee, and Accomplish"** the following goals: [1]

> 1) To recruit individual Muslims, who live in non-Muslim lands, and transform them into collective units by establishing cultural centers, educational programs, mosques, and other organizations, in order to stop assimilation in non-Muslim nations;
>
> 2) These collective units can influence non-Muslim host nations by shifting the demographic scale due to their population growth in favor of the Saudi agenda;

---

[1] *A Strategic Plan to Spread 'Sharia Law' Worldwide,* Memorandum by Saudi King Fahd bin Abdul Aziz, Reaud, Saudi Arabia, 2002

3) A gradual implementation of "Sharia Law" will ensure that Islam will become a major revolutionary powerhouse;
4) These will tilt the host nation in favor of Muslims due to their increase as a population;
5) This is a transformation which encourages the host nation to gradually begin to implement Wahhabi-style Sharia Law; and
6) The host state will then join the "Muslim Commonwealth."

Portions of the 2002 Memorandum are translated into English below.

"The Muslim societies in all the continents of all the world exist either as 'Muslim Nations' or 'Muslim Minorities.' The assessment to determine what constitutes a 'state' vs. a 'minority state' is done based on numerous measures. First, the numbers scale: if the number of Muslims in a nation exceeds half its population and its constitution states (declares) that Islam is its official religion and that Islamic 'Sharia Law' is its source of (its) law, this state is considered an Islamic state." [ln 1: p 29]

"The number of Muslims has risen greatly in the last years to where their population now exceeds 1.3 billion. Of these more than 900 million reside in Muslim nations and an additional 400 million live as communities and as Muslim minorities in non-Muslim nations." [ln 1: p 31]

"In Africa, 250 million Muslims reside; and in Europe, 60 million Muslims reside; and in North and South America 10 million Muslims reside. Extrapolating from these statistics, it is expected that the number of Muslims world-wide will reach 2.6 billion within a short time span."

"The Muslims will then become a mighty and effective power in the world, shifting the demographic balance in their favor." [ln 1: p 32]

As Muslim populations have increased in countries throughout Africa, Asia, Europe, and the Western Hemisphere, they have become natural targets for ISIS and ISIS affiliates to recruit new Jihadi terrorists. ISIS has been effective in utilizing the Internet and US social platforms to spread their hatred and gain support for their cause of **"World Dominance."**

Since 2015, a slick monthly magazine has been broadcast by ISIL around the world on the Internet. The focus is to recruit citizens from within Western nations to become active combatants within their own nations or to join ISIL in the armed fight throughout the Middle East and around the globe.

Failed Islamic states (i.e., Afghanistan, Libya, Pakistan, Somalia Syria, Yemen, and Kosovo) plus the Balkan countries of Macedonia and Bosnia Herzegovina have become training grounds for Islamic fighters.

ISIL ... the Islamic State in Iraq and the Levant

Under the leadership of the Trump administration and with the military prowess of America, great progress has been made in diminishing the influence of ISIL in Iraq and Syria. Most of the area in these two countries once occupied by ISIL is now free of terrorist threats.

While the reduction in ISIL forces in Iraq and Syria has been significant, one cannot ignore the fact that Jihadi terrorists frequently fight from the shadows of residential neighborhoods, so they can retreat and reorganize after skirmishes with local military or police.

In addition, ISIL has expanded the scope of their theater of operation by officially declaring the 3rd Caliphate to be operational from Morocco to Southeast Asia and from Southern Europe to the Congo. They believe that this declaration gives them governing authority over the entire area. A more complete discussion of these developments is presented in Chapter IX, pages 79 - 88.

POLITICAL CORRECTNESS WILL DESTROY AMERICA

The Muslim Brotherhood and its affiliated entities have already made great strides in accomplishing the aforementioned goals in America. Utilizing the practice of *"taqiyya"* (lying to infidels, as they are required by the Koran), Islamic Supremacists have:

1) Impacted the US Military and Military Chaplains;
2) Impacted the Prison System and Prison Chaplains;
3) Forced the re-writing of FBI Training Manuals & Interrogation Procedures Manuals;
4) Created at least 32 "No Go Zones" in America;
5) Transformed Public Education;
6) Affected the Media;
7) Begun to transform our legislative system:
   a) to compromise the principles of the US Constitution;
   b) to embrace Sharia Law; and
   c) to implement the cultural mores of Islam; and
8) Attempted to replace the federal, state, and local court systems with "Sharia Law Courts."

America must institute "Constitutional Discipline" in each of these areas!!

"THE CALL TO ACTION" on pages 145 & 146

"America Must Be Awakened !!"

Chapter VIII

"March to World Dominance"

20-Year Strategic Plan for World Dominance: 2001 - 2020 [1]

1. **"The Awakening"**   **2001 to 2003**
   Attacks on high-value, US targets on 9/11, after many years of planning and a series of smaller attacks on non-US targets, designed to make al-Qaeda a central player on the global scene;
2. **"Opening The Eyes"**   **2003 to 2006**
   Transformation of al-Qaeda into a "Global Movement";
3. **"The Arising and Standing Up"**   **2007 to 2010**
   Focus on terrorist destabilization of "Western Friendly, Islamic Regimes";
4. **"The Toppling of the Western Friendly, Islamic Regimes";**
                                                            2010 to 2013
   Egypt, Libya, Turkey and other Islamic states
5. **"The Formation of a New World Order"**   **2013 to 2016**
   "The Third Islamic Caliphate", becomes a world power, operating from the Middle East, North Africa and beyond;
6. **"Global Confrontation"**   **2016 to 2020**
   Between Islam and the Western cultures of Europe and America;
7. **"Decisive Global Victory for Islam"**   **2020 !!!**

---

[1] "The Zawahiri Letter and the Strategy of Al-Qaeda"; July 9, 2005, from Ayman al-Zawahari to Abu Musah, outlining the stages of action, leading to the establishment of "The Third Caliphate" & "The Ultimate Victory of Islam over Western Civilization;" *Current Trends in Islamist Ideology*, vol. 3, February 16, 2006 by Shmuel Bar and Yair Minzilil, Hudson Institute.

Detailed Plans of
"March to World Dominance"

PHASE #1: "THE AWAKENING" 2001 TO 2003

"The Making of al-Qaeda a Central Player on the Global Scene"

Events over the past century have set the stage for "Civilization Jihad" to be successful on the European continent and the North American continent.

In Europe, two devastating wars eliminated much of two generations from the population. Infrastructure and production assets were destroyed and rebuilt; only to be destroyed and rebuilt again. In the second half of last century, the confluence of three events created a situation, particularly favorable to "Islamic Supremacists:" 1) a decline in birth rates in all European countries, well below the 2.1 per couple needed to maintain population stability; 2) an enormous Muslim immigration to assist in the reconstruction of war torn Europe; and 3) the use of "Civilization Jihad" by "Islamic Supremacists" to infiltrate all aspect of life in these countries.

Progressivism of the late 19th century and early 20th century had its nexus in **Marxism,** and then morphed into the totalitarian governmental forms which appeared in Europe (i.e., **Communism; Fascism; Nazism; and Socialism).** In America, progressivism had its start in the administration of President Woodrow Wilson and then gained momentum during the Presidencies of FDR and BHO.

Today, liberals have co-opted the name and redefined it to mean "progress." This allows them to throw of the negative connotations their big government objectives and "forcefully state" that they stand for the melioration of the "out dated" US Constitution and the "American way-of-life."

Following the death of Communism, totalitarian "State Controlled Islam" has gained prominence as the preeminent threat to freedom.

With the direct assistance from the liberal media and from progressive academia, the American public has been lied to and conditioned to accept Islam as a "peaceful religion" rather than the "brutal state system," governing all aspects of society: culture; education; business; banking; government; and religion.

Four research organizations have conducted extensive surveys on the opinions of Muslims in America and Muslims around-the-world to attain better understanding of the sentiments of Muslims towards: Islamic Supremacy, The Muslim Brotherhood, Sharia Law, and Jihad. The Pew Research Foundation, The Polling Company, Wenzel Strategies, and World Public Opinions obtained valuable information through numerous surveys from 2007 to 2015. (see Appendices G & H)

Islamic Supremacist Attacks Against American Interests

Since 1981, The Muslim Brotherhood and its affiliates (Al-Qaeda; Egyptian Islamic Jihad; Hezbollah; Hamas; & many others) have attacked American interests with increasing boldness. Finally, they did the "unimaginable" to government officials, by attacking America on American soil with the coordinated attacks of September 11, 2001.

These violent acts against civilian and military targets, reaffirmed Osama bin Laden's "1995 Declaration of War against the United States." With these attacks, The Muslim Brotherhood and al-Qaeda positioned themselves on the world stage as global terrorist organizations, capable of destroying Western targets anywhere at any time. (see list of Attacks on America Interests which follows)

The 3rd Jihad Attacks American Interests (partial list)

1972   a Pan Am 747 was hijacked by Muslims, diverted to Cairo and Blown up shortly after landing

1974   ***"The Phased Plan"*** issued by The Muslim Brotherhood

1979   Iranian Terrorists overthrew the Shah of Iran and occupied the US Embassy in Tehran, Iran for 444 days

1979   The Organization of the Islamic Revolution in the Arabian Peninsula declaration ... "the people all over the Islamic countries are with the Iranians. The people in the Arabian Peninsula are sharing with the rest of the Muslim peoples their will in establishing "The ISLAMIC GOVERNMENT of the WHOLE UNIVERSE"

1981   Assassination of Egyptian President Anwar Sadat by Egyptian Islamic Jihad and The Muslim Brotherhood.

1982   *"The Project"* issued by The Muslim Brotherhood.

1983   Bombing of Marine Barracks in Lebanon by Hezbollah & The Muslim Brotherhood.

1983   Bombing of US Embassy in Beirut, Lebanon by Hezbollah & The Muslim Brotherhood.

1983   SAAR Foundation established by The Muslim Brotherhood as Umbrella organization over a cluster of 100 charities & think tanks.

1988   Pan Am flight 103 was bombed by The Muslim Brotherhood.

1988   **International Institute of Islamic Thought (IIIT)** Think tank committed to the "Islamization of Knowledge," founded by **The Muslim Brotherhood.**

1991   **"Explanation Memorandum on the General Strategic Goals of the Group"** issued by The Muslim Brotherhood.

1991   Al Taqwa Bank (Lugana, Switzerland with branches in Italy, Liechtenstein and the Bahamas) founded by leaders of The Muslim Brotherhood.

1993   Bombing of World Trade Center, New York City, USA by al-Qaeda.

1995   Osama Bin Laden declares war on the United States by al-Qaeda.

1996   Bombing of Khobar Towers Marine Barracks, Saudi Arabia by Hezbollah and Iranian Revolutionary Guard Corps.

1998   Bombing of US Embassies in Kenya and Tanzania by al-Qaeda.

2000   Attack on the destroyer, US Cole by al-Qaeda.

2001   9-11 Attack on World Trade Center and Pentagon by al-Qaeda.

2002   The *"Memorandum"* by the King of Saudi Arabia to spread Islam through-out the United States; to implement Sharia Law in America.

2005   *"March to World Dominance"* Ayman al-Zawahiri letter to Abu Musab: "The Third Caliphate" 20 Year Strategic Plan for World Dominance: 2001 – 2020.

PHASE #2: "OPENING THE EYES" 2003 TO 2006

"Transforming al-Qaeda into a 'Formative Global Movement'."

Islamic Supremacists -- War in Europe

In 2002, a German constitutional court ruled that the German school system in Berlin must teach its Muslim students, who are the majority population in a particular elementary school district, a Muslim curriculum. [2]

On 11 March 2004, a Muslim terrorist group, inspired by al-Qaeda, attacked the public train system in Madrid with 10 bombs, killing 191 persons and most assuredly effected the outcomes of the elections held just days later. [3]

On 2 November 2004, the murderer of Theo Van Gogh on a street in Amsterdam, [4] left a letter pinned with the knife to the victim's chest, stating, "I surely know that you, Oh America, will be destroyed: I surely know that you, Oh Europe, will be destroyed …" [5]

On 7 July 2005, a succession of four coordinated suicide bombings rocked London, exploding in three locations on the London Underground and at street level on a double-decker bus. [6]

In the fall of 2005, the French experienced a series of riots by Muslims on the streets of Paris and 270 other cities in France. Martial law restored peace: 2,888 arrests; 126 police injured; 8973 cars damaged; 200 million Euros in damage. [7] [8]

---

[2] *Why German Public Schools Now Teach Islam*, by Isabella de Pommereau, The Christian Science Monitor, Jan. 20, 2010.

[3] ibid #1

[4] *Reconstructing the Death of Theo Van Gogh*, NOVA, 25 Jan 2005.

[5] *Terror on Trial in the Netherlands,*"Aing. Org, 20 November 2005.

[6] *"7/7 Anniversary: The UK's Risks of Terror Attack Higher Now Than Days of London Bombing"*: Yorkshire Post, 4 July 2015.

[7] *"Ethnicity, Islam and les banlieues: Confusing the Issues,* Jocelyne Cesari, November 2005.

[8] *France's Burning Issue: Understanding the Riots of November 2005,* Canet, R; L. Pench; M. Stewart, November 2008.

Islamic Supremacists -- War in Africa

In Nigeria and the Sudan, Muslims regularly target and kill Christians and burn their churches and villages, with the support of the respective federal governments. Sudan has been infamous in the brutality of the attacks, killing refugees in UN camps established for their safety. Public crucifixion of Christians is still being used to terrorize the people. [9]

When the 2002 Miss World Beauty Pageant was held in Nigeria, Muslims protested the event. When a western journalist wrote a response which some Muslims deemed offensive, the newspaper office was burned down, 200 people were killed and 500 injured. [10]

Islamic Supremacists -- War in the Middle East

Hamas (Gaza) and Hezbollah (Lebanon) continue their relentless rocket attacks and string of homicide bomber attacks against the people of Israel.

On September 19, 2006, the President of Iran, Mahmoud Ahmadinejad, while addressing the UN General Assembly, prayed for the arrival of the twelfth Iman (the Islamic messiah) to usher in an era of "world peace" through the conversion of all people to Islam. He openly admitted that as many as two billion people could be killed. Muslim etiology, the study of end times prophesy, claims that the appearance of the "Islamic messiah" must be proceeded by a worldwide conflict to cleanse the earth of all "infidels." [11]

Islamic Supremacists -- War Against America

The mismanagement of wars in Afghanistan and Iraq has cost America thousands of lives and trillions of dollars. We also have lost the trust of our allies and the respect of our enemies. Our leaders have failed to understand our enemies. Therefore, we failed to appropriately attack the enemy; and to destroy them.

---

[9]   www.catholic.org/news/international/africa, September 25, 2009.

[10]   *The Miss World Riots: Continued Impunity for Killings in Kaduna,* Human Rights Watch, July 2003

[11]   Transcript of Ahmedinejad UN Speech 16/9/06, www.npr.org/templates/story.

America has experienced an even bigger loss at home. Our leaders failed to **"KNOW OUR ENEMIES,"** and therefore, caused us to **"FAIL"** in our ability to effectively counter the stealth and violent attacks against us.

Unspoken alliances have been formed between Islamic Supremacists and the "Blame American First" Movement:

> American Left
> Mainstream Media
> Progressive Academia

The hatred spread through many entities has re-enforced this cooperation and amplified its impact:

> Mosques and Islamic Cultural Centers
> Islamic Charitable Organizations
> Prisons and Islamic "No Go Zones"

RECALL:

**"Killing the infidels is our religion;
Slaughtering them is our religion;
Until they convert to Islam or pay us tribute."** [12]
-- Abu Musab al-Zarqawi, 2005

---

[12] ibid #1

PHASE #3:"THE ARISING AND STANDING UP"
2007 TO 2010

"Terrorist Destabilization of Western Friendly, Islamic Regimes"

Since 2008, America's image in the eyes of the people of the Middle East, North Africa and Central Asia has changed. The spread of anti-American sentiment, fostered by surging Islamic Supremacists, has widened and deepened.

In spite of the assassination of terrorist leader Osama bin Laden, al-Qaeda has not declined. It's organization, and its affiliates, have increased in overall influence; in specific political control; and in violent intimidation.

Prior to 2006, many of the countries in the Middle East and North Africa were led by Western friendly regimes. By 2012, that all had changed dramatically, with The Muslim Brotherhood and its surrogates dominating the political capitals of most countries.

Muslim Persecution of Christians Continues

Lebanon: Recall from chapter IV, that prior to 1960, Lebanon was a Christian-majority nation. Over the past 50 years, hundreds of thousands of Christians have been massacred, displaced or exiled, due to the so called "civil war." [13]

The **Sudan:** Since the Islamic take over in 1989, more than one million Christians have been killed because of their faith. [14]

Syria: A century ago, there were more than one million Christians living there. Today there are fewer than 1,000 Christians. [15]

Egypt: A century ago, there were also more than one million Christians living there. Today there are fewer than 50,000. [16]

---

[13] *"Drip-Drip Genocide; Muslim Persecution of Christians Continues;"* Gatestone Institute, Feb. 2017.

[14] ibid #1

[15] ibid #1

[16] ibid #1

Indonesia: More than half-million Christians have been displaced. [17]

Kosovo and **Chechnya** are other examples of how The Muslim Brotherhood and its surrogates have driven Christians out of a nation and gained control of many countries.

---

[17] ibid #1

PHASE #4: "TOPPLING OF WESTERN FRIENDLY, ISLAMIC REGIMES"   2010 – 2013+

The "Arab Spring" was a movement to over throw Pro-Western leaders in countries which the Islamist Supremacists wanted to control. Recall: The Muslim Brotherhood has at least three separate geographic strategies to spread Islam and to establish the "Global Caliphate." In the Middle East and North Africa, the Brotherhood does not view these countries as being individual countries, with unique boundaries and identities. They believe that these countries are opportunities to liberate the people from foreign occupation and to unite them under "Sharia Law." Placing new Islamic Supremacist leaders in these countries is part of establishing the "Global Caliphate."

The "Arab Spring" has had several different waves depending on the country: 1) uprising by local citizens with limited organization; 2) intensified demonstrations with participation by The Muslim Brotherhood, other Islamist groups, with Communist involvement; 3) pressure by foreign governments and the Obama administration; and 4) takeover by the new political leadership with establishment of a new Islamic government.

Chronological Order of Over Thrown Governments   [18]

Tunisia --- Nahda & Salafists (al-Qaeda): **2011 - 2012**
Ben Ali regime (western friendly), suppressed political institutions and democratic opposition for years. Nahda and Salafists were given access to the White House and to the US State Department and were provided assistance from US-funded non-governmental organizations for their political efforts.

Egypt --- Muslim Brotherhood & Salafists (al-Qaeda): **2011 - 2012**
The western friendly, Mubarak administration was politically helpful to US on many occasions. The Obama administration did not support student/worker demonstrators in first wave; but moved quickly to endorse The Muslim Brotherhood 2nd wave; and the Communists 3rd wave. Mubarak resigned under extreme pressure from President Obama. New elections were ordered. The Muslim Brotherhood won a plurality, but not majority, and had to form a coalition government, with Mohamed Morsi of The Muslim Brotherhood as President.

---

[18] *TimeLine of the Arab Spring*, Wikipedia

Libya --- Salafists (al-Qaeda) & Muslim Brotherhood: **2011 - 2012**

From the very beginning, US supported the rebels in the over throw of the western friendly, Gaddafi regime. US supplied weapons, ammunition, advisers to the rebels through Benghazi.

Yemen --- Islah Party (MB) & Salafists (al Qaeda): **2011 - 2013**

Demonstrations for resignation of President Ali Abdallah Saleh. The army killed or jailed more than a thousand. When soldiers quit and joined rebels, the Communists & Salafists filled the political void.

Algeria --- Islamists: **2011 - 2012**

Discontent swelled as President Bouteflika sought fourth term. United States championed special elections in 2012. Islamists gained power in new Parliamentary coalition.

Syria --- al-Qaeda and The Muslim Brotherhood: **2012 - 2014**

The regime of Bashar al-Assad was under attack by Free Syria Army (al-Qaeda) supported by arms shipments by US.

Sudan --- Salafists and Muslim Brotherhood: **2011 - 2014**

Sudan is two separate nations; Arab Republic of Sudan in the north (under control of Salafists & The Muslim Brotherhood) and Republic of South Sudan in the south (Christian). The south has been under continuous attack by the military forces of Omar al Bashir's Islamic regime (north). Two million South Sudanese have been killed or relocated to UN refugee camps.

Morocco --- Justice Party (MB) & Salafists (al Qaeda): **2014**

United States called for King Mohammed to reduce his control and to accept a new power-sharing with Islamists controlled Parliament.

President Obama's support, on numerous occasions, for the ouster of a US ally in the Middle East and North Africa, and his support for replacement leaders, with radical Islamic Supremacist ideologies, has been a great detriment to US foreign policy and has reduced our effectiveness in containing and defeating radical Islam. The Western friendly leaders had been supported for many decades by previous US administrations (Kennedy; Johnson; Nixon; Ford; Reagan; G. H. W. Bush; Clinton; and G. W. Bush).

PHASE #5: "THE FORMATION OF A NEW WORLD ORDER"   2013 TO 2016

"The Third Islamic Caliphate of the Middle East, North Africa & Beyond"

The proclamation of the establishment of "The Third Caliphate" has been decreed by ISIL (see chapter IX). The Muslim Brotherhood and its affiliate organizations, including ISIL, continue to exercise considerable influence over political and economic developments in the region from Pakistan to Morocco and from Turkey to Nigeria (see map of The 3rd Caliphate on page 84). They continue to ferment tensions and frequently justify violence to advance their ideology and/or to keep people groups in line. The violence is usually carried out by the local terrorist group, so as to allow The Muslim Brotherhood to keep its distance and to play more acceptable political roles.

Conversion to Islam is paramount.

Implementation of Sharia Law in all countries is the "Absolute Goal".

ISIS (Islamic State of Iraq and Syria) was formed in 2013 by an off shoot of al-Qaeda in Syria. These individuals didn't think that al-Qaeda was violent enough in attacking the Syrian regime of Bashar al-Asad. In 2014, ISIS crossed into Iraq, invading cities/towns and occupying large areas of northern Iraq.

In June 2014, ISIS announced the formation of the "Islamic Caliphate of Syria and Iraq," covering eastern Syria and northwestern Iraq, declaring that it was now a separate country. Raqqa (major city in Syria) was proclaimed as their capital.

All "Islamic Supremacist" groups have been, and will continue to be, embolden by the actions of ISIL. The lack of an effective foreign policy response by the United States under the Bush and Obama administrations has been judged as weakness and indifference by Muslims world-wide.

PHASE #6: "GLOBAL CONFRONTATION BETWEEN ISLAM AND THE WESTERN CULTURES OF EUROPE & AMERICA" 2016 – 2020

World Government Summit

February 11-14, 2018, the Sixth Annual World Government Summit was held in Dubai, United Arab Emirate, sponsored by the Organization for Economic Co-Operation and Development (Paris, France). The purpose was to once again bring together top globalists, Communists, and Islamists. [19]

World Government Summit Chairman, Mohammed Abdullah Al Gergawi, who also serves as "Minister of the Future," boasted that the Summit was a "permanent knowledge platform" for *Governance of the Future*. This will prepare all governments to participate in a movement toward a new world order. "Through the World Government Summit, we seek to create new models of international cooperation," he continued, touting the agenda of "His Highness Sheikh Mohammed bin Rashid Al Maktoum." The goal is to "prepare for the future within the framework of global efforts to achieve common goals." [20]

In an official press release issued at the end of the Summit, organizers said the event ended with "a plea for institutions to realign with the **'New World Order'**." [21]

This was a very anti-American, three-day globalist summit," reported WorldNetDaily, pointing to various anti-American, anti-Trump rants by celebrities and globalist bigwigs, that made America the "number 1 enemy." Beyond promoting the government takeover of healthcare – a key goal of "Progressives," Communists, and NWO globalists everywhere – a number of speakers also promoted a radical restructuring of government education to help centrally plan the economy. Sheikh Abdullah bin Zayed, Minister of Foreign Affairs and

---

[19] https://amac.us/creepy-world-government-summit-targets-america-freedom; March 11, 2018.

[20] ibid #1

[21] ibid #1

International Co-operation, UAE stated, "We should rethink (education) in unprecedented manner and break old molds." "We need a new system of education that looks into a country's future economic requirements." [22]

The Muslim Brotherhood Organizations in U.S.

An Egyptian government website features a warning that The Muslim Brotherhood has "a lobby in the U.S. disguised as a network of civil society organizations." The United Arab Emirates has made similar statements. Both Egypt and the UAE have officially declared The Muslim Brotherhood as a terrorist entity. [23]

The Egyptian government's State Information Service has an entire section (branch) devoted to documenting the world-wide violence and terrorism of The Muslim Brotherhood. Egypt is furious with the U.S. for its stance on the Brotherhood.

In December 2013, Egyptian President El-Sisi, then serving as Defense Minister, told the Washington Post, that the U.S. has turned its back on Egypt and was misunderstanding the Islamist group. The official U.S. response in 2013, represented the position of President Obama, a Muslim sympathizer. [24]

The international Muslim Brotherhood designated representative in America is Amin El-Ara. "He is responsible for re-establishing the connection between The Muslim Brotherhood and the West, which was significantly broken in 2013, after the fall of former Egyptian President Mohammed Morsi (member of The Muslim brotherhood). El-Ara belongs to one of the most respected families of Hamas, the ruling political party in Gaza. His father was one of the founders of Hamas in Gaza, along with arch-terrorist Ahmed Yassin. [25]

[22] ibid #1
[23] https://clarionproject.org/egypt-warns-muslim-brotherhood-organizations-us/January 15, 2015.
[24] ibid #5
[25] ibid #5

While President Trump has on several occasions expressed his concerns about The Muslim Brotherhood, even going so far as to imply that they are a supporter of violent Jihad, he has not followed through on a promise he made to have the Brotherhood officially declared a terrorist organization by the U.S. State Department.

Muslim Brotherhood Calls for Uprising Against U.S.

In response to President Trump's recognition of Jerusalem as Israel's capital, The Muslim Brotherhood has been fomenting anti-America sentiment. They have "launched a solidarity call with all Palestinian factions and other Islamic movements to ignite an uprising throughout the Islamic world against the Zionist occupation and the American administration in support of the occupation and against the rights and freedoms of the Muslim peoples." [26]

---

[26] https://clarionproject.org/muslim-brotherhood-declares-us-enemy/

PHASE #7: "DECISIVE GLOBAL VICTORY FOR ISLAM: DECLARED"   2020 !!!

Since the 7th century, in the time of Muhammad, Islamic Supremacists have envisioned World Dominance, over every aspect of peoples' lives. This led them to forcibly establish the 1st Caliphate (634 – 1145 AD) and the 2nd Caliphate (the Ottoman Empire 1278 – 1920 AD). [27] [28] [29] [30]

With the founding of The Muslim Brotherhood in 1928 by Hassan Al-Banna, the vision has transitioned from planning to specific action plans for selected regions of the globe. In 1984, the Muslim Brotherhood printed the "Five Phased Plan" for taking over any country in the world. In 1991, they printed the "Explanation Memorandum on the General Strategic Goals of the Group" … "A Strategic Plan for America." [31] [32]

In 2002, Saudi King Fahd bin Abdul Aziz issued a Memorandum entitled: **"A Strategic Plan to Spread 'Shari'a Law' Worldwide."** [33]

On July 9, 2005, Ayman al-Zawahari wrote a letter to Abu Musah, outlining the stages of action, leading to the establishment of "The Third Caliphate" & "The Ultimate Victory of Islam over Western Civilization."

---

[27] *German Soldiers in the Ottoman Empire, 1835-1918*; Oliver Janz, Freie Universitat Berlin

[28] Ibid #1

[29] A Century of War: Anglo-American Oil Politics and the New World Order; William Engdahl

[30] Turkey, The Great Powers and the Bagdad Railway; Edward Meade Earle: Russell and Russell; 1923 (reprint 1966)

[31] *Phases of the World Underground Movement Plan,* paper specifying Five Phases of The Muslim Brotherhood Movement in North America, obtained in raid on Elbarassee home (Virginia),

[32] "Explanation Memorandum on the General Strategic Goals of the Group" … "A Strategic Plan for America;" Moham Okrom, May 1991.

[33] *A Strategic Plan to Spread 'Sharia Law' Worldwide,* Memorandum by Saudi King Fahd bin Abdul Aziz, Reaud, Saudi Arabia, 2002

In July 2014, the 3rd Caliphate was declared by ISIS. It spans fifteen time-zones from Morocco to the Philippines and from southern Europe down to the Congo, including all of northern Africa.

"The March to World Dominance is Making Progress."

Chapter IX

ISIS ... ISIL ... "The 3ʳᵈ Caliphate"

Since the end of World War II, turmoil has reigned throughout the Middle East (from riots; to revolts; to civil wars) with the various sectarian factions fighting among each other. ISIS claims that this "partitioning of Muslim lands by the crusader power" ignored tribal alliances and lead to sectarian and ethnic divisions. [1]

ISIS has set forth a goal of "redrawing" the map of the Middle East "to liberate" Muslims in these occupied areas. Their goal was outlined in an article from the weekly ISIS web magazine, *The Islamic State Report*, a professionally, designed mouth-piece meant to recruit would-be Jihadi Fighters from the West. The fourth issue of this weekly web magazine, claimed to rectify the results of these past "injustices" and offers "justification" for redrawing the boundaries of the Middle East. [2]

History of al-Qaeda

al-Qaeda is a global militant, Islamic Supremacist organization founded by Osama bin Laden, Abdullah Azzam and other militants in late 1978. Its origins can be traced to the Soviet war in Afghanistan of the 1970's. [3]

al-Qaeda operates as a network comprised of both multi-national, stateless armies and radical Wahhabi Muslim movements, calling for strict interpretation of Sharia Law and Jihad. It has been designated as a terrorist organization by the United Nations Security Council, NATO, the European Union, the United States, Russia, India, Australia, Japan

---

[1] *The Master Plan: ISIS, al-Qaeda and the Jihadi Strategy for Final Victory,* Brian Fishman, Yale University Press, 2016.

[2] *The Islamic State Report,* ISIS website magazine (weekly), vol 1. #4.

[3] Al-Qaeda, Wikipedia & Wikipedia references.

and other countries. [4]

al-Qaeda has attacked civilian and military targets in various countries including: the 1998 US Embassy; 9/11 2001 attacks on the World Trade Center & The Pentagon; and the 2002 Bali bombings. The US government responded to the 9/11 attacks by launching in Afghanistan the poorly defined "War on Terror." [5]

With loss of key leaders, including Osama bin Laden, al-Qaeda's operations have evolved from actions that were controlled from the top down, to actions by "franchise associated groups" and by "lone wolf" operators, inspired by al-Qaeda terrorist propaganda.

al-Qaeda currently operates numerous training camps in Afghanistan, Pakistan, Iraq, Sudan and other countries. [6]

al-Qaeda ideologues envision the complete break from all foreign influences in Muslim countries and the establishment of a new "World-wide Islamic Caliphate." Among their beliefs is the conviction that a Christian-Jewish alliance is conspiring to destroy Islam. As Salafist Jihadists, they believe that the killing of civilians is religiously sanctioned. They ignore any aspect of religious scripture which might be interpreted as forbidding the murder of "infidels" (Muslim and non-Muslims), who do not practice "Sharia Law" as set forth in the Koran.

al-Qaeda also opposes all man-made laws. Man-made laws must be replaced with a strict form of "Sharia Law."

History of ISIS

ISIS is a Sunni, extremist Jihadist organization with no recognized state. They claimed Raqqa, Syria as their capital. They have declared the formation of "The 3rd Caliphate," which calls all Muslims to recognize ISIS authority over these lands. [7]

---

[4] ibid #3

[5] ibid #3

[6] ibid #3

[7] ISIS, Wikipedia & Wikipedia references.

The group originated as Jama'at al-Tawhid wal-Jihad in 1999 and was the forerunner of Tanzim Qaidat al-Jihad fi Bilad al-Rafidayn, commonly known as al-Qaeda in Iraq (AQI). Following the 2003 invasion of Iraq by coalition forces, AQI took part in the Iraqi insurgency against coalition forces and against Iraqi security forces. [8] In 2008, AQI joined other Sunni insurgent groups to form the Mujahideen Shura Council, which consolidated shortly afterwards into ISIS. [9]

In April 2013, ISIS changed its name to ISIL, the Islamic State of Iraq and the Levant, and extended their geographical area to encompass southern Turkey, all of Syria, northwestern Iraq, Jordan, Lebanon, Israel, Gaza, Cyprus and northern Saudi Arabia. [10]

Under the leadership of Abu Bakr al-Baghdadi, ISIL gained support throughout the Levant because of the perceived extended economic and political power. After entering the Syrian Civil War, ISIL established an even larger presence in the Syrian region of Raqqa. [11]

ISIL had close links to AQI until February 2014, when, after an eight-month power struggle, al-Qaeda cut its ties with ISIL, citing its failure to consult with AQI leadership and its notorious, violent acts against infidels.

Recently, ISIL and AQI have indicated a mutual desire to rejoin forces and to define common objectives. ISIL and al-Qaeda have been designated as terrorist organizations by the United Nations Security Council, NATO, the European Union, the United States, Australia, Canada, Turkey, Saudi Arabia, Indonesia, Israel and many other countries. [12]

History of Khorasan

Khorasan is a small group of 100-250 experienced Jihadist, high-ranking members of al-Qaeda from various countries, who have separated themselves from al-Qaeda in Iraq (AQI) and operate in Syria with autonomy from AQI.

---

[8]   ibid #7
[9]   ibid #7
[10] ibid #7
[11] ibid #7
[12] ibid #7

The group is reported to be led by Muhsin al-Fadhli, a prominent al-Qaeda member who went from Pakistan to Iran after the 2001 US invasion of Afghanistan. Khorasan members are particularly proficient in bomb making.

US intelligence sources state that Khorasan Jihadists have worked with bomb-makers from al-Qaeda Yemen, including Ibrahim al-Asiri, to target civilian aircraft heading to the United States and other western targets. Frenchman David Drugeon (Khorasan leader and bomb-maker) was killed in Syria by a missile from a US drone on 5 November 2014. Another high-level Khorasan leader, Abu Yusuf Al-Turki, a Turkish national and Jihadist, was reported to have been killed on 23 September 2014 by air strikes in Syria. [13]

It is reported that Khorasan has as its goal, to identify targets in the United States and to participate in the implementation of "Sharia Law" in America. On 5 October 2014, FBI Director James Comey stated, "I can't sit here and tell you whether their plan is tomorrow or three weeks or three months from now," but that "we have to act as if it's coming tomorrow." [14]

THE 3RD CALIPHATE

In June 2014, Abu Bakr al-Baghdadi, Caliph, leader of ISIL, proclaimed a world-wide caliphate, starting with The Levant and expanding to liberate all lands form Southern Europe to the Congo River and from Western bulge of Africa to India, extending on to Thailand, Singapore, Indonesia and the Philippines.

(see map of the **The 3ʳᵈ Caliphate**; page 84)

---

[13]   Khorsan, Wikipedia,& Wikipedia references.

[14]   ibid #13

ISIS has also announced ten new "nation state identities," covering more than forty regional areas of the 3rd Caliphate, baring ancient Islamic tribal names and uniting tribal groups with similar ancestry. [15] [16]

ANDALUS	Iberian Peninsula (Spain & Portugal)
MAGHREB	Western bulge of Africa
The LAND of HABASHA	Central Africa across to Somalia
The LAND of ALKINANA	Libya, Sudan, Egypt, Southern Sudan
YAMAN	Yemen
HIJAZ	Saudi Arabia & Qatar
SHAM	Lebanon, Jordan, Israel, Gaza
IRAQ	Iraq
ANATHOL	Turkey
KHURASAN	Afghanistan, Pakistan, India, Iran, Kazakhstan, Turkmenistan, Uzbekistan

(partial list of national identities declared by ISIS to be the 3rd Caliphate: not all inclusive)

---

[15] *From Paper State to Caliphate: The Ideology of the Islamic State,* Cole Bunzel, The Center for Middle East Politics, Brookings Institute, March 2015.
[16] *Does Abu Bakr al-Baghdadi and his Caliphate Mark the Beginning of the Third World War?,* Sheldon Filger, Huffington Post, September 2014.

The 3rd Caliphate (declared by ISIS 2015)

ISIS HAS MORE THAN 43 AFFILIATES WORLDWIDE

On February 5, 2016, United Nations Secretary-General Ban Ki-moon said, "… more than 34 terrorist organizations have pledged allegiance to ISIS.

The recent expansion of the ISIS sphere of influence, across western & northern Africa; the Middle East; and southern & southeastern Asia, demonstrates the speed and scale at which the gravity of the ISIS threat has evolved in just 18 months."

In 2017, Intel Center, a counter-terrorist company, put the number of ISIS affiliates and ISIS supporter organizations at more than 43.

Afghanistan:	al-Tawheed Brigade in Khorasan Heros of Islam Brigade in Khorasan
Algeria:	al-Huda Battalion in Maghreb of Islam The Soldiers of the Caliphate in Algeria al-Ghurabaa Djamaat Houmat ad-Da'wa as-Salafiya Al-Ansar Battalion
Egypt:	Jamaat Ansar Bait al-Maqdis Jund al Khilafah in Egypt Mujahideen Shura Council in the Environs of Jerusalem
India:	Ansar al-Tawhid in India
Indonesia:	Jemaah Anshorut Tauhid Mujahideen Timot
Iraq:	Ansar al-Islam
Lebanon:	Liwa Ahrar al-Sunna in Baalbek
Libya:	Islamic Youth Shura Council Islamic State Libya Shura Council of Shabab al-Islam DarnahLions of Libya
Nigeria:	Boko Haram
Pakistan:	Jundullah Tehreek-e-Khilafar Mujahid in Khorasan

Philippines:	Abu Sayyaf GroupAnsaral-Khilafah
	Bangsamoro Islamic Freedom Fighters
	Bangsamoro Justice Movement
	Jemaah Islamiyah
Russia:	Central Sector of Kabardino-Balakria of the
	Caucasus Emirate
	The Nokhchico Wilayat of the Caucasus
	Emirate
Somalia:	al-Shabaab Jubba Region Cell Bashir Abu
	Numan
Syria:	Jasish al-Sahabah in the Levant
	Martrs of al-Yarmouk Brigade
	Faction of Katibar al-Iman Bukhari
Saudi Arabia:	Supporters of the Islamic State in the
	Land of the Two Holy Mosques
Sudan:	al-I'tisam of the Koran and Sunnah
Tunisia:	Okba Ibn Nafaa Battalion Jund al-Khilafah
	in Tunisia Mujahideen of Tunisia of
	Kairouan
Uzbekistan:	Islamic Movement of Uzbekistan
Yemen:	Mujahideen of Yemen
	Supporters for the Islamic State in Yemen

ISIS Inroads into America

During the first quarter 2018, ISIS had been driven out of Iraq and Syria, but they and their affiliates are now well organized and aggressively active in more than 34 other countries.

As of February 2018, the FBI has more than 1,000 active investigations into ISIS terrorist activities in America, at least one in all fifty states. Federal prosecutors have charged 159 individuals in 28 states and the District of Columbia with plotting domestic terrorist attacks or with traveling/attempting to travel abroad to participate in terror attacks in America. 107 individuals have pleaded guilty or have been found guilty at trial.

ISIS IN AMERICA
FROM RETWEETS TO RAQQA

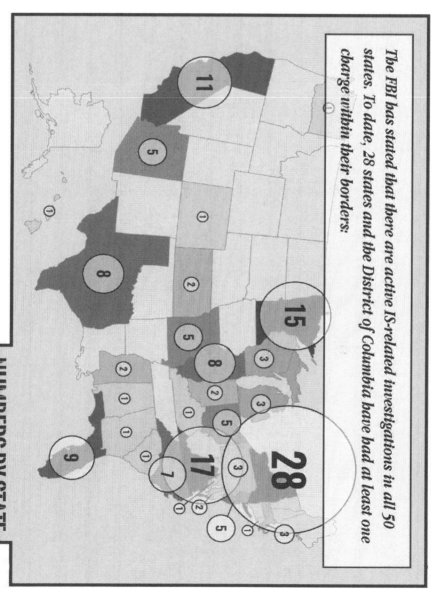

The FBI has stated that there are active IS-related investigations in all 50 states. To date, 28 states and the District of Columbia have had at least one charge within their borders:

NUMBERS BY STATE

Chapter X

"The Evil Within" - The United States Government

"A nation can survive its fools, and even their ambitions. But it cannot survive treason from within. An enemy at the gates is less formidable, for he is known and carries his banners openly. But the traitor moves among those within the gates freely, his sly whispers rustling through all the alleys, heard in the very halls of government itself. For the traitor appears not traitor, he speaks in accents familiar to his victims, and he wears their face and their garments, and he appeals to the baseness that lies deep in the hearts of all men. He rots the soul of a nation, he works secretly and unknown in the night to undermine the pillars of the city, he infects the body politic so that it can no longer resist. A murderer is less to be feared."

Marcus Tullius Cicero - Roman orator & statesman, circa 45 BC

TREASON: the offense of acting to overthrow one's government or to harm or kill its sovereign.

Webster's Universal College Dictionary

(**Author's Note:** The Islamist factions in this country are all continually exhibiting treasonous behaviors. They claim to be citizens, but, for the most part, they are clearly, under cover militants, committed to the total overthrow of the existing government of the United States.
Their long standing treasonous efforts were confirmed in 1995 when Osama Bin Laden and al-Qaeda declared war on the United States. The attacks of 9/11 were the first wave of that declaration of war.
Those Islamists, currently operating in this country, are aligned with those who attacked us on that fateful day)

The Muslim Brotherhood, Fountain of Islamic Violence

by Cynthia Farahat
Middle East Quarterly: **Spring 2017 - Vol XXIV: No. 2, page 3**

This text may be reposted or forwarded so long as it is presented as an integral whole with complete and accurate information provided about its author, date, place of publication, and original URL

(see **Appendix C, page 156** for complete article)

During the Obama years, it became common place for the US Administration and its Western Acolytes to portray The Muslim Brotherhood as a "moderate option" to more radical Muslim groups. Thus, for example, US Director of National Intelligence, James Clapper, incredibly described the group as "largely secular," [1] while John Esposito of Georgetown University claimed that the "Muslim Brotherhood affiliated movements and parties have been a force for democratization and stability in The Middle East." [2]

On the other hand, in 2014, the United Arab Emirates formally designated the Muslim Brotherhood and its local and international affiliates, including its US based Council on American-Islamic Relations, as international terrorist groups. [3] [4]

A British government review, commissioned the same year, similarly asserted that ... parts of the Muslim Brotherhood have a highly ambiguous relationship with violent extremism. Both as an ideology and as a network, it has been a rite of passage for some individuals and groups who have gone on to engage in violence and terrorism. [5]

---

[1]   *ABC News*, February 10, 2011

[2]   John Esposito, "The Muslim Brotherhood, Terrorism and US Policy," The Huffington Post (New York), March 22, 2016.

[3]   Reuters, November 15, 2014.

[4]   The Washington Post, November 17, 2014.

[5]   Reuters, December 17, 2015.

THE QUESTION IS WHICH IS CORRECT ?
WITHOUT A DOUBT, THE SECOND ONE IS !

The Muslim Brotherhood has been a militaristic organization from its inception and has operated as a terrorist entity for almost a century. It influenced the establishment of most modern Sunni terrorist organizations, including al-Qaeda, al-Gama'a al-Islamiya (GI) Hamas, and the Islamic State (ISIS). These organizations have either been founded by current or former Brotherhood members or have been directly inspired, indoctrinated, or recruited by MB members and literature. Contrary to what the MB propagates to Westerners, MB violence is not just in the past but is an ongoing activity. [6]

CONCLUSION

The deadly Muslim Brotherhood cult is responsible for almost a century of terror, since the young al-Banna engaged in the intimidation and harassment of his Christian and moderate Muslim neighbors. Since then: 1) The Muslim Brotherhood established Hamas as its Palestinian wing; 2) Three Muslim Brotherhood activists established al-Qaeda; 3) The Muslim Brotherhood leaders, from inside their prisons, founded al-Gama'a al-Islamiyya; and Egyptian Islamic Jihad; 4) The Muslim Brotherhood members recruited the founder of Jama'at al-Tawhid wa-l-Jihad, which started the trend of video decapitations; and 5) one of its former operatives is currently acting as the Caliph of Islamic State. The Muslim Brotherhood also has other connections to organizations on the U.S. government's list of foreign terrorist organizations.

The Muslim Brotherhood has stated its intentions to destroy the West's "miserable house" by infiltrating Western society and institutions and by subverting them from within. [7] Designating The Muslim Brotherhood as a foreign terrorist organization will stop its operatives from reaching sensitive positions in the intelligence community and in other powerful US government positions. It will also stop Brotherhood operatives in America from funding terrorism operations world-wide.

---

[6] Rep. Dave Brat press release, Brat.House.gov, July 19,2016.

[7] *The Muslim Brotherhood's Strategic Plan for America—Court document*, The Clarion Project, Washington, D.C., accessed Sep. 1, 2016.

Council on American-Islamic Relations (CAIR)

Official Mission of CAIR: "To enhance understanding of Islam, encourage dialogue, protect civil liberties, empower American Muslims, and build coalitions that promote justice and mutual understanding."

Purpose: To function as public relations organization for The Muslim Brotherhood, the most powerful terrorist organization in the world.

CAIR: ISLAMISTS FOOLING THE ESTABLISHMENT

by Daniel Pipes and Sharon Chadha
Middle East Quarterly: **Spring 2006 – Vol. XIII No. 2, page 3**

This text may be reposted or forwarded so long as it is presented as an integral whole with complete and accurate information provided about its author, date, place of publication, and original URL

(see **Appendix D, page 170** for the complete article)

The Council on American-Islamic Relations (CAIR), headquartered in Washington, is perhaps the best-known and most controversial Muslim organization in North America. CAIR presents itself as an advocate for Muslims' civil rights and the spokesman for American Muslims. "We are similar to a Muslim NAACP," says its communications director, Ibrahim Hooper. [8]   The Official Mission — "to enhance understanding of Islam, encourage dialogue, protect civil liberties, empower American Muslims, and build coalitions that promote justice and mutual understanding" — suggests nothing problematic [9]

---

[8]   Columbus Dispatch (Ohio); January 1, 2002.
[9]   *What's CAIR's Vision and Mission*, CAIR website, accessed January 13, 2006.

Starting with a single office in 1994, CAIR now claims thirty-one affiliates, including a branch in Canada, with more steadily being added. In addition to its grand national headquarters in Washington, it has impressive offices in other cities; the New York office, for example, is housed in the 19-story Interchurch Center located on Manhattan's Riverside Drive.

But there is another side to CAIR that has alarmed many people in positions to know.

The Department of Homeland Security refuses to deal with it. Senator Charles Schumer (Democrat, New York) described it as an organization "which we know has ties to terrorism." [10] Senator Dick Durbin (Democrat, Illinois) observed that CAIR is "unusual in its extreme rhetoric and its associations with groups that are suspect." [11] Steven Pomerantz, the FBI's former chief of counterterrorism, noted that "CAIR, its leaders, and its activities effectively give aid to international terrorist groups." [12]

The family of John P. O'Neill, Sr., the former FBI counter-terrorism chief who perished at the World Trade Center, named CAIR in a lawsuit as having "been part of the criminal conspiracy of radical Islamic terrorism" [13] responsible for the September 11 atrocities. Counterterrorism expert Steven Emerson calls it "a radical fundamentalist front group for Hamas." [14]

---

[10] FDCH Political Transcript, September 10, 2003.

[11] *Bad CAIR Day: Ex-staffer pleads guilty to terror charges, Senate asks questions on 9/11 Anniversary,* accessed January 9, 2006.

[12] Joseph Farah, *Between the Lines, The Real CAIR, WorldNetDaily,* April 23, 2003; Steve Pomerantz, *Counterterrorism in a Free Society, the Journal of Counterterrorism and Security International;* Spring 1998.

[13] *Estate of John P. O'Neil, Sr. et al. vs. Al Baraka Investment and Development Corporation,* DanielPipes.org, accessed January 9, 2006.

[14] Steven Emerson, *Re: Terrorism and the Middle East Peace Process,* prepared testimony before the U.S. Senate Foreign Relations Committee, Subcommittee on Near East and South Asia, Mar. 19, 1996

International Institute of Islamic Thought (IIIT)

Official Mission of IIIT: "The subordination of scientific inquiry to 'the mere implementation of the assorted teachings of the Shari'a'. "

Purpose: To function as a think tank, committed to the "Islamization of Knowledge."

IIIT: ISLAMIST INFILTRATION OF AMERICAN UNIVERSITIES

by Ryan Mauro
Shillman Fekkow at the Clarion Project: March 19, 2018

This text may be reposted or forwarded so long as it is presented as an integral whole with complete and accurate information provided about its author, date, place of publication, and original URL

(see **Appendix L, page 247** for the complete article)

In 1988, an FBI source inside the Muslim Brotherhood revealed that the Islamist group's proxies in America had a six-phase plan to "institute the Islamic Revolution in the United States."[15]

Over the last three decades, IIIT's part in the Brotherhood's plan has met remarkable success. The institute has made itself an indispensable resource for Islamic scholarly studies: It has provided funding for over 70 active researchers based at institutions across America; it has spent millions of dollars on endowing chairs in Islamic studies;[16] and it has publicized the research of hundreds of like-minded academics at its Summer Institute for Scholars.[17]

---

[15] "Islamist Infiltration of American Universities." Clarion Project, 21 Mar. 2018, clarionproject.org/islamists-infiltration-american-universities/#_ftn1.

[16] ibid #15

[17] ibid #15

IIIT's activities are integral to the Brotherhood's broader strategy of inciting an international Islamic revolution. As an official IIIT handbook notes:

> *At a time when we are forced to fight and defend ourselves on political, economic and military fronts … (these efforts) can be accomplished by developing (the **Ummah's**, that is, the Muslim community's) ideological power and the power of the "islamization of knowledge (sic)" to effectively harness its full potential.*[18]

In other words, the long-term success of the Islamists' revolution is dependent not only on success on the battlefield and at the ballot, but also on the cooptation of education in order to foment popular sympathy for the Brotherhood's objectives.

While IIIT's actions are ostensibly nonviolent, it has not hesitated to cultivate ties to international terrorists. In 2002, an anti-terrorism taskforce raided the IIIT's office. Based on the evidence obtained in this investigation, U.S. Customs Service Special Agent David Kane said in a sworn affidavit that IIIT co-founder and former vice president for research, Jamal Barzinji, was "not only closely affiliated with PIJ [Palestinian Islamic Jihad] . . . but also with Hamas."[7]

While IIIT is unapologetic about its links to violent Islamism, it is less forthright about the sources of its generous revenue. It is clear that the Brotherhood provided the start-up money for IIIT in 1988, when the aforementioned FBI memo notes that the organization had almost "unlimited funds" at its disposal.[19] That was 30 years ago. Nevertheless, today, IIIT's assets appear undiminished. Yet IIIT's website does not solicit donations; indeed, a search for "donate" on the site returns no relevant information.

This raises the question:

Who is supporting IIIT today?

---

[18] ibid #15

[19] The website http://www.iiit.org/ provides The International Institute for Islamic Thought's description of its own activities. For IIIT's association with the Muslim Brotherhood, see FBI Memo, "An Analysis of Religious Divisions in the Muslim Community of Toronto," 1988. The document was obtained through FIOA by The Investigative Project on Terrorism (www.investigativeproject.org).

THE MYTHS SURROUNDING ISLAMIC SUPREMACY

Myth #1: "Only A Negligible Minority of Muslims Are Islamists."

It's simply not true. The vast, vast majority of Muslim [do] believe in the goals of Islamic Supremacists, even if they are unwilling to participate themselves in Jihad. Bernard Lewis explains, significant numbers of Muslims are ready to approve Jihad; and many of them to apply, the Jihad interpretation of their religion." [20]

Myth #2: "Not everyone who is 'Non-Violent' is Non-Islamist."

American groups like the Council of American-Islamic Relations and the Islamic Society of North America also reflect an Islamist worldview. Dr. Jalal Zuberi, Director of the Center for Islamist Pluralism states, 'that they support Hamas and The Muslim Brotherhood.' Yet, these organizations are routinely utilized as points of contact for governments at local, state and federal levels. The seed-bed of terrorism is a far larger community of people who agree with the terrorist views and 'tut-tut' their means." [21]

Myth #3: "The West Has No Part in Pushing Islamic Reform."

The notion here seems to be that only the Islamic world can produce reforms inside Islam. That's largely true. But the US federal government, and Western governments around the world, have an obligation to help identify reformers & moderates and to provide them support" … while resisting Islamic Supremacists. [22]

---

[20] *Fighting Islamism will Require Destroying these 3 Myths,* Ben Shapiro, Daily Wire, June 5, 2017.
[21] ibid #1
[22] ibid #1

"The Perception that We Can't Kill Enough Terrorists to Make a Difference is Wrong."

We Certainly Can: We Must !!

We must take All Measures to Protect Ourselves at home, including "Extreme Vetting!"

Bill Clinton Administration

PERSONNEL SYMPATHETIC TO ISLAMIC SUPREMACY

Partial List (see **Appendix E, page 197** for more details)

Huma Abedin, who served as Hillary Clinton's longtime Deputy Chief of Staff and has worked with her for more than 20 years, has known ties to The Muslim Brotherhood - an organization bent on destruction of western civilization and the United States. [23]

Abedin grew up in a family where her father, Sayed Z. Abedin, served on the Board of Directors of The Muslim Brotherhood. Her mother, Shelab Abedin, was a founding director of The Muslim Sisterhood and continues to be active in the organization. Her brother, on faculty at Oxford University, is an active member of the Muslim Brotherhood. She had to be significantly influenced by the beliefs and philosophies of the Brotherhood. [24]

She was assistant editor for a dozen years of the Journal of Muslim Minority Affairs for the Institute of Muslim Minority Affairs. The Institute -- founded by her late father and currently directed by her mother -- is backed by the Muslim World League, an Islamic organization headquartered in the Saudi holy city of Mecca, also founded by Muslim Brotherhood leaders. [25]

The 2002 Manifesto by Saudi King Fahd shows that, "Muslim Minority Affairs - the mobilizing of Muslims communities to spread Islam instead of assimilating into the population - is a key strategy in the ongoing effort to establish Islamic rule in the United States and a global Sharia or "Islamic law", the 3rd Caliphate of modern times. The Manifesto, commissioned by the ruling Saudi Arabian monarchy, places the work of an institute that employed Abedin at the forefront of a

---

[23] Huma Abedin, Wikipedia and Wikipedia Resources.

[24] ibid #1

[25] ibid #1

grand plan to mobilize U.S. Muslim minorities to transform America into a Saudi-style Islamic state, according to Arabic-language researcher Walid Shoebat." [26]

Abedin also was a member of the executive board of the Muslim Student Association, which was identified as a Muslim Brotherhood front group in a 1991 document introduced into evidence during the terror-financing trial of the Texas-based Holy Land Foundation. [27]

Abdurahman Alamoudi served in the Clinton Administration:

Goodwill Ambassador to the Muslim Community:
Advisor to Israel-Palestinian Peace Talks:
Advisor to Military & Prison Chaplain Oversight Committee.

American Muslim Council

1990: Alamoudi founded the American Muslim Council as a tax-exempt 501(c)(4) organization, described as a de facto front of The Muslim Brotherhood. The AMC's affiliate, the American Muslim Foundation, is a 501(c)(3) group to which contributions are tax-deductible.

1993 WTC Attack [28]

1993 March: Alamoudi assailed the federal government's case against Mohammed Salameh, who was arrested ten days after the first World Trade Center bombings in February: "All their [law enforcement] facts are - they are flimsy." Salameh was convicted in the bombing plot and is currently serving a life sentence in prison."

1994: Alamoudi complained that the judge picked on the 1993 World Trade Center bombers trail was picked because of their religion: "I believe that the judge went out of his way to punish the defendants harshly, and with vengeance, and to a large extent, because they were Muslim."

---

[26] ibid #1
[27] ibid #1
[28] Abdurahman Alamoudi, Wikipedia and Wikipedia Resources.

1996: Alamoudi called on President Clinton to "free Sheikh Omar Abdul Rahman," the Egyptian Islamic Jihad leader, serving a life sentence for his role in the early 1990s of bombings and the attempted bombings in New York, and for plotting to destroy civilian airliners.

Chaplains, the Wahhabi Lobby and The Muslim Brotherhood

From about 1993 to 1998, the Pentagon retained Alamoudi on an unpaid basis to nominate and to vet Muslim chaplain candidates for the U.S. military. [29]

The process for becoming a Muslim chaplain for any branch of the U.S. military, currently involves two separate phases. First, individuals must complete religious education and secondly, they must receive an ecclesiastical endorsement from an approved body. Federal investigators long have suspected three key groups in the chaplain program; 1) the Graduate School of Islamic & Social Sciences; 2) the American Muslim Armed Forces and Veterans Affairs Council; and 3) the Islamic Society of North America, each have strong links to terrorist organizations.

Support of Hamas

1994: Alamoudi began a public defense of Hamas: "Hamas is not a terrorist group ... I have followed the good work of Hamas ... they have a wing that is a violent wing. They have had to resort to some kind of violence." [30]

1995: Alamoudi continued his Hamas defense, arguing that "Hamas is not a terrorist organization. The issue for us (the American Muslim Council) is to be conscious of where to give our money, but not to be dictated to where we send our money." [31]

1996: Alamoudi spoke out in response to the arrest at New York's JFK Airport of his admitted friend, Hamas political bureau leader, Mousa Abu Marzook. Months after the arrest, Alamoudi blamed the

---

[29]   ibid #6

[30]   ibid #6

[31]   ibid #6

February 25th Hamas suicide bombings of Israeli citizens on Marzook's detention: "If he was there, things would not have gone in this bad way. He is known to be a moderate and there is no doubt these events would not have happened, if he was still in the picture." [32]

Grover Norquist introduced Abdurahan Alamoudi to President Clinton and was influential in securing positions in the Clinton 1992 Presidential Campaign and later in the Clinton Administration.

Norquist works as a lobbyist /consultant for many different organizations. He is particularly favored by Islamic entities, which prefer that he represent them. In addition, he is married to Samah Alrayyes, a Muslim. Norquist's sister, Loraine, is married to Majad Tomeh, also a Muslim. Both women graduated Harvard School of Business with MBA degrees.

Norquist founded:
> ATR Americans for Tax Relief
> CRC Center Right Coalition

Norquist co-founded with **Abdurahman Alamoudi and Majad Tomeh**:
> II Islamic Institute

Norquist co-founded with **Abdurahman Alamoudi** and **Khail Suffari**:
> Islamic Free Market Institute (IFMI)

---

[32] ibid #6

George W. Bush Administration

PERSONNEL SYMPATHETIC TO ISLAMIC SUPREMACY

Partial List (see **Appendix E, page 197** for more details)

Abdurahan Alamoudi

In 1998, leadership of The Muslim Brotherhood realized that they had very few contacts within the Republican party and that the 2000 US elections was up for grabs. They understood it is most likely that Al Gore would be the Democratic party nominee, but the Republican field was wide open. [33]

The Muslim Brotherhood asks Abdurahan Alamoudi to reach out through Jack Abramoff and Grover Norquist in order to establish himself with the Republican Party. It is well known that Abdurahan Alamoudi was the founder and president of the American Muslim Council and had been an effective fund raiser for the Democrats and for al-Qaeda. [34]

In spite of these troublesome associations, Abdurahan Alamoudi was invited to join the GW Bush campaign team as a liaison to the Muslim committee. After Bush won the election, Abdurahan Alamoudi was:

2001 Appointed to select, train & credential Muslim military & prison chaplains; and

2003 Tried, convicted and served time in federal prison (Al-Qaeda fund raiser). [35]

---

[33]   ibid #6
[34]   ibid #6
[35]   ibid #6

Legal Notes on Abdurahan Alamoudi

Abdurahan Alamoudi was arrested in late September 2003 at Dulles International Airport after law-enforcement authorities stopped him with $340,000 in cash, that he was trying to take to Syria. US officials allege that the money may have been destined for Syrian-based terrorist groups to attack Americans in Iraq. Charges include illegally receiving money from the Libyan government, passport and immigration fraud, and other allegations of supporting terrorists abroad and here in the United States.

As of 2018, Abdurahan Alamoudi is in jail, convicted on federal terrorism-related charges.[36]

Kaled Suffuri

Campaign Coordinator for Outreach to Muslims for GWB 2000.[37]

Ali Tulbah

Associate Director, White House Office of Cabinet Affairs;

President Bush Liaison to Arab/Muslim American communities;

President Bush Liaison to Arab/Muslim Int'l organizations. [38]

Sami Al-Arian

Enlisted Grover Norquist to lobby President Bush to abolish "Secret Evidence" law. The purpose of the cancelled White House meeting (scheduled: 9/11/2001) was to abolish this law;

Founded National Coalition to Protect Political Freedom (renamed Defending Dissents Foundation).

Al-Arian was tried and convicted of raising money for the Holy Land Foundation. He was deported. [39]

---

[36] ibid #6
[37] Kaled Sufri, Wikipedia and Wikipedia Resources.
[38] Ali Tublah, Wikipedia and Wikipedia Resources.
[39] Sami Al-Arian, Wikipedia and Wikipedia Resources.

Huzammil Siddiqui

Selected by Bush Administration to represent Muslim faith in the Ecumenical Memorial Service at the National Cathedral. He gave copy of Koran to President Bush, who responded, "the teachings of Islam are the teachings of peace and good." [40]

Grover Norquist

Introduced Abdurahan Alamoudi to President George W. Bush and was influential in securing positions for Alamoudi in the Bush 2000 Presidential Campaign and later in the Bush Administration.

From his earlier involvement in the founding of The Islamic Institute (II) and The Islamic Free Market Institute (IFMI) during the 1990's (Clinton Administration; page 99), Norquist extended his involvement with Islamic organizations to include the founding of:

CIC	The Conservative Inclusion Coalition
MFA	Muslims for America
ACDA	American Conservative Defense Alliance
CNAPI	Campaign for a New American Policy on Iran
NIAC	National Iranian American Council
OSPC	Open Society Policy Center (founded with George Soros)
IPS	Institute for Policy Studies (founded with Russian involvement)

---

[40] Huzammil, Siddiqui, Wikipedia and Wikipedia Resources.

On 9/11/2001, President George W. Bush was to Meet with Representatives of The Muslim Brotherhood & Affiliated Organizations

In early 2015, the Clarion Project received, long hidden, documents which listed who was to attend these 2 meetings with President Bush at the White House on 9/11/2001, upon his return from a trip to Florida. These meetings were arranged by Grover Norquist and Karl Rove. [41]

The purpose of these 2 meetings was to encourage President Bush to fulfill the commitment he had made during the 2000 Presidential Campaign. During one of the debates with Al Gore, President Bush stated that he would direct the US Department of Justice not to use "secret evidence" in the prosecution and subsequent deportation of terrorists. If such "secret evidence" was used, then it would be made public. [42]

3:05PM MEETING IN THE WHITE HOUSE OVAL OFFICE

President George W. Bush
Sec. Spenser Abraham: US Department of Energy
        additional administrative staff most likely present
Dr. Muzzamil Siddiqui: president, Islamic Society of North
        America
Khaled Saffuri: co-founder, Islamic Free Market Institute
Talat Othman: chairman, Islamic Free Market Institute
Dr. Yahya Basha: president, American Muslim Council
Dr. Amanullah Khan: vice-chairman, American Muslim Council
George R. Salem: president, Arab-American Institute and 1988
        Chairman Arab-Americans for George H. W. Bush

---

[41]   *G. W. Bush was to Meet Muslim Brotherhood Affiliates on 9/11*, Meira Svirsky, Clarion Project, April 2, 2015.

[42]   ibid #1

These meetings had originally been scheduled for March 5, 2001. Ironically, when they were cancelled, they were re-scheduled for September 11, 2001.

3:30PM MEETING IN THE ROOSEVELT ROOM

President Bush

John Dilulio: Director, Office of Faith-Based & Community
    Initiatives
Ali Tulbah: Associate Director, Office of Cabinet Affairs
Suhail Khan: staff official, Office of Public Liaison
Nina Shokrail Rees: Dep Assistant, Office of the Vice-President
Randa Fahmy Hudome: Counsel, US Dept. of Energy
    additional administrative staff most likely present

16 Additional Representatives of The Muslim Brotherhood

Dr. Siddiqui, Mr. Saffuri, Mr. Talat, Dr. Basha, Dr. Khan, and
    Mr. Salem (all from the 3:05 meeting) plus
Abdulwahab Alkebsi: Executive Director, Islamic Free Market
    Institute
Omar Ahmed: Co-founder and Chairman, Council on American
    Islamic Relations (CAIR)
Dr. Maher Hathout: Co-founder, Muslim Public Affairs Council
Salam Al-Marayati: President, Muslim Public Affairs Council
Azizah Al-Hibri: Founder, Muslim Women Lawyers for Human
    Rights
Dr. Agha Saeed: Chairman, American Muslim Political
    Coordinating Council
Eric Vickers: Board Member, American Muslim Alliance
Zaid Asail: President, Arab Anti-Discrimination Committee
W. Deen Mohammed: American Society of Muslims
Peter Tanous: President, American Task Force for Lebanon

Sources: Center for Security Policy
and
The Clarion Project

9/11 Events Caused Major Problems for Islamic Supremacists

The events of 9/11 and the cancellation of these White House meetings created two major problems for the Islamic Supremacists, who had planned to meet with President Bush to resolve both:

1) How were they going to move ahead on the "secret evidence" issues; and

2) What could they do to distance themselves from the terrorist attacks which had just occurred. [43]

To strategize on both these issues, the Islamic Supremacists immediately went to the offices of Americans for Tax Relief (ATR and Grover Norquist) on 'K' Street, Washington, DC. ATR had leased an entire floor of the building, and subsequently sublet about 1/3 of the floor to the Center for Security Policy, led by Frank Gaffney, former Assistant Secretary, US Department of Defense. [44]

The Islamic Supremacists gathered in the ATR conference and spent almost five hours discussing the two situations. Unbeknownst to them, on the other side of the wall partition separating the two office spaces, was a staff work room of Center for Security Policy. When CSP personnel overheard conversations in Arabic, they quickly summoned employees who were fluent in the Farci languages. CSP personnel even pushed up the ceiling tiles so they could hear better. [45]

For these five hours CSP staff took meticulous notes. This "chance" strategic planning meeting of the Islamic Supremacists provided a treasure trove of intelligence and acted as a wakeup call to the "Stealth Jihad" plans of The Muslim Brotherhood to destroy America and Western civilization.

---

[43] *The Muslim Brotherhood in America*, Frank Gaffney, Center for Security Policy.
[44] ibid #1
[45] ibid #1

Center for Security Policy staff used this September 11th date as pivot point to research the past and to build ("cold case style") data files of information about Islamic Supremacist organizations wanting to overthrow the United States government. [46]

Information gleaned from the CSP notes was given to the intelligence agencies of the Bush administration.

RAID ON ISLAMIC SUPREMACISTS OFFICES

On March 20, 2002, a major raid was initiated by a joint task force of the FBI, CIA and Homeland Security, at two five-story office buildings in Herndon, VA. More than 200 different Islamic Supremacist organizations, with interlocking directorates, were housed in these two office buildings. Each of these organizations had been established by The Muslim Brotherhood and was being funded by The Muslim Brotherhood. [47]

More than 800 banker boxes of files and materials were taken from the offices of these 200+ organizations.

Until this time, US intelligence agencies had been uninformed of the plans of The Muslim Brotherhood to utilize "Civilization Jihad" against America.

Eventually, President Bush assigned control and responsibility for the collected information to the FBI and Director Robert Mueller. However, senior government officials, with top secret security clearances, (including: Congress; FBI; CIA; Homeland Security; Department of Defense; and Department of State), were prohibited from reading the treasure trove of data or analyzing the information for many years.

---

[46]   ibid #1

[47]   *Operation Green Quest,* Interagency Joint Task Force Raid on Islamic Supremacists Offices, Herdon, VA, March 20, 2002.

RAID ON THE ELBARASSE RESIDENCE IN ANNANDALE, VIRGINIA

"In August 2004, an alert Maryland Transportation Authority police officer observed a woman wearing traditional Arabic garb, videotaping the support structures of the Chesapeake Bay Bridge, and conducted a traffic stop. The driver of the vehicle was identified as Ismail Elbarasse. Elbarasse was detained on an outstanding material witness warrant issued in a Chicago Hamas case." [48] [49]

"The FBI's Washington Field Office raided Elbarasse's residence in Annandale, Virginia. In the basement of the suspects home, the FBI found a hidden sub-basement. In the sub-basement, agents found the archives of The Muslim Brotherhood in North America." [50] [51]

"The documents confirmed what investigators and counter-terrorism experts had previously suspected, that the myriad of Muslim-American associated groups in the United States were nearly all controlled by The Muslim Brotherhood and, therefore, as Sharia Law dictates, were hostile to the United States, its constitution, and our freedoms." [52] [53]

"The documents make clear that the strategic objective of The Muslim Brotherhood in North America is to implement Sharia Law in the United States, in furtherance to establish a 'Global Caliphate'." [54] [55]

---

[48] *FBI: The Muslim Brotherhood Deeply Rooted inside U.S.,* WorldNetDaily, February 21, 2015.

[49] *Destroying Western Civilization From Within,* The Tribune Papers, August 23, 2013.

[50] ibid #6

[51] ibid #7

[52] ibid #6

[53] ibid #7

[54] ibid #6

[55] ibid #7

"TEAM B" PROJECT

In May 1974, President Gerald Ford initiated the "Team B Project", by inviting a group of outside experts to evaluate classified intelligence on the Soviet Union. Team B was a "competitive analysis exercise", commissioned by the Central Intelligence Agency (CIA) and approved by then Director of CIA, George H. W. Bush, to analyze threats the Soviet Union posed to the security of the United States.

Team B was created, in part, due to a 1974 publication by Albert Wohlstetter, who accused the CIA of chronically underestimating Soviet military capability. For years "Team A," (code name for the CIA itself), had reached erroneous conclusions on National Intelligence Estimates, which were demonstrated to be very wrong. [56]

At that time the CIA was in the process of putting together its own assessment for 1974. Team B concluded that the "National Intelligence Estimates" on the Soviet Union, generated yearly by the CIA, underestimated the military power of the Soviet Union and "misinterpreted the strategic intentions of the Soviet Union." [57]

During the 1976 Republican Primary, Ronald Reagan extolled the findings of the "Team B Report." He promised, if elected President, he would alter the old foreign policy of appeasement towards the former Soviet Union, to one forceful intervention. He lost the primary race to George H. W. Bush.

Four years later in 1981, shortly after his inauguration, President Reagan implemented a new foreign policy that ended "appeasement" and "forcefully challenged" the Soviet Union, at all times. This led to Reagan's 1982 demand during his speech in Berlin, "Mr. Gorbachev, tear down this wall."

---

[56] *Shariah: the Threat to the America,* Report issued by Team B2, Center for Security Policy, Washington, DC., August 22, 2010.
[57] ibid #14

"TEAM B II" PROJECT

In 2010, the "Team B II Project" was commissioned by The Center for Security Policy, to bring together a group of "outside experts" to evaluate non-classified information on the threat of Islamic Supremacists and "Sharia Law" to the United States. Team B II was so named in recognition of the important findings identified 35 years earlier by Team B.

Team B II was also considered a "competitive analysis exercise" in that it dared to expose the facts that the intelligence agencies of the US government (code name: Team A II) had been systematically "misinterpreting the strategic intentions" of The Muslim Brotherhood, CAIR and other affiliated organizations. The nineteen-person team of intelligence, military and legal experts was co-chaired by Lt. Gen. William G. "Jerry" Borkin and Lt. Gen. Harry Edward Soyster. [58]

Shariah: The Threat to the America, the Team B II report published by the Center for Security Policy in August 2010, reflects a consensus of the following four points.

1) Islamic Supremacists, who adhere to the tenants of Shariah Law, constitute a mainstream, dynamic movement in Islam. [59]

There are more than one billion Muslims in the world. The understandings of this belief system, and the practice of these beliefs, varies within different sects of Islam and in different countries around the world. In this light, there may not be a "true Islam."

However, Islamic Supremacists from countries like Saudi Arabia and Iran have been well financed and have been successful in propagating their "dominate the world image" of Islam, through organizations such as The Muslim Brotherhood, the Organization of the Islamic Conference and the Council of American Islam Relations.

---

[58] ibid #14
[59] ibid #14

2) It is vital to Western civilization that we recognize the differences between Islamic Supremacists & the authentic moderates of Islam. [60]

Many moderate Muslims only want to practice the personal religious tenants of their faith. We must no longer follow the failed strategy of fictionalizing one picture of Islam as a "religion of peace", when more than 60 percent of its followers adhere to the goals of the Islamic Supremacists and/or are willing to be controlled by these Supremacists.

3) It is vital to the national security of the United States that we recognize our obligation to protect our nation from all enemies domestic and international. [61]

The Muslim Brotherhood and CAIR are only two of the many organizations which mean to overthrow our government by implementing "Civilization Jihad" against us. Their intent is to: a) implement Sharia Law to replace the US Constitution; b) dominate public education in America; c) gain control of the American media; d) implement Zakat in our banking system; and e) eliminate our protected rights to worship as we choose.

4) Sharia Law is incompatible with the US Constitution. [62]

We must move expeditiously to implement in every state, on a nation-wide basis the objectives of "American Laws for American Courts."

In a letter dated April 26, 2011 to all Members of Congress, the authors of the Team B II Report called on the legislative branch to do something the Obama administration seemed determined not to do:

"A rigorous investigation of the extent to which The Muslim Brotherhood's 'Stealth Civilization Jihad' had gained access to and influence over the US government." [63]

---

[60]   ibid #14

[61]   ibid #14

[62]   ibid #14

[63]   *Team B II Letter to Congressional Leaders on The Muslim Brotherhood,* www.shariahthetreat.org.

Barrack Hussein Obama Administration

PERSONNEL SYMPATHETIC TO ISLAMIC SUPREMACY
Partial List (see **Appendix E, page 197** for more details) [64]

Huma Abedin

Deputy Chief of Staff to Secretary of State Hillary Clinton
Many direct associations with The Muslim Brotherhood

Oborn'go Malik Obama

Step Brother of President Obama
President of the Barack Hussain Obama Foundation.
Member of The Muslim Brotherhood.

Valerie Jarrett

Senior Advisor to President Obama and Assistant to the President for Public Engagement & International Affairs. She held many other powerful positions of responsibility at the White House. Many recognize her as being the most influential advisor to the President.

She was born in Shiraz, Iran to American citizens Dr. John E. Bowman and Barbara Taylor Bowman, both African-American of the Muslim faith.

In the 1977 Stanford year book, Jarrett stated, **"I am an Iranian by birth and of my Islamic Faith. I am also an American citizen and I seek to help change America to become a more Islamic country. My faith guides me and I feel like it is going well in the transition of using freedom of religion in America against itself."**

She has frequently reaffirmed her strong Muslim faith.

---

[64] Obama Administration Personnel Sympathetic to Islamic Supremacy, Wikipedia & Wikipedia Resources, Accessed July 2017.

Rashad Hussain

Deputy Associate Counsel to President Obama.

Special Envoy to the Organization of the Islamic Conference (OIC), the second largest inter-governmental organization after the United Nations.

Member of The Muslim Brotherhood.

Mehdi K. Alhassini

Member of the National Security Council (NSC).

Member of The Muslim Brotherhood.

Arif Alikhan

Assistant Secretary for Policy Development for the US Department of Homeland Security.

Mohamed Elibiary

Homeland Security Advisory Council.

Member of The Muslim Brotherhood.

Kareem Shora

Homeland Security Advisory Council

Iman Mohamed Magid

"Sharia Czar" to President Obama Council of Czars.

Member of The Muslim Brotherhood.

Member of the Islamic Society of North America

Salam al-Marayati

Special Advisor to the President Obama

Founder & Current Executive Director of the Muslim Public Affairs Council

Nawar Shora

Senior Advisor to the Civil Rights and Liberties Office, Transportation Security Administration

Luoay Safi

Former Advisor to US Department of Defense

Barrack H. Obama Administration Policies

"SUPPORTING ISLAMIC SUPREMACY OBJECTIVES"

The United States has been fighting wars in Afghanistan and Iraq for more than ten years. We have been in a cold war with Iran, over its nuclear weapons program, for more than 25 years.

The naivety and miscalculations by the George W. Bush administration lead us into wars in Afghanistan and Iraq for different reasons. The imprudent continuation of both military actions represented misunderstandings of **"Who is The Enemy"** by both President Bush and President Obama.

We are not at war with terror, ie "A War on Terror." We are at war with Islamic Supremacists, who use (and will continue to use) all approaches and all methodologies (violent and non-violent) to accomplish their ends; the establishment of **"A Global Islamic Caliphate"** under the rule of Sharia Law as dictated by the Koran.

In each of these countries, President Obama had his own ideas of how he wanted to end all three conflicts. From the beginning, he ignored how we entered each war; what has transpired over the years since its beginnings; and where we are today. His only concern was to achieve three goals:

1) to end the war in Afghanistan and bring all troops home;

2) to end the war in Iraq and bring all troops home; and

3) to reach an agreement with Iran, however flawed.

Each of these goals, and their respective strategies, reveals President Obama's lack of understand in **"Knowing The Enemy."**

Author's Opinion: President Obama carried out his plans in a manner of an "Islamic Sympathizer," frequently contrary to America's best interest.

OBAMA EXECUTIVE ORDERS AND EXECUTIVE MEMORANDUM FAVORING ISLAMIC SUPREMACISTS

(partial list)

On numerous occasions, President Obama's supported positions and programs which were not only counter intuitive to the US Constitution, but seem to favor positions aspired by Islamic Supremacists. These actions reduced our effectiveness in containing and defeating radical Islam.

$770 million to Save Mosques Overseas

A CBS news investigation found that the Obama State Department sent hundreds of millions of dollars overseas to refurbish mosques and save other Islamic sites. The State Department displayed before and after pictures of mosques refurbished with U.S. tax dollars.

(see **Appendix J, page 222**)

Muslim Federal Holidays

"President Obama, through an executive order, declared both "Eid al-Fitr" and "Eid al-Adha" federal holidays, until Congress was able to take legislative action. The White House felt strongly that since the Christian holiday of Christmas is a federally recognized holiday, Muslim holidays should also be recognized." said Jay Carney, White House Press Secretary. Congress did not take legislative action to make them permanent Federal holidays. (see **Appendix J, page 222**)

Muslims are Excluded from Forcible Participation in The Affordable Care Act (ACA or Obamacare)

Muslims have been given the right of "dhimmitude," to separate themselves from non-Muslims, by allowing Muslims to elect not to participate in the ACA nor to have to pay the "penalty tax" for not participating. One can conclude that President Obama is an Islamic sympathizer.

(see **Appendix J** for details and examples of other Obama Executive Orders and Executive Memorandum favorable to Islamic Supremacists).

Obama White House Responded to Requests from CAIR

FBI Training Curricula Purged of Material Deemed 'Offensive to Muslims' by CAIR [65] [66]

"Judicial Watch has released hundreds of pages of FBI memos and other documents, revealing that in 2012, the agency purged their anti-terrorism training curricula of material determined by an undisclosed group of "Subject Matter Experts" (SME) to be "offensive" to Muslims ..." [67]

"The purged material included references linking The Muslim Brotherhood to terrorism; tying al-Qaeda to the 1993 World Trade Center and Khobar Towers bombings; and suggested that 'young male immigrants of Middle Eastern appearance ... may fit the terrorist profile best." [68] [69] [70]

"Judicial Watch obtained the materials on January 15 and on April 16, 2013, pursuant to a Freedom of Information (FOIA) lawsuit, originally filed on March 7, 2012 and later re-filed on July 18, 2012." ... "It sought access to records detailing a February 8, 2012 meeting between FBI Director Robert Mueller and various Islamic organizations.[71] [72] [73]

---

[65] *FBI Removes Hundreds of Training Documents After Probe on Treatment of Islam*, FoxNews, February 21, 2012.

[66] *Obama Orders Government to Cleanup Terror Training Materials*, Wired, November 29, 2013.

[67] *US Government Purges Law Enforcement Training Material "Deemed Offensive" to Muslims*, Judicial Watch, September 1, 2015.

[68] ibid #1

[69] ibid #2

[70] ibid #3

[71] ibid #1

[72] ibid #2

[73] ibid #3

The FOIA request also asked for any and all records setting criteria or guidelines for FBI curricula on Islam or records identifying potentially offensive material within FBI curricula on Islam,' as well as any directives to withdraw FBI presentations and curricula on Islam." [74] [75] [76]

"During the February 8 meeting, Mueller reportedly assured the Islamic groups in attendance that the agency had ordered the removal of presentations and curricula on Islam from FBI offices around the country that were deemed 'offensive.' As reported by NPR: 'The FBI has completed a review of offensive training materials and has purged 876 pages and 392 presentations, according to a briefing provided to lawmakers." [77] [78] [79]

The FBI acquiesced to all requests from CAIR and from the White House (392 presentations were purged plus an additional 876 pages eliminated.)

Author's Note: The "Subject Matter's Experts" included representatives of CAIR, The Muslim Brotherhood and other Islamic Supremact's groups.

---

[74] ibid #1

[75] ibid #2

[76] ibid #3

[77] ibid #1

[78] ibid #2

[79] ibid #3

Mosques, Cultural Centers & "No Go Zones"

Since the 1970's, the construction of mosques & cultural centers and the creation of "No Go Zones" in America can be traced back to The Muslim Brotherhood, the Muslim Student Association, and the North America Islamic Trust.

More than 80% of the funding for these mosques and cultural centers has been provided by Middle Eastern Islamic countries, primarily Saudi Arabia.

More than 75% of these mosques and cultural centers are owned by the North American Islamic Trust, a wholly owned subsidiary of the Muslim Student Association, which was founded by The Muslim Brotherhood. (chapter VII, pages 52 - 54: chronology of organizations).

For the past 35 years, US administrations have looked the other way, naively ignoring the purposes and the ever increasing threats, associated with the Islamic Supremacy organizations in America.

SEDITION: the incitement of discontent or rebellion against the government or any action promoting such discontent or rebellion.

Webster's Universal College Dictionary

(**Author's Note:** These Islamists are continually bringing legal cases against US citizens and entities who oppose their view of things. And their view of things is inimical to the best and proper interests of the US. They are often in opposition to our civil authorities. And they use our legal system against us because they search for and find Islamic sensitive judges to rule against our own people. But we must continue to try to have them found guilty of what they have seditiously done and get rid of them by deporting them)

Embedding the Enemy in Our Military

In 2010, Obama issued an executive order to expedite immigrant visa requests from Islamic countries. A person from a Muslim country could become a U.S. citizen in as little as ten weeks, with no I.D. and no declaration of allegiance to the U.S. Constitution (see **Appendix J, pg 222**)

"No Go Zones." in America

In many countries around the world, the federal and state governments have abrogated their political and legal authority to leaders in the Muslim communities. These governments have generally allowed:

1) "Sedition" to be preached in mosques and Islamic cultural centers;

2) "Sharia Law" courts to replace "State Law" courts;

3) Islamic religious/history to take president over state history subjects;

4) Unprecedented access to government officials; and

5) Acquiesced to unfounded claims of Islamic religious persecution.

More specifically, governments allowed **"No Go Zones"**, small geographic areas (suburban and/or rural) to be established by Muslims, and cordoned off, instructing local/federal officials not to enter under, the consequence of death. In France there are more than 1,000 "No Go Zones." [80]

In America, the FBI has identified more than 32 "No Go Zones" and continues to investigate the activities of more than 1,000 ISIS connected individuals in every state throughout the United States. While the FBI has been monitoring these seditious activities from a distance, it is doubtful that the FBI has infiltrated every zone. [81]

At least 22 of these "No Go Zones" have become paramilitary in nature. Is the FBI doing enough to thwart the seditious activities of these "religious communities?" The stage has been set for more Jihad attacks on US soil, under the watchful eyes of the FBI. [82]

Many of these paramilitary communities are operated by Jamaat al-Fuqra, a Pakistan-based organization, operating in America as a series

---

[80] *Sharia Law Muslim "NO GO" Zones in France*, FoxNews
[81] *Did You Know There are Muslim "NO GO" Zones in the USA?*, truthuncensored.net, Jan 29, 2015.
[82] ibid #2

of private schools, offering educational services under the umbrella of Muslims of the Americas (MOA). Sherikh Mubarak Ali Gilani, a Pakistan cleric, given asylum by the United States in 1947, leads the organization from their headquarters in Islamberg, New York. Other communes, operated by Jamaat al-Fuqra, are located in remote areas of: California, Georgia, Michigan, New York, South Carolina, Tennessee, Texas, Virginia and West Virginia. More than likely, there are other unknown communes. [83]

"Islamberg" (Hancock County, NY) and "Mohmoudberg" (Brazoria County near Sweeney, TX) are two of the more notorious "No Go Zones." [84] [85]

According to the Clarion Project, three of the more dangerous mosques, preaching sedition in America, are: Dar Al Hijarh Islamic Center (Falls Church, VA); mosque of radical Iman, Siraj Wahhaj (Brooklyn, NY); and the Islamic Circle of North America (Queens, NY). [86] [87]

Other cities with Islamic mosques & Islamic cultural centers, teaching sedition include: New York City; Boston; Tampa; Chicago; Pittsburg; Patterson and Middletown, NJ; Alexandria and Herndon, VA; Lexington, KY; Plainfield, IN; Oak Brook, Bridgeview, Palos Hills and Orland Park, IL; Irving, TX; Tucson, AZ; West Covina and Sacramento, CA. [88] [89]

The Clarion Project has possession of two video tapes; one of secret MOA footage, showing female members receiving paramilitary training at Islamberg (featured on the Kelly File, FOX News) and second showing a MOA spokesman declaring America to be a Muslim-majority nation.

---

[83] ibid #2

[84] ibid #2

[85] Muslim "NO GO Zones" in the USA?, Israelvideonetwork.com, April 9, 2017.

[86] ibid #2

[87] ibid #6

[88] ibid #2

[89] ibid #3

A 2007 FBI report states:

"MOA members have been involved in at least 10 murders, one disappearance, three fire bombings, one attempted firebombing, two explosive bombings and one attempted bombing."

The 2007 FBI report also states:

"The documented propensity for violence by this organization supports the belief that the leadership of MOA extols membership to pursue a policy of Jihad or holy war against individuals or groups it considers enemies of Islam, which includes the US government. Members of Muslims of America are encouraged to travel to Pakistan to receive religious and military training from Sheikh Gilani."

The 2007 report concludes:

"The Muslims of America is now an autonomous organization which possesses an infrastructure capable of planning and mounting terrorist campaigns overseas and within the US."

An earlier FBI 2003 report described MOA in similar ways, stating:

"Investigation of the Muslims of the Americas is based on specific and articulate facts, giving justification to believe they are engaged in international terrorism..."

The 2003 report also claims that:

"Muslims of America members believe the holiest Islamic site in America is located at their Islamville commune in South Carolina. Other MOA entities include: International Quranic Open University; United Muslim Christian Forum; Islamic Post; Muslim Veterans of America and American Muslim Medical Relief Team."

159 individuals have been charged in the U.S. with offenses related to the Islamic State (also known as IS, ISIS, and ISIL)–since the first arrests in March 2014.
(As of March 5, 2018)

102 individuals have pleaded or were found guilty.

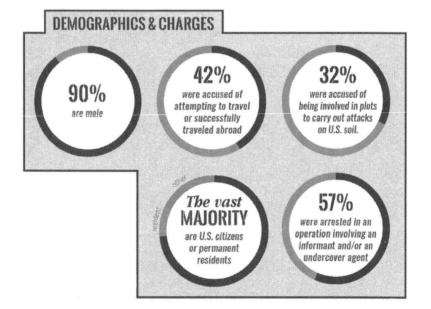

DEMOGRAPHICS & CHARGES

90% are male

42% were accused of attempting to travel or successfully traveled abroad

32% were accused of being involved in plots to carry out attacks on U.S. soil.

other

resident

The vast **MAJORITY** are U.S. citizens or permanent residents

57% were arrested in an operation involving an informant and/or an undercover agent

new research & analysis from the
Program on Extremism
THE GEORGE WASHINGTON UNIVERSITY

Benghazi:
The Attacks and the Cover-Up

On numerous occasions, President Obama supported the ouster of a US ally in the Middle East or North Africa. His support of Islamic Supremacists to replace Muammar Gaddafi in Libya was one of those situations.

In 2011, the United States established the "special mission" and the CIA annex in Benghazi without giving formal notice to the Gaddafi government. Weapons, supplied by the US, were carefully purchased through extremist middlemen. They used financing in Saudi Arabia, Qatar and Turkey, so as to avoid US government accountability ... to US citizens and to US allies around the world." [90]

In March 2012, the US State Department, with the approval of Sec. Clinton, awarded a one-year contract to the Blue Mountain Group, a small British firm located in Wales, to protect the US mission in Benghazi, despite the fact that the company had only limited experience in Libya. [91]

On August 15, 2012, Ambassador Steven requested in writing that security and fortification of the "special mission" be increased. Secretary of State Clinton denied the request. Instead, her office reduced the number of personnel in the security force at the mission on August 31st. [92]

On September 11, 2012 the **First Wave** of the attacks began at 9:41 pm (local time; 3:41 pm EDT) and lasted most of the night. The **Second Wave** began at 5:15 am (local time: 11:15 pm EST). Both waves were well-planned; well-coordinated; and carried out by well-armed Jihadists. [93]

---

[90] *"The Real Benghazi Story"*; Aaron Klein, WND Books, 2014
[91] *Daily Telegraph,* October 2012
[92] ibid #1
[93] ibid #1

At all times the physical whereabouts of the President, the Secretary of Defense and the Secretary of State are known and are recorded. These records are known as their respective "Time Lines".

The recorded "Time Line" of the Secretary of Defense, reveals that Secretary Leon Panetta was made aware of the attack in its early stages. He started watching it in his office at the Pentagon at approximately 3:42 pm (recall the 1st wave attack began at 3:41 pm). Secretary Panetta left the Pentagon; continued to watch the attack through communications equipment in his government car; and went to the White House, for a scheduled weekly meeting. Upon arrival at the White House, he went to the Oval Office and there continued to watch the attack with President Obama and Vice-President Biden.

(see **Appendix K, page 234** for detailed discussion on Benghazi)

American Laws for American Courts

To counteract the seditious movements of Islamic Supremacists in America, each of the 50 states must pass state laws, requiring all courts to use only applicable federal, state, and/or local laws. In addition, US law must limit US courts to using only the US laws; no international laws.

As of the Spring 2017, only 28 states had passed laws in their respective state to require, and to limit, these applications of law. In the state of Florida, the Florida House of Representatives has passed the necessary bill on 3 occasions, only to have Florida Senate vote against it.

Many Florida state representatives and state senators have received election contributions from CAIR and other Islamic Supremacists groups, encouraging them to vote against the ALAC legislation.

AMERICA RETURNS $400 MILLION TO IRAN

Throughout the reign of the Shah of Iran, the country of Iran purchased military equipment from the United States. In the late 1970's, Iran entered into another such purchase agreement with the America and sent an initial payment of $400 million to secure the deal. Before the equipment could be delivered, the government of the Shah was overthrown, and a new nation created, The Islamic Republic of Iran.

In all similar situations throughout history, when a government is overthrown through a revolt, all prior contractual agreements are voided, and cash obligations are absolved. On several occasions, Iran has tried to get new US administrations to reconsider the consist position of prior administrations. While the new revolutionary government of Iran might not want to accept this traditional outcome, the United States has maintained the consistent position (1979-2014) of not returning the $400 million payment to Iran.

However, many of the foreign policy positions, dealing with Iran and consistently administered by the Reagan - Bush - Clinton - Bush Administrations, were reversed by President Obama through executive orders. In one of these critical situations, President Obama not only authorized the repayment of a $400 million deposit for the purchase of the military equipment, agreed to by the United States before the Shah was overthrown on 16 January 1979, but Obama approved the inclusion of an additional $1.3 billion in accrued interest on the deposit.

To repeat, precedence has established that deposits made by the overthrown country, and held by the receiver country, become the sole property of the receiver country. No refund of the deposit nor accrued interest was required.

Chapter XI

Iran -- World Dominate Terrorist Funding Nation

FAILED U.S. POLITICAL RELATIONS WITH IRAN

Since January 1979, through six different administrations, the United States has failed repeatedly in our attempts to establish successful, political relations with Iran. This has not been without our trying to deal with a very obstinate nation.

Our approaches to enlist help from the Europeans have been unsuccessful. Our willingness to acquiesce to UN demands, that the UN be given absolute control over negotiations, were naïve and foolish.

Hope of a new beginning, with the return of our hostages in January 1981, was unfounded.

One thing is known. "Iran has constantly negotiated in bad faith." Every time Iran has outwitted their opponent; whether the UN or the European Union or the USA. They have repeatedly held out for terms and conditions which were unreasonable or unenforceable. Each time with another agreement, year after year for more than 40 years, Iran has increased its nuclear capabilities and has moved closer to producing nuclear weapons with the capability to deliver them throughout the Middle East; Europe; Asia; or to the Western Hemisphere.

TERMINATION OF U.S. FUNDING OF IRANIAN FREEDOM FOUNDATION

In 2009, President Obama terminated the funding by the United States to the Iranian Freedom Foundation. These moneys were used to support demonstrators, freedom fighters and other dissents in Iran, striving to overthrow the current regime and to establish a democratic nation.

In addition, The Obama Administration reversed the foreign policy positions of the Clinton and G. W. Bush Administrations and discontinued support of Iranian dissents against Ayatollah Ruhollah Khomeini.

Stealth Drone on Secret Mission Down in Iran

On December 2, 2011, US Air Force Flight Command, located in Oklahoma, lost control of a stealth drone flying over Afghanistan. The stealth drone, one of only three stealth drones in the US fleet, crash landed in one piece in Iran. The Iranians were not aware of our surveillance nor that our drone had crashed. [1] [2]

Secretary of Defense Leon Panetta immediately notified President Obama of the problem and articulated the three possible courses of action that were approved if such a problem occurred:

1)   Send in a missile to destroy the drone on the ground, so that the Iranians could not gain any scientific/engineering knowledge;

2)   Send in a manned team to destroy the drone on the ground, so that successful destruction of the drone could be verified; or

3)   Send in a manned team with a 2nd heavy lift helicopter to extract the drone without the Iranians knowing we had penetrated their airspace and to assure they would gain no knowledge.

President Obama decided to do none of the three pre-approved options.

Instead, President Obama elected to do nothing, knowing that the Iranians would eventually discover the drone. Yes, they would gain knowledge of all our cutting-edge technology through reverse engineering of the drone. This would enable them and/or other nations to manufacture clones of our aircraft. [3] [4]

---

[1]   *Exclusive: Iran Hijacked US Drone*, says Iranian Engineer," compositor.com, December 23, 2011

[2]   *Iran Aires Footage of Downed US Drone*, Presstv.ir, December 9, 2011

[3]   *Russia, China seek info on US Drone held by Iran*, FoxNews, April 19, 2012.

[4]   *Officials Challenge Iran Claims on US Drone - Despite Concerns About Value to Russia & China*, FoxNews, April 23, 2012.

Iran did discover our stealth drone and notified the Russians and the Chinese of their successful recovery of our drone in one piece. They invited Russia and China to send representatives to Tehran to inspect the aircraft. [5]

When President Obama asked for them to return it, they just laughed at his stupidity. Eventually, they mocked him, by returning a toy drone. [6]

Because of the traitorous actions of President Obama, now all three of our enemies have gained the technology to build stealth drones and the engineering capabilities to spy on the United States. [7]

---

[5]   ibid #4

[6]   *Obama Appeals to Iran to give back downed US Drone*, New York Tomes, December 2012.

[7]   ibid #6

"The Iranian Nuclear Accord"
Joint Comprehensive Plan of Action
(JCPoA)

(Detailed Explanation: **Appendix K, page 234**)

The latest ineptness, or complicity, was demonstrated by the Obama administration in the Joint Comprehensive Plan of Action (JCPoA). Democrats have hailed President Osama's "Iranian Nuclear Deal" as a hallmark of his presidency. However, the truth is that the agreement did virtually nothing to stop Iran from acquiring a nuclear weapon(s).

At the very best, it simply delayed Iran. At the worst, it actually accelerated the development of nuclear weapons, because it stabilized their economy with an infusion of cash ($150 Billion) and lifted all economic sanctions. The country was now no longer strapped for cash.

In addition, the JCPoA omitted any consideration on restricting missile delivery systems, which could be used to deliver conventional and/or nuclear weapons to targets throughout the Middle East, Central Asia, Europe and more distant locations.

With new financial capabilities, Iran has been able to pursue both development programs with renewed vigor. They also have new capacity to fund terrorist programs around the globe.

The Obama Administration also failed to establish any pre-conditions on the release of American prisoners, being held by the Iranian government on false charges, before negotiations would begin.

Thus, the "Agreement" has heavily favored Iran, with no concessions given to the United States and its partners. It also allowed the United Nations to undermine the false premise of the negotiations, that of claiming to reduce the world-wide threat of a nuclear capable Iran.

THE JCPoA ALLOWED THE ECONOMY OF IRAN TO RECOVER WHEN:

1) international trade/banking sanctions were lifted. [8] [9]

2) $150 Billion was paid directly to Iran out of funds, formerly frozen assets of Iran, held because of sanctions against Iran, for their continued violation of UN nuclear restrictions. [10]

The US agreed to both these actions, without establishing realistic constraints on the nuclear development program, which could be monitored objectively by independent authorities. With Iran's poor history of living up to prior agreements, Iran once again played the leaders of the Western World as fools. [11]

SANCTIONS LIFTED

International reductions in purchases of Iranian oil and reductions in selling refined petroleum products (i.e., gasoline) back to Iran, had squeezed its economy in recent years. The restricting of many other business activities by foreign nations, and by foreign business, had further insolated Iran. Lifting of these sanctions brought major financial rewards to Iran.

In the Iran Nuclear Accord, the United States, the European Union and the UN agreed to lift nuclear-related sanctions on the Iranian economy -- a priority for Iran -- after the UN atomic energy commission verified that Iran had taken key steps to comply with UN resolutions and with the Accord. All parties understood that if Iran violated the terms of the Accord, the sanctions would snap back into place. (see **Appendix K, page 234**)

---

[8]   *Iran Nuclear Deal: Key Details,* BBC News, January 16, 2016
[9]   *Six Shocking Details from the Iran Nuke Deal,* Washington Times, July 12, 2016.
[10]   *What's in the Iran Nuclear Deal? 7 Key Points,* Eric Bradner, CNN, April 2, 2015.
[11]   ibid #2

CASH PAYMENTS TO IRAN BY UNITED STATES

As one of the conditions of The Iran Nuclear Accord, the United States agreed to release $150 Billion up front to Iran.

Sharia Law, through the process of *zakat*, requires that Iran use 12% ($18 B) of this amount to support the spread of Islam around the world. Zakat further stipulates that 3% of the moneys handled through banking system (25% of the 12% or $4.5 B), must be used for violent jihad! [12]

Because Sharia Law requires *"zakat"*, the $4.5 Billion payment qualifies the United States to be considered as the "The *Largest Single Donor of Violent Islamic Terrorism"* in the World. [13]

The lengths to which President Obama and his administration went, to make sure the Iranian deal happened, were suspicious.

First, he approved the release of Iranian prisoners held by US. He misled the America public over the severity of their crimes. Each of the prisoners had been convicted of serious terrorist activities not the felony criminal activities President Obama eluded to in public statements to the press and to the American people. [14]

Second, the son of the Iranian Foreign Minister was the best man at the wedding of Secretary of State Kerry's daughter to an Iranian doctor. The same Iranian Foreign Ministry was adversary to Secretary Kerry at the negotiation table. Secretary Kerry's first wife, their daughter, and other family members visited Iran prior to the wedding, as special guests of the country.

Third, President Obama and his administration didn't disclose the cyberattacks, orchestrated by Iran, against the US Department of State and against Israel, during the period of deal negotiations.

---

[12]   ibid #1

[13]   ibid #3

[14]   *Obama's Hidden Iran Deal Giveaway,* Jose Meyer, POLITICO, April 24, 2017.

From the Washington Free Beacon:

THE ATTACK TOOK PLACE WITHIN DAYS OF THE DEAL OVERCOMING OPPOSITION IN CONGRESS IN LATE SEPTEMBER THAT YEAR. THAT SAME WEEK, IRANIAN OFFICIALS AND NEGOTIATORS FOR THE UNITED STATES AND OTHER WORLD POWERS WERE BEGINNING THE PROCESS OF HASHING OUT A SERIES OF AGREEMENTS ALLOWING TEHRAN TO MEET PREVIOUSLY DETERMINED IMPLEMENTATION DEADLINES.

CRITICS REGARD THESE AGREEMENTS AS "SECRET SIDE DEALS" AND "LOOPHOLES" INITIALLY DISCLOSED ONLY TO CONGRESS.

SOURCES FAMILIAR WITH THE DETAILS OF THE ATTACK SAID IT SENT SHOCKWAVES THROUGH THE STATE DEPARTMENT AND THE PRIVATE CONTRACTOR COMMUNITY WORKING ON IRANIAN-RELATED ISSUES.

[...]

THE OBAMA ADMINISTRATION KEPT QUIET ABOUT THE CYBER-ATTACKS AND NEVER PUBLICLY ACKNOWLEDGED CONCERNS THE ATTACK CREATED AT STATE, RELATED AGENCIES AND WITHIN THE PRIVATE CONTRACTOR COMMUNITY THAT SUPPORTS THEIR WORK.

CRITICS OF THE NUCLEAR DEAL SAID THE OBAMA ADMINISTRATION DID NOT PUBLICLY DISCLOSE THE IMPACT OF THE CYBER-ATTACK OUT OF FEAR IT COULD UNDERMINE SUPPORT RIGHT AFTER THE PACT HAD OVERCOME POLITICAL OPPOSITION AND CLEARED A CRITICAL CONGRESSIONAL HURDLE.

[...]

IN THE WEEK LEADING UP TO THE DEADLINE, SENATE DEMOCRATS BLOCKED SEVERAL ATTEMPTS TO PASS A GOP-LEAD RESOLUTION TO DISAPPROVE THE NUCLEAR DEAL. THE RESOLUTION OF DISAPPROVAL NEEDED 60 VOTES TO PASS, BUT THE MOST IT GARNERED WAS 58.

UNITED NATIONS SIDE AGREEMENT WITH IRAN

Unbeknownst to the United States the (International Atomic Energy Agency (IAEA) of the United Nations, had been negotiating a "Special Nuclear Side Agreement" with Iran, to address some of the same problems and concerns of the Iranian Nuclear Accord. President Obama and Secretary of State John Kerry have stated that they were unaware of the IAEA agreement with Iran and the requirements and conditions of this side agreement. [15]

This IAEA- Iran Agreement allows for Iran to self-select and to self-inspect their own facilities for violations to the "Special Nuclear Side Agreement." Iran will give 24-day notice to the IAEA in a written report with video pictures and files of the sites with violations. [16]

AMERICAN HOSTAGES RELEASED BY IRAN - $400 MILLION RANSOM PAID

On 16 January 2016, four US citizens were released from an Iranian prison in exchange for seven Iranians held by United States on espionage/terrorist convictions. The four US citizens had been convicted by Iran on false charges of spying. The seven Iranian prisoners had been convicted of terrorist and/or espionage charges and were serving felony convictions.

President Obama justified that prisoner exchange, by falsely claiming that the seven Iranians were serving minor misdemeanor charges. [17] [18]

President Obama stated that the cash payment was not a ransom payment, resulting from negotiations with terrorists (Iranian authorities). The Administration claimed the moneys were a return of a contested cash payment of $400 million made by Iran to the United

[15] *US Sent Cash to Iran as Americans were Freed.* WSJ, August 3, 2016.
[16] ibid #8
[17] ibid #8
[18] *US Sent Plane with $400 Million in Cash to Iran,* CNNPolitics.com, August 3, 2016.

States in the late 1970's, to purchase military equipment under the authority of the former Shah of Iran, before his overthrow in 1979. The equipment purchase was never fulfilled. [19] [20]

The cash payment ($400 million equivalent) was made in Euros, Swiss francs and other foreign currencies to avoid current US law prohibiting direct payment of US dollars to Iran for any purpose. The currency was shrink wrapped on wooden pallets and transported by private chartered jets. [21] [22]

The departure of these hostages from the Tehran, Iran airport was delayed because of the arrival of the US airplane bringing the $400 million cash payment from Switzerland was late. Upon receipt of $400 million payment, Iranian officials immediately claimed it was a ransom payment for release of the hostages. [23] [24] [25]

The Obama Administration had also approved an additional cash payment of $1.3 billion to represent accrued interest since April 1, 1979 on the unfulfilled equipment purchase. Since the former Iran government of Shah was dissolved and a new governmental state, The Islamic Republic of Iran, was established by the revolution, all prior contracts and obligations, debts and credits were absolved. The Obama Administration reversed the US position recognized by all administrations since the Carter Presidency. The $1.7 billion dollars is from the US treasury and represent US tax payer moneys. [26] [27]

---

[19]   ibid #11

[20]   *State Department Admits Obama Lied - $400 Million Paid as Ransom,* www.zerohedge.com, August 18 2016

[21]   ibid #11

[22]   ibid #13

[23]   ibid #9

[24]   ibid #11

[25]   ibid #13

[26]   ibid #11

[27]   ibid #13

Iranian Designs to Overthrow Saudi Arabian Government

The Muslim religion, the Islamic "religious code of conduct," is made up of two major sects (Shia & Sunni). Their split can be traced back in religious history to both claiming to be the true successors of Muhammad. The Wahhabi sect of Saudi Arabia broke away from the Sunni sect. The Baath sect is an Arab socialist sect that also broke away from the Sunni. The Kurds are a smaller independent sect. (Chapter II)

Against this background of religious and political differences, the Muslim people groups have been fighting amongst themselves for fifteen hundred years.

Since 1997, Iran has had its sights on participating in the overthrow of the Saudi Arabian government. It was Iranian sponsored terrorists who attacked the USS Cole on October 12, 2000 in Aden Harbor, Yemen.

In 2015, Iran funded and participated in the coup which toppled the Yemen government. Iran now uses the terrorist bases in Yemen to systematically attack southern Saudi Arabian cities and villages.

When the Saudi government asked President Obama for assistance, Obama sided with the Iranians, in an effort to garner favor for the flawed "Iranian Nuclear Accord."

(see **Chapter II, page 21**)

Chapter XII

"The Way Forward"
Changes in Priorities to:
Right "The Ship of State"

NEW TRUMP MIDDLE EAST DOCTRINE

In May 2017, President Trump made his first international trip, visiting Saudi Arabia, Israel, The Vatican, Brussels, and Sicily (the G-7 meeting). While in Saudi Arabia, he addressed a combined meeting of leaders from more than 50 Arab countries. He announced a new US policy towards The Middle East, reversing the Obama Administration position of supporting Iran and its affiliates. He drew a new line in the sand, asking all Muslim nations to join together in the fight against Iran and Iranian supported terrorist organizations (al Qaeda; Hezbollah; Hamas; ISIS/ISIL; Boko Roham & others).

This new Middle East policy was well received: by Saudi Arabia; by the leaders of more than 50 Muslim majority nations; and by Israel.

However, when, President Trump spoke out about "the nature of Islamism," he ignored the Saudi objective of spreading Wahhabism all over the planet. In doing so, he lumped Islamic Supremacists in with moderates, a crucial misjudgment that he needs to be aware of.

The Wahhabi sect of Islam, based in Saudi Arabia, is one of the most fundamental in it beliefs, including strict adherence to "Sharia Law." They justify their financial support of Islamic Supremacists causes, both violent and non-violent, in that the ends justify the means; "World Domination" is the goal of Wahhabism.

"A STRATEGIC PLAN TO SPREAD 'SHARIA LAW' WORLDWIDE."

2002 Memorandum by Saudi King Fahd bin Abdul Aziz of Saudi Arabia. (see **Chapter VII, page 57**)

The Fight Against Islamic Supremacists

To win the war against Islamic Supremacists, President Trump has implemented new international trade and banking policies:

1) To pursue and to destroy the enemy;

2) Wherever they hide and whenever they attack.

This is the antithesis of President Obama's policies of appeasement and accommodation.

IN-COUNTRY MILITARY "RULES OF ENGAGEMENT"

When the US initially went into Afghanistan (late 2001 and early 2002), the primary objective was to wipe out as many Taliban and al-Qaeda fighters as possible. The strategy was to conduct an aerial bombing campaign of three to five months, using approximately "special ops" team members on the ground to identify bombing targets. Once the operation was successfully completed, the special ops personnel would be withdrawn, and the campaign would be terminated. It was anticipated that there would be no "boots-on-the-ground."

The objective of the original, "short-term" bombing operation was to destroy the Taliban and al-Qaeda.

It appears that the White House and the State Department had a different plan from the beginning. In 2002, they began finalizing operational plans to move from the air bombing campaign to one of "Nation Building." This new objective would require hundreds of thousands of "boots on the ground."

With the transition to the new strategy (nation building), also came for the first time the implementation of "rules of engagement" for the US military and coalition forces, to conduct themselves when engaging the enemy in Afghanistan. The old rules of engagement, negotiated by the Bush & Obama administrations with local government authorities, put our military at extreme disadvantage when trying to: 1) **"eliminate the enemy;"** and 2) **"win the war."**

Politicians and lawyers in Washington were more interested in acquiescing to local government authorities than protecting our troops.

As the years past and the war dragged on, more and more stringent "rules of engagement" were insisted by Afghan authorities. First the Bush Administration and then the Obama Administration acquiesced and implemented the additional limitations on engagement. The more stringent rules forced on our military personnel were so unrealistic, that many men and women unnecessarily lost their lives.

One example of the unreasonable Obama era rules was that in order to initiate actions against the enemy, ground leaders had to get approval from the Defense Department and the State Department in Washington, DC before attacking their targets. This approval process was cumbersome and always delayed action. Some potential attack opportunities were lost completely.

Another example was that all US military personnel had to have their weapons unloaded when on base. When off base and on a mission, they could load their weapons, but **"fire only when fired upon."**

President Trump, in consultation with his military advisors, has reversed all the unrealistic "rules of engagement" established by the Obama administrations.

TAKING THE FIGHT TO ISIL AND AL-QAEDA

Coalition forces now have a new strategy to "win the war" against ISIS and al-Qaeda. The Trump policy is to pursue and destroy, by eliminating them wherever they hide. We no longer have the Obama strategy of appeasement and accommodation.

Coalition forces have greatly reduced the number of ISIL fighters in Iraq and Syria. Coalition forces (Kurds and United States) now control Raqqa, the former ISIL capital, and the neighboring region.

Under the new Trump policy, special ops personnel are actively seeking ISIL and al-Qaeda fighters in more than 70 countries in Africa, the Middle East and Asia. Since January 2017, more than 75,000 ISIL and al-Qaeda fighters have been killed.

DECLARING "THE MUSLIM BROTHERHOOD" A TERRORIST ORGANIZATION

The US State Department has officially declared al-Qaeda, Hamas and Hezbollah each a terrorist organization. Having founded and funded each of these entities, The Muslim Brotherhood is the parent organization. Therefore, the Trump administration must declare The Muslim Brotherhood, CAIR and all its other affiliates as terrorist organizations. (see **Chapter VII, page 57**)

In the past, under previous administrations, the US State Department has placed foreign founding organizations on the official terrorist list, after declaring their subsidiaries as terrorist organizations. These declarations of the Communist Party, made in the 1940's, 1950's and 1960's, should require individuals to:

1) make a commitment to permanent residency; 2) recognize and accept our laws and institutions; 3) become fluent in English; and 4) accept all conditions for US citizenship.

For eight long years, the Obama Administration took extreme measures to encourage, and to facilitate, illegal migration into the United States. More than 90,000 "unaccompanied minors" from Mexico, Central America and other countries, were brought into the United States, without "complete vetting." They were quickly, and secretly, distributed across America in all lower 48 states, without notifying local officials. If local officials asked about these immigrants, they were denied information. When their school systems and medical facilities were over run with immigrants demanding services, the counties were not given any additional federal funds.

In addition, the Obama Administration implemented other policies which facilitated the immigration of hundreds of thousands of individuals from Muslim majority countries (i.e., Syria, Lebanon, Gaza), with incomplete vetting processes: 1) information data bases don't exist; and 2) tens of thousands of blank invalid passports, visas and driver's licenses from Syria were known to exist and were in the possession of ISIS/ISIL Jihadists.

TRUMP TRAVEL BAN AND EXTREME VETTING

The vetting of individuals, applying for immigration status into the United States, must include all measures necessary to: 1) verify the identity of each individual; and 2) to validate the statements made in their application.

This process should stipulate that information provided by some individuals, traveling from certain countries, may require special scrutiny because of the country of origin. Within his authority, President Trump has signed an Executive Order #13769, establishing the procedure that all individuals from six Muslim majority countries (i.e., Iran; Somalia; Sudan; Syria; Libya; & Yemen), must be processed with extra scrutiny. The list of six countries was identified in 2016 by the Obama Administration.

US 9th Circuit Court of Appeals has held up the implementation of the Trump Executive Order.

Build the Wall Along the Southern Border

The US southern border with Mexico, and the northern border with Canada, are currently being monitored by the Border Patrol, with the aid of sophisticated equipment. Border walls, specifically designed for differing terrains, will greatly enhance the current effectiveness of the Border Patrol.

In addition, thorough and absolute enforcement of existing immigration laws must be adhered to. If new laws are necessary, then the administration and Congress must pass the additional legislation. However, new legislation can only be planned if existing laws are properly enforced for a period of time and deficiencies are identified.

We must not interfere with the effective, efficient enforcement of our immigration laws, by limiting or restricting the authority of any personnel in the Department of Homeland Security. The Obama Administration took action on many occasions, which prohibited DHS personnel from exercising their full responsibility.

The result was greatly reduced security during the Obama years, which has greatly increased our exposure to terrorism today.

We do not need "comprehensive immigration reform." This is just a falsehood put forth by the Democrat party "to blame America first" for the problems we, as a country, have because so many illegal immigrants have been allowed into America; 1) the result of lax enforcement of immigration laws; and 2) the continuing efforts by some government officials and many misguided private organizations to allow them to stay.

THE "INHERENT DANGERS" OF UNCONTROLLED CHAINED IMMIGRATION

The 14th Amendment was ratified on July 9, 1868, to provide US citizenship to children born of non-citizen slaves, living in the United States. Since then US courts ruled that the same principle could be applied to the civil rights of any person(s), citizen or non-citizen, residing in the United States, including foreign nationals giving birth inside the United States.

President Trump was correct when, during the 2016 campaign, he stated that the current practice of automatically granting US citizen to any baby born in the US to a non-citizen, is not protected by the 14th Amendment. He added that this policy is a great magnet for illegal immigration.

Congress passed the Immigration Act of 1990, under which the Diversity Visa Lottery program is operated. Created in 1987, the first diversity visa program benefited mainly Ireland, Canada and Great Britain. In 1989, legislation was passed by Congress which caused the diversity program to transition to its second phase, with a shift in recipients to the countries of Bangladesh, Pakistan and Egypt. From 1991 to 1994, during its third phase, the program became a true lottery system, open to many more countries.

Legislation passed by Congress and signed by the President will be sufficient to change the 14th Amendment and the Immigration Act. Congress and President Trump can correct each of these situations.

"THE CALL TO ACTION"

RESPONSIBILITIES OF THE US FEDERAL GOVERNMENT

To gain control of our future, the United States Federal government must institute the following:

1) Must immediately end the lottery system used to select foreign nationals for migration to the United States. This system was authorized by the US Department of State, but is implemented and controlled by the foreign government;
2) Must immediately end chained migration;
3) Must immediately designate The Muslim Brotherhood, CAIR and all of its affiliates as terrorist organizations. Terrorist organizations such as Al-Qaeda, Hamas and Hezbollah, all founded and funded by The Muslim Brotherhood, have already been designated;
4) Must immediately return to full enforcement of all Federal Immigration Laws;
5) Must immediately end sanctuary cities and states;
6) Must immediately dissolve all "No Go Zones" and assure the prevention of any new ones being formed, even secretly. These "No Go Zones" preach sedition and train militants in terrorism methodologies. Sometimes they serve as half-way houses for prisoners, recently released from jails/penitentiaries. They frequently disguise themselves as religious organizations;
7) Must immediately evaluate the curriculum and policies of charter schools, established by foreign governments in the United States; and
8) Must encourage all state legislatures to pass legislation, limiting all judicial proceeding and actions to "American Laws for American Courts." Congress must pass legislation which will require that all judicial proceedings in Federal courts will be based on US laws. No international laws shall ever take precedence over state or federal laws.

RESPONSIBILITIES OF INDIVIDUALS

To understand your future and influence its outcome, individuals must commit to the following:

1) **Get Involved** - Accept Personal Responsibility.

2) **Get Informed** - about "Sharia Law" and The Muslim Brotherhood's "Civilization Jihad."

3) **Get Trained** - in how to counter "Civilization Jihad."

4) **Develop a Network of "THE INFORMED:"** Church family; schools; friends; neighbors; colleagues; and bio-family

5) **Elected Representatives Know the Facts** - about The Muslim Brotherhood in America and how Strongly you are committed to Defeating The Muslim Brotherhood

6) **Engage the Media** - Traditional and Social

7) **Join an Organization** - there is strength in numbers

RESPONSIBILITIES FOR GROUPS

To understand the future of America and influence its outcome, groups must commit to the following:

1) **Raise Awareness** - about Islamic Supremacy, "Civilization Jihad" and The Muslim Brotherhood

2) **Exercise Free Expression**

3) **Oppose Preferential Treatment for Islamists**

4) **Prevent Islamic "Dawa"** (Islamic evangelism in American schools)

5) **Oppose one-way "Interfaith Dialogue"**

6) **Challenge government support** for complicity in "Sharia Compliant Finance"

7) **Demand** that each state pass legislation requiring **"American Laws for American Courts"**

8) **Hold officials accountable** on Islamic influence operations

Source: Center for Security Policy

Appendices

Referenced Citations for each Appendix are listed at the end of each Appendix, respectively.

Appendix A

GLOSSARY OF TERMS

Allah Akbar: "god is great".

Caliphate: Sharia compliant government structure to rule Islamic lands.

Caliph: The Ayatollah (leader) who rules the Caliphate

Civilization Jihad: "Non-militant over throw of infidel government"; education; and by infiltrating: the administration; legislature; courts; police; military media.

Dawa: "invitation" (form of evangelism).

Dhimmitude: Islamic system of controlling non-Muslim people conquered through Jihad, specifically taxing them in exchange for tolerating their presence and as a coercive means to convert them to Islam.

Fatwa: A legal opinion or ruling issued by an Islamic scholar

Hafiz: Someone who has completely memorized the Koran.

Infidel: Any person (Muslim or non- Sharia Law as set forth in the Muslim) not following Koran.

Islamic Jihad: Violent Jihad.

Islamic Supremacist: Person who follows strict "Sharia Law".

Jizya tax: The tribute (tax) that must be paid by all infidels (people of scripture, Christians, Jews, & others) to Islamists for sparing their life.   Koran 9:29 Surah al-Tawbah

Mutaween: "Religious Police" employed to enforce "Sharia Law" and other moral codes in Muslim countries (ie Afghanistan; Iran; Indonesia; Malaysia; Saudi Arabia; Sudan; and others).

No Go Zones: "geographic or political areas where local authorities and other citizens are afraid to go".

Shahaadah: A declaration of faith; one of the five pillars of Islam.

Shahada: "There is no god but Allah and Mohammed is his messenger."

Sharia compliant finances: "banking transactions which follow 'zakat'," the requirement that 12% of every Banking transaction must be paid to the state Government for support of Islam.

Stealth Jihad: "Civilization Jihad"

Taqiyya: The "Justification for Lying" to infidels; and the "Requirement to Lie" to infidels, as set forth in the Koran.

Violent Jihad: "Islamic Terrorism"

Zakat: "Sharia Law" requires that every banking transaction be subject to a 12% tax for the "advancement of Islam." The government must apply "zakat" to all bank accounts. 3% (25% of the 12%) must go to "Violent Jihad" (i.e., "Islamic Terrorism")

Appendix B

VERSES FROM THE KORAN CALLING FOR JIHAD (WAR AGAINST INFIDELS)

Koran (2:191-193): "And kill them wherever you find them, and turn them out from where they have turned you out. And al-Fitnah [disbelief or unrest] is worse than killing ... And fight them until there is no more Fitnah [disbelief] and worship is for Allah alone."

Koran (2:216): "Fighting is prescribed for you, and ye dislike it. But it is possible that ye dislike a thing which is good for you, and that ye love a thing which is bad for you. But Allah knoweth, and ye know not."

Koran (3:118): "O you who believe! Do not take for intimate friends from among others than your own people; they do not fall short of inflicting loss upon you; they love what distresses you; vehement hatred has already appeared from out of their mouths; and what their breasts conceal is greater still; indeed, we have made the communications clear to you, if you will understand.

Koran (3:151): "Soon shall we cast terror into the hearts of the unbelievers for that they joined companions with Allah, for which He had sent no authority."

Koran (4:76): "Those who believe, fight in the cause of Allah."

Koran (4:101): "And when you (Muslims) travel in the land, there is no sin on you if you shorten your Salat (prayer) if you fear that the disbelievers may attack you, verily, the disbeliever are ever unto you open enemies."

Koran (5:33): "The Punishment of those who wage war against Allah and his Messenger and strive to make mischief in the land is only this, that they should be murdered or crucified or their hands and their feet should be cut off on opposite sides or they should be imprisoned; this shall be as a disgrace for them in this world, and in the hereafter they shall have a grievous chastisement."

Koran (5:51): "O you who believe! Do not take the Jews and the Christians for friends; they are friends of each other; and whoever amongst you takes them for a friend, then surely he is one of them; surely Allah does not guide the unjust people."

Koran (8:12): "Remember when your Lord inspired the angels ... 'I will cast terror into the hearts of those who disbelieve. Therefore, strike off their heads and strike off every fingertip of them'."

Koran (8:39): "And fight with them until there is no more Fitna [unbelief] and religion should be only Allah."

Koran (8:57): "If thou comest on them in the war, deal with them so as to strike fear in those who are behind them, that happily they may remember."

Koran (8:59-60): "And let not those who disbelieve suppose that they can outstrip Allah's purpose. Lo! They cannot escape. Make ready for them all thou canst of force and horses tethered, that thereby ye may dismay the enemy of Allah and your enemy."

Koran (8:67): "It is not for a Prophet that he should have prisoners of war until he had made a great slaughter in the land."

Koran (9:29): "Fight those who believe not in Allah nor the Last Day, nor hold that forbidden which hath been forbidden by Allah and His Messenger, nor acknowledge the religion of Truth, even if they are of the People of the Book, until they pay the Jizya with willing submission, and feel themselves subdued."

Koran (9:30): "And the Jews say: Ezra is the son of Allah; and the Christians say: The Messiah is the son of Allah; these are the words of their mouths; they imitate the saying of those who disbelieved before; may Allah destroy them; how they are turned away!"

Koran (9:38-39): "O ye who believe! What is the matter with you, that, when ye are asked to go forth in the cause of Allah, ye cling heavily to the earth? Do ye prefer the life of this world to the Hereafter? But little is the comfort of this life, as compared with the Hereafter. Unless ye go forth, He will punish you with a grievous penalty, and put others in your place."

Koran (9:73): "O Prophet! Strive hard against the unbelievers and the hypocrites and be unyielding to them; and their abode is hell, and evil is the destination."

Koran (9:88): "But the Messenger, and those who believe with him, strive and fight with their wealth and their persons: for them are all good things: and it is they who will prosper."

Koran (48:29): "Muhammad is the Messenger of Allah. And those with Him are hard (ruthless) against the disbelievers and merciful among themselves."

Koran (61:10-12): "O you who believe! Shall I guide you to a commerce that will save you from a painful torment. That you believe in Allah and His Messenger, and that you strive hard and fight in the Ca use of Allah with your wealth and your lives, that will be better for you, if you but know!"

Koran (66:9): "O Prophet! Strive against the disbelievers and the hypocrites, and be stern with them. Hell will be their home, a hapless journey's end."

Sources:

The Truth About Islam - Traditional Values Coalition, 2016

Appendix C

THE MUSLIM BROTHERHOOD
CREED OF THE MUSLIM BROTHERHOOD (MB)

"Allah is our Objective

The Prophet is our Leader

The Qur'an is our Law, Jihad is our Way

Dying in the Way of Allah is our highest Hope" [1]

Philosophy and Authority

"It is the nature of Islam to dominate, not to be dominated: to impose its laws on all nations & extend its power to entire planet."

"Killing the infidels is our religion, slaughtering them is our religion, until they convert to Islam or pay us tribute." Abu Musab al-Zarqawi [2]

Al-Qaida in Iraq warned Pope Benedict XVI that its war against Christianity and the West will go on until Islam takes over the world, and Iran's supreme leader called for more protests over the pontiff's remarks on Islam. "You and the West are doomed"... Ayatollah Ruhollah Khomeini [3]

"...[W]e will stand against the whole world and will not cease until the annihilation of all [infidels]. Either we shake one another's hands in joy at the victory of Islam in the world, or all of us will turn to eternal life and martyrdom." Ayatollah Ruhollah Khomeini [4]

THE MUSLIM BROTHERHOOD, FOUNTAIN OF ISLAMIC VIOLENCE

by Cynthia Farahat
Middle East Quarterly: **Spring 2017 - Vol XXIV: No. 2, pg 3**

What to make of the Muslim Brotherhood (MB)? During the Obama years, it became commonplace for the U.S. administration and its Western acolytes to portray the Muslim Brotherhood as a moderate option to "more radical" Muslim groups. Thus, for example, U.S. director of National Intelligence James Clapper incredibly described the organization as "largely secular" [5] while John Esposito of Georgetown University claimed that "Muslim Brotherhood affiliated movements and parties have been a force for democratization and stability in the Middle East." [6]

On the other hand, in 2014, the United Arab Emirates formally designated [7] The Muslim Brotherhood and its local and international affiliates, including the U.S. based Council on American-Islamic Relations (CAIR), [8] as inter-national terrorist groups. A British government review commissioned the same year similarly asserted that parts of the Muslim Brotherhood have a highly ambiguous relationship with violent extremism. Both as an ideology and as a network it has been a rite of passage for some individuals and groups who have gone on to engage in violence and terrorism. [9]

In the United States, Sen. Ted Cruz (R-Tex.) and Rep. Mario Diaz-Balart (R-FL) have recently introduced legislation to designate The Muslim Brotherhood as a terrorist organization. In February 2016, the U.S. House Judiciary Committee approved a house bill that calls on the State Department to designate The Muslim Brotherhood as a foreign terrorist organization. In July 2016, Rep. Dave Brat (R-VA) introduced the "Naming the Enemy within Homeland Security Act," a bill that prohibits the Department of Homeland Security from funding or collaborating with organizations or individuals associated with The Muslim Brotherhood. [10]

The Muslim Brotherhood has operated as a terrorist entity for almost a century.

The question is—which view is correct? Without doubt, the second one is.

It influenced the establishment of most modern Sunni terrorist organizations, including al-Qaeda, al-Gama'a al-Islamiyya (GI) Hamas, and the Islamic State (ISIS). These organizations have either been founded by current or former Brotherhood members or have been directly inspired, indoctrinated, or recruited by MB members and literature. Contrary to what the MB propagates to Westerners, MB violence is not just in the past but is an ongoing activity.

Historical Background

The Muslim Brotherhood was founded in 1928 by Hassan al-Banna (1906-49), an Egyptian schoolteacher and sometime watch repairer from a small rural town north of Cairo. Reared in a deeply devout household steeped in the Hanbali school of Islamic jurisprudence popular among Wahhabi and Salafi Jihadists, [11] al-Banna engaged in Islamist activities from a young age, joining a local group that intimidated and harassed Christians and non-observing Muslims in his hometown. [12] He was also fascinated by secret societies, cults, and fraternal orders, which flourished in Egypt at the time, and this obsession drove him to form the Brotherhood as a fraternity cult with its own secret militia—al-Tanzim al-Khass (the Special Apparatus, also known as the Secret Apparatus)—charged with strategizing, funding, and executing military training and terror activities. [13] The MB infiltrated the Egyptian army with a group that overthrew the monarchy in a bloodless coup in July 1952. During the first few decades of its existence, the Special Apparatus carried out numerous acts of political violence in Egypt, notably the 1947 assassination of Judge Ahmed Khazinder Bey and the 1948 assassination of Prime Minister Mahmoud Nuqrashi Pasha, who reportedly considered outlawing the MB. [14] At that time, according to a secret U.S. intelligence memorandum, the Brotherhood's "commando units" were estimated to possess "secret caches of arms ... reported to have 60,000 to 70,000 rifles." [15] This military buildup was ac-companied by infiltration of the Egyptian army, including the conspiratorial group of Free Officers, who in July 1952 overthrew the monarchy in a bloodless coup. [16]

The Secret Apparatus was not only involved in assassinations but also carried out a large wave of terrorism and bombings. [17] Thus, for example, on Christmas Eve 1945 it bombed the British Club in Egypt, and in December 1946 bombed eight police stations in Cairo. Two years later, the Brotherhood bombed several Jewish homes in Cairo and many Jewish owned businesses and cinemas. [18] The Brotherhood also bombed trains in Sharqia and Ismailia, as well as the King George Hotel in Ismailia. In a 1948 raid on one of the organization's Cairo offices, the police confiscated 165 bombs. [19]

After al-Banna's assassination in 1949, Hassan Hudaybi, who succeeded him as MB general guide (al-Murshid al-Amm), claimed to have dissolved the Secret Apparatus in order to ease the government's persecution of the "movement," [20] only to be arrested in 1965 alongside other MB leaders for forming a new militia that engaged in military training with a view to assassinating President Gamal Abdel Nasser. [21] Hudaybi managed to escape with a three-year prison sentence (the MB's foremost ideologue Sayyed Qutb was executed in 1966 together with two other leaders); his false denial of the MB's military wing was to become a standard tactic of the Brotherhood to date.

Laying Infrastructure

This denial notwithstanding, the late 1960s and early 1970s saw the formation of a number of MB terror groups under ostensibly independent banners. The first such group was Gama'at al-Muslim in, commonly known as Takfir wa-l-Hijra (Excommunication and Emigration), formed by two leaders of the Secret Apparatus released from prison: Shukri Mustafa and Sheikh Ali Ismael, brother of MB leader Fattah Ismael who was executed alongside Sayyed Qutb. [22] Another terrorist group created by The Brotherhood at the time was al-Gama'a al-Islamiyya (GI, the Islamic group), which was responsible for the October 1981 assassination of Egyptian president Anwar Sadat. Both groups were founded by active leaders of the Brotherhood, who never claimed to have left the organization or their leadership positions therein.

Indeed, in his last speech, one month before his assassination, Sadat equated the GI with the Brotherhood and expressed regret for having released many Brotherhood operatives from prison. [23]

Omar Abdel Rahman ("The Blind Sheikh") and nine others were convicted of seditious conspiracy in connection with the 1993 bombing of the World Trade Center.

During the 1990s, the Egyptian authorities battled against a sustained wave of Islamist terrorism involving attacks on government officials and the country's Coptic minority, the murdering of foreign tourists as well as an audacious attempt on the life of President Hosni Mubarak while he was in Ethiopia in June 1995. [24] In the same year, GI's leader and MB spiritual authority, Omar Abdel Rahman, known as "The Blind Sheikh," and nine others were convicted of seditious conspiracy in connection with the 1993 bombing of the World Trade Center. Abdel Rahman is currently serving a life sentence in a federal prison in North Carolina, and in Muhammad Morsi's first speech as Egyptian president in Tahrir Square, he called for Abdel Rahman's release and acknowledged the sheikh's family who was present in the audience. [25]

No less important was the formation of the movement's International Apparatus by al-Banna's son-in-law Said Ramadan. Having fled Egypt to Saudi Arabia in 1954, Ramadan moved to Geneva in 1958 where he established the International Apparatus under the guidance of Mustafa Mashour, head of the Secret Apparatus, future MB general guide, and author of its militant manifesto "Jihad Is the Way." [26] The International Apparatus was not fully operational until the mid-1980s when Mashour, who fled Egypt after Sadat's assassination, settled in West Germany [27] in 1986 where he reestablished the Apparatus.

The MB's International Apparatus is involved in operating and funding terrorist groups responsible for attacks on American soil. The International Apparatus is not just responsible for the Brotherhood's public operations, but is also involved in operating and funding terrorist groups responsible for attacks on American soil. Thus, for example, Chakib Ben Makhlouf, one of the most prominent leaders of the MB's Geneva office, is also the president of the Federation of Islamic Organizations in Europe. He has been described by Egyptian member of parliament and terrorism expert Abdel Rahim Ali as "one of the most dangerous operatives of the Brotherhood's International Apparatus." [28] Likewise, according to Egyptian general Fouad Allam, who investigated the MB's operations in the 1960s-70s, the Geneva office funneled funds that helped establish al-Gama'a al-Islamiyya. [29]

Later Influences

The International Apparatus's most critical mission, though, has been to infiltrate, subvert, and recruit operatives from within the armies, governments, educational systems, and intelligence agencies of the MB's targeted states, especially in the West, in what is called "civilization jihad."

This term dates to a 1991 document titled The Explanatory Memorandum, drafted in a meeting that outlined the Muslim Brotherhood's strategic goals for North America and entered as evidence in the Holy Land Foundation (HLF) terror funding trial in 2008—the largest terror financing case in U.S. history. [30] In 2009, five MB leaders were charged with providing material support to Hamas, the Brotherhood's Palestinian branch and a designated foreign terrorist organization.

The 1980s and 1990s were the two most important decades for the "civilization jihad." During this time, Hamas was transformed from an essentially missionary and charitable organization seeking to win Palestinian hearts and minds into a fully-fledged terror group during the first intifada (December 1987-September 1993), and the seeds were sown for the advent of al-Qaeda through the newly-formed Maktab al-Khidamat (MAK, the Services Bureau), also known as Maktab Khidamat al-Mujahidin al-Arab (the Services Bureau of Arab Jihadists) and the Afghan Services Bureau.

As jihadists flocked to Afghanistan and Pakistan to fight the Soviet occupation, the Brotherhood was busy running recruitment, jihadist services through its MAK offices throughout the Middle East. In 1984, MB operative Abdullah Azzam established the MAK office in Jordan. [31] Azzam's philosophy helped establish and organize the Brotherhood's "global jihad" movement, which earned him the alias, "The Father of Global Jihad." [32] No less important, this philosophy inspired GI and Egyptian Islamic Jihad (EIJ) to try to export their terrorism and greatly inspired Osama bin Laden, whom Azzam taught at a Saudi university. [33]

In 1985, MB operatives Abdullah Azzam (L), bin Laden, and Ayman Zawahiri (R) founded MAK in Pakistan, which evolved into al-Qaeda. The Amman MAK recruited Abu Musab Zarqawi, who founded

Jama'at al-Tawhid wa-l-Jihad, which evolved into al-Qaeda in Iraq and eventually into ISIS.

In 1985, Azzam, bin Laden and Ayman Zawahiri, leader of Takfir wa-l-Hijra who fled Egypt after the Sadat assassination, founded MAK in Pakistan, which subsequently evolved into al-Qaeda. Meanwhile, the Amman MAK office recruited one of the world's most brutal terrorists of modern time, Abu Musab Zarqawi. [34] Mentored by Jordanian former MB leader Abu Muhammad Maqdisi, in 1999, Zarqawi founded Jama'at al-Tawhid wa-l-Jihad (Organization of Monotheism and Jihad), which six years later, evolved into al-Qaeda in Iraq (AQI) after Zarqawi pledged allegiance to bin Laden in late 2004. This group eventually morphed into ISIS after Zarqawi's death in June 2006. Indeed, in a 2014 interview reported in Al-Arabiya News, the Muslim Brotherhood spiritual guide Yusuf Qaradawi admitted that ISIS leader Abu Bakr Baghdadi was a member of the Muslim Brotherhood. [35] For their part, several MB leaders publicly announced their support for ISIS, including the Qatar-based Sheikh Wagdy Ghoneim. [36]

The nature of al-Qaeda's current relationship with the Brotherhood is somewhat unclear. While Zawahiri argued that bin Laden's affiliation with the MB was severed in the 1980s due to differences over the anti-Soviet Afghanistan campaign, [37] this claim was discounted by Tharwat Kherbawy, the highest ranking MB member to have defected from the organization, [38] and also by evidence suggesting that the Brotherhood is still organizationally involved with al-Qaeda. Thus, for example, after Morsi's July 2013 ouster from power, Zawahiri issued a videotaped statement on his behalf where he criticized Egyptian Salafi jihadists for not formally joining the Muslim Brotherhood's Freedom and Justice Party to help it uphold Sharia law. [39] In another statement, Zawahiri criticized the deposed MB president for having played politics with opponents, [40] but eventually prayed for his release and supported him while he was facing trial for inciting the killing of regime opponents and for espionage for foreign militant groups including Hamas, Hezbollah, and Iran's Revolutionary Guard Corp. [41]

A Political Party or a Jihadi Group?

The Obama administration's stubborn support for the Morsi regime and its tireless attempts to cast the MB as a moderate organization are preposterous—not only because the Brotherhood is the bedrock of some of the worst terror groups in today's world but also because violence is endemic to the movement's raison d'être: restoring the caliphate via violent jihad. Were the Brotherhood to give up this foundational goal, it would lose its legitimacy and sole reason for existence. This is why al-Banna used military terminology in structuring the MB, calling the organization "Allah's battalion," [42] a term used to this very day to denote the MB's governing core; this is why the current Brotherhood leadership includes operatives who personally engaged in violent jihad and terror activities such as Abdel Moneim Abul Futuh. [43]

Osama Yassin, a former minister in Muhammad Morsi's cabinet, revealed that members of the MB's 95 Brigade militia engaged in the abduction, beating, and torture of "thugs" during riots leading to Mubarak's downfall.

Furthermore, the organization's Secret Apparatus remains intact and operational with new recruits required to undergo military training by such militias as the 95 Brigade, [44] which was established in 1995 and which played an active role in the January 2011 riots leading to Mubarak's downfall. In a series of interviews with al-Jazeera TV, Osama Yassin, a former minister in Morsi's cabinet, revealed that members of the brigade engaged in the abduction, beating, and torture of "thugs" and threw Molotov cocktails at their opponents. [45] Asked by an Egyptian newspaper to clarify these revelations," [46] the MB dismissed them as a joke. Still, the brigade operatives were later implicated in the killing of anti-Brotherhood protestors. In March 2014, for example, two operatives were sentenced to death after an online video clip showed them killing a teenager by throwing him from a building. [47]

According to the Brotherhood's own standards and internal bylaws, [48] there are ten solid, unchangeable thawabit (precepts) in their organization's bai'a (Islamic oath of allegiance) process. The fourth of these precepts is violent jihad and martyrdom, [49] which the Brotherhood states is an obligation of every individual Muslim, as well as the collective obligation of their organization.

The current Brotherhood leadership includes operatives who personally engaged in violent jihad and terror activities. Unfortunately, many American specialists either receive foreign funding or are otherwise oblivious to these facts and actively engage in a disinformation campaign. For example, a Brookings Institute article turned the meaning of the "fourth precept" of the Brotherhood's bylaws on its head, stating that it stipulated that "during the process of establishing democracy and relative political freedom, the Muslim Brotherhood is committed to abide by the rules of democracy and its institutions." [50]

Reality, of course, was quite different. When after Mubarak's downfall the Muslim Brotherhood rose to power in a sham presidential election, [51] which brought its operative Mohamed Morsi to the presidential palace, its violent [52] and undemocratic rule triggered, in short notice, mass protests throughout the country that brought millions of protestors to the streets and enabled the military to overthrow Morsi in a bloodless coup.

Islamic Reformers

Indeed, the sheer brutality of ISIS and various Brotherhood-affiliated or inspired terror groups across the Middle East has led to the advent of a mainstream Islamic reformist movement that draws on vastly more popular support than the Brotherhood itself. This unprecedented revival of a reform-oriented movement has received too little attention in the West. For example, Islam Behery, one of the movement's heroic leaders, was incarcerated for a year for blasphemy for insulting al-Azhar University and the Sunni doctrine on his television show. [53] For two years, that show had been dedicated daily to exposing the brutality and terrorism of Sunni doctrine while offering a non-theocratic, liberal interpretation of Islam that pushes for separation of mosque and state. Behery received a presidential pardon in December 2016, which was unprecedented in Egyptian history. Another supporter of reformation and freedom of thought is Ibrahim Issa, a popular Egyptian commentator, television host, and owner and editor-in-chief of the independent opinion newspaper Al-Maqal. Earlier this year, Issa announced that he would end his TV show due to "current events," kindling speculation that the cancellation was related to Saudi pressure on the Egyptian regime because of Issa's criticism of the kingdom's violent Wahhabi sect.[54] Issa's reformist stance has placed him on terrorist hit lists since 1992, and he has been living under tight security ever since. His opposition to the Muslim Brotherhood has made him one of the organization's high-profile targets, and in 2015, he became the subject of an official fatwa declaring him an "infidel." [55]

Another heroic figure of Islamic reform currently facing the possibility of incarceration for blasphemy is the popular author and prominent secular figure Sayyed Qemani. His sin: stating that al-Azhar University should be designated a terrorist organization. [56] Behery, Qemani, and their like have the support of the most mainstream media figures in Egypt and across the Middle East, and they have dramatically changed the Islamic political discourse. Yet Western audiences have almost never heard of their heroic efforts. The war of ideas is highly dynamic in today's Middle East. The vast majority of the region's peaceful Muslims are marginalized by Western support for the Brotherhood and the West's refusal to designate the MB as a terrorist organization.

Conclusion

The deadly Brotherhood cult is responsible for almost a century of terror since the young al-Banna engaged in the intimidation and harassment of his Christian and moderate Muslim neighbors. Since then, the Brotherhood established Hamas as its Palestinian wing. Three Brotherhood activists established al-Qaeda. Brotherhood leaders, from inside their prisons, founded al-Gama'a al-Islamiyya and Egyptian Islamic Jihad. Brotherhood members recruited the founder of Jama'at al-Tawhid wa-l-Jihad who started the trend of video decapitations, and one of its former operatives is currently acting as the Caliph of Islamic State. The MB also has other connections to organizations on the U.S. government's list of foreign terrorist organizations.

The majority of the region's peaceful Muslims are marginalized by Western support for the Brotherhood. Neither Washington, nor any capital, can hope to counter Islamic terrorism successfully without allying with Muslim figures fighting on the forefront of the battle of ideas. Washington can give these moderate Muslims a voice by designating the Muslim Brotherhood as a terrorist organization.

The Brotherhood has stated its intention to destroy the West's "miserable house" by infiltrating Western society and institutions and subverting them from the inside. [57] Designating the Muslim Brotherhood as a foreign terrorist organization will stop its operatives from reaching sensitive positions in the intelligence community and in other powerful U.S. government positions. It will also stop Brotherhood operatives in the United States from funding terrorism operations worldwide.

Cynthia Farahat, a Middle East Forum Writing Fellow and columnist for Al-Maqal daily newspaper, is currently working on a book about the Muslim Brotherhood.

REFERENCES CITED FOR APPENDIX C

[1] *The Muslim Brotherhood's Conquest of Europe;* Middle East Quarterly, Winter 2005

[2] *Fear The Muslim Brotherhood;* National Review, Andrew C. McCarthy, Jan. 31, 2011.

[3] *The Muslim Brotherhood in Egypt: Historical Evolution and Future Prospective;* K. Helaby; 2006.

[4] Quote from 11th grade Iranian schoolbook, Bernard Lewis, 2006.

[5] ABC News, Feb. 10, 2011.

[6] John Esposito, "The Muslim Brotherhood, Terrorism and U.S. Policy," The Huffington Post (New York), Mar. 22, 2016.

[7] Reuters, Nov. 15, 2014.

[8] The Washington Post, Nov. 17, 2014.

[9] Reuters, Dec. 17, 2015.

[10] Rep. Dave Brat, press release, Brat.House.gov, July 19, 2016.

[11] Abdallah Aqeel, "Al-Sheikh al-Muhadith Ahmad Abdel Rahman al-Banna al-Sa'ati," AlaqeelAbuMostafa.com, accessed Aug. 30, 2016.

[12] Hassan al-Banna, Mudhakkirat al-Da'wa wa'l-Da'iyah (Cairo: Maktabat al-Shihab, 1979), pp. 17-18 & pp. 25-26; Misr al-Balad TV (Cairo), Mar. 19, 2014.

[13] Mahmoud Sabbagh, Haqiqat al-Tanzim al-Khass (Cairo: Etisam Publishing, 1989).

[14]] Abdel Rahim Ali, "Abdel Rahman Sendi: Mu'asis al-Tanzim al-Khass bi'l-Ikhwan," Islamists-Movements.com, Nov. 12, 2015.

[15] "Assessing the Islamist Threat, circa 1946," Middle East Quarterly, Summer 2006, pp. 76-82; FrontPage Magazine (Sherman Oaks, Calif.), Feb. 13, 2006.

[16] Khaled Mohieddin, Al'an Atakkalam: Mudhakkirat al-Thawra (Cairo: American University of Cairo Press, 1995), p. 45; Hassan Ashmawy, Mudhakkirat Harib (Cairo: Islamic Publishing House, 2000), p.15.

[17] Farouk Taifour, "Al-Juz' al-Rabi: al-Ikhwan wa'l-Tanzimat al-Sirriya," Egyptian Institute for Political and Strategic Studies, Cairo, EIPSS-EG.org, Feb. 24, 2016.

[18] "Profile: Egypt's Muslim Brotherhood," BBC, Dec. 25, 2013.

[19] Al-Wafd (Cairo), Dec. 14, 2013.

[20] Salah Shadi, Safahat min al-Tarikh (Cairo: Islamic Publishing House, 1987), p. 79.

[21] Ahmad Abdel Majid, Al-Ikhwan wa Abdel Nasser: Al-Qissa al-Kamila li-Tanizm 1965 (Cairo: al-Zahra for Arabic Media, 1991), p. 33.

[22] Tharwat Kharbawi, Sirr al-Ma'bad (Cairo: Nahdet Misr Publishing, 2012), p. 220.

[23] YouTube, "Al-Sadat Yatahadath an al-Gama'a al-Islamiya wa'l-Ikhwan," May 9, 2012.

24 Efraim Karsh, Islamic Imperialism: A History (New Haven and London: Yale University Press, 2013; rev. ed.), chap. 12.

25 TV News (Cairo), June 29, 2012.

26 Mustafa Mashour, "Al-Jihad huwa al-Sabil," The Official Muslim Brotherhood Encyclopedia, IkhwanWiki.com, accessed Aug. 31, 2016; idem, "Jihad Is the Way," trans. Palestinian Media Watch, Jerusalem, Feb. 9, 2011.

27 Daniel Pipes, "How Islamists Came to Dominate European Islam," National Review Online, May 25, 2010.

28 Al-Bawabah News (Cairo), Mar. 11, 2014.

29 Rifaat Sayed, Hassan al-Banna, al-Sheikh al-Musalah (Cairo: Akhbar al-Youm Publishing, 2004), p. 198

30 "The Muslim Brotherhood's Strategic Plan for America—Court document," The Clarion Project, Washington, D.C., accessed Sept. 1, 2016.

31 Farouk Taifour, "Hal Kharajat Daesh min Rahm Fikr al-Ikhwan al-Muslimin?" Egyptian Institute for Political and Strategic Studies, Cairo, EIPSS-EG.org.

32 "Abdullah Azzam: Overview," Counter Extremist Project, New York, accessed Feb. 9, 2017.

33 Karsh, Islamic Imperialism, chap. 13.

34 Elaph (London), July 18, 2005.

35 Al-Arabiya News Channel (Dubai), Oct. 14, 2014.

36 "Al-Sheikh Wagdy Ghoneim: La li'l-Tahaluf al-Salibi dudd al-Dawla al-Islamiya," You Tube, Sept. 19, 2014.

37 Stephen Lacroix, "Osama bin Laden and the Saudi Muslim Brotherhood," Foreign Policy, Oct. 3, 2012.

38 Al-Aan TV (Cairo), Apr. 19, 2014.

39 "Ta'kib al-Sheikh Ayman al-Zawahiri ala Azl Morsi wa-Tahdid al-Jaish," You Tube, July 5, 2013.

40 "Ayman al-Zawahiri Yuwajih Risalat Itab li-Morsi wa-Yadou Allah an Yafuku Asrahou," You Tube, Feb. 11, 2014; Erich Follath, "Political Stability Eludes Polarized Egypt," Der Spiegel (Hamburg), July 29, 2013.

41 Reuters, Dec. 17, 2015.

42 al-Banna, Mudhakkirat al-Da'wa, p. 144.

43 "Abdel Moneim Abul Futuh Yajtami ma'a Haraket Taliban Afghanistan," You Tube, June 8, 2013.

44 Al-Wafd (Cairo), Jan. 11, 2013.

45 Al-Jazeera TV (Cairo), Nov.-Dec. 2011.

46 Al-Watan (Cairo), Jan. 3, 2013.

47 Al-Arabiya News, Mar. 29, 2014.

48 "Bylaws of the International Muslim Brotherhood," June 1928.

49 Muhammad Kandil, "Al-Thabit al-Rab'i: al-Jihad Salbiluna," The Official Muslim Brotherhood Encyclopedia, IkhwanWiki.com, accessed Sept. 1, 2016; "The Muslim Brotherhood: Understanding its Roots and Impact, 1. Overview," Foundation for Defense of Democracies, Washington, D.C., accessed Feb. 9, 2017.

50 Umar Ashur, "Hal Ya'ud al-Ikhwan al-Muslimun fi Masr ila'l-Unf al-Siyasi?" Brookings Institute, Washington, D.C., July 30, 2014.

51 Daniel Pipes and Cynthia Farahat, "Egypt's Sham Election," National Review Online, Dec. 6, 2011; Shuruk News (Cairo), Mar. 22, 2016.

52 Amb. Yahia Najm, Akhbar al-Yom TV (Cairo), in Cynthia Farahat, "CairoGate: Egyptian Diplomat Survives MB Torture Says 'It was like a Nazi camp,'" Dec. 9, 2012.

53 Al-Ahram (Cairo), Dec. 29, 2015.

54 Bawabat al-Qahira (Cairo), Jan. 1, 2017.

55 Bawabat al-Haraqat al-Islamiya (Cairo), Mar. 18, 2015. The fatwa was subsequently broadcast on the official Muslim Brotherhood television channel Rabaa, broadcasting from Turkey. See Al-Arabiya News, Dec. 5, 2017.

56 Al-Dustur (Cairo), Jan. 3, 2016.

57 "The Muslim Brotherhood's Strategic Plan for America—Court document," The Clarion Project, Washington, D.C., accessed Sep. 1, 2016.

Appendix D

COUNCIL ON AMERICAN-ISLAMIC RELATIONS (CAIR)

Official Mission: "To enhance understanding of Islam, encourage dialogue, protect civil liberties, empower American Muslims, and build coalitions that promote justice and mutual understanding."

Purpose: To function as public relations organization for The Muslim Brotherhood, the most powerful terrorist organization in the world

CAIR: ISLAMISTS FOOLING THE ESTABLISHMENT

by Daniel Pipes and Sharon Chadha
Middle East Quarterly: **Spring 2006, Vol XIII: No. 2, pg 3-20**

The Council on American-Islamic Relations (CAIR), headquartered in Washington, is perhaps the best-known and most controversial Muslim organization in North America. CAIR presents itself as an advocate for Muslims' civil rights and the spokesman for American Muslims. "We are similar to a Muslim NAACP," says its communications director, Ibrahim Hooper. [1] Its official mission ... "to enhance understanding of Islam, encourage dialogue, protect civil liberties, empower American Muslims, and build coalitions that promote justice and mutual understanding" [2] ... suggests nothing problematic.

Starting with a single office in 1994, CAIR now claims thirty-one affiliates, including a branch in Canada, with more steadily being added. In addition to its grand national headquarters in Washington, it has impressive offices in other cities; the New York office, for example, is housed in the 19-story Interchurch Center located on Manhattan's Riverside Drive.

But there is another side to CAIR that has alarmed many people in positions to know. The Department of Homeland Security refuses to deal with it. Senator Charles Schumer (Democrat, New York) describes it as an organization "which we know has ties to terrorism." [3] Senator Dick Durbin (Democrat, Illinois) observes that CAIR is "unusual in its extreme rhetoric and its associations with groups that are suspect." [4] Steven Pomerantz, the FBI's former chief of counterterrorism, notes that "CAIR, its leaders, and its activities effectively give aid to international terrorist groups." [5]

The family of John P. O'Neill, Sr., the former FBI counterterrorism chief who perished at the World Trade Center, named CAIR in a lawsuit as having "been part of the criminal conspiracy of radical Islamic terrorism" [6] responsible for the September 11 atrocities. Counterterrorism expert Steven Emerson calls it "a radical fundamentalist front group for Hamas." [7]

Of particular note are the American Muslims who reject CAIR's claim to speak on their behalf. The late Seifeldin Ashmawy, publisher of the New Jersey-based Voice of Peace, called CAIR the champion of "extremists whose views do not represent Islam." [8] Jamal Hasan of the Council for Democracy and Tolerance explains that CAIR's goal is to spread "Islamic hegemony the world over by hook or by crook." [9] Kamal Nawash, head of Free Muslims Against Terrorism, finds that CAIR and similar groups condemn terrorism on the surface while endorsing an ideology that helps foster extremism, adding that "almost all of their members are theocratic Muslims who reject secularism and want to establish Islamic states." [10] Tashbih Sayyed of the Council for Democracy and Tolerance calls CAIR "the most accomplished fifth column" in the United States. [11] And Stephen Schwartz of the Center on Islamic Pluralism writes that "CAIR should be considered a foreign-based subversive organization, comparable in the Islamist field to the Soviet-controlled Communist Party, USA." [12]

CAIR, for its part, dismisses all criticism, blaming negative comments on "Muslim bashers" who "can never point to something CAIR has done in its 10-year history that is objectionable." [13]

Part of the Establishment

When President George W. Bush visited the Islamic Center of Washington several days after September 11, 2001, to signal that he would not tolerate a backlash against Muslims, he invited CAIR's executive director, Nihad Awad, to join him at the podium. Two months later, when Secretary of State Colin Powell hosted a Ramadan dinner, he, too, called upon CAIR as representative of Islam in America. [14] More broadly, when the State Department seeks out Muslims to welcome foreign dignitaries, journalists, and academics, it calls upon CAIR. [15] The organization has represented American Muslims before Congress. The National Aeronautics and Space Agency hosted CAIR's "Sensitivity and Diversity Workshop" in an effort to harmonize space research with Muslim sensibilities. [16]

Law-enforcement agencies in Florida, Maryland, Ohio, Michigan, New York, Arizona, California, Missouri, Texas, and Kentucky have attended CAIR's sensitivity-training sessions. [17] The organization boasts such tight relations with law enforcement that it claims to have even been invited to monitor police raids. [18] In July 2004, as agents from the FBI, Internal Revenue Service, and Homeland Security descended on the Institute of Islamic and Arabic Sciences in America, a Saudi-created school in Merrifield, Virginia, a local paper reported that the FBI had informed CAIR's legal director, Arsalan Iftikhar, that morning that the raid was going to take place.

CAIR is also a media darling. It claims to log five thousand annual mentions on newspapers, television, and radio, including some of the most prestigious media in the United States. [19] The press dutifully quotes CAIR's statistics, publishes its theological views, reports its opinions, rehashes its press releases, invites its staff on television, and generally dignifies its existence as a routine part of the American and Canadian political scenes.

CAIR regularly participates in seminars on Islamic cultural issues for corporations and has been invited to speak at many of America's leading universities, including Harvard, Stanford, Johns Hopkins, and Columbia. American high schools have invited CAIR to promote its agenda, as have educationally-minded senior citizens. [20]

Terrorists in Its Midst

Perhaps the most obvious problem with CAIR is the fact that at least five of its employees and board members have been arrested, convicted, deported, or otherwise linked to terrorism-related charges and activities.

Randall ("Ismail") Royer, an American convert to Islam, served as CAIR's communications specialist and civil rights coordinator; today he sits in jail on terrorism-related charges.

In June 2003, Royer and ten other young men, ages 23 to 35, known as the "Virginia jihad group," were indicted on forty-one counts of "conspiracy to train for and participate in a violent jihad overseas." The defendants, nine of them U.S. citizens, were accused of association with Lashkar-e-Taiba, a radical Islamic group designated as a foreign terrorist organization by the U.S. Department of State in 2001. They were also accused of meeting covertly in private homes and at the Islamic Center in Falls Church to prepare themselves for battle by listening to lectures and watching videotapes. [21]   As the prosecutor noted, "Ten miles from Capitol Hill in the streets of northern Virginia, American citizens allegedly met, plotted, and recruited for violent jihad." [22] According to Matthew Epstein of the Investigative Project, Royer helped recruit the others to the jihad effort while he was working for CAIR. The group trained at firing ranges in Virginia and Pennsylvania; in addition, it practiced "small-unit military tactics" at a paintball war-games facility in Virginia, earning it the moniker, the "paintball jihadis." [23] Eventually members of the group traveled to Pakistan.

Five of the men indicted, including CAIR's Royer, were found to have had in their possession, according to the indictment, "AK-47-style rifles, telescopic lenses, hundreds of rounds of ammunition and tracer rounds, documents on undertaking jihad and martyrdom, [and] a copy of the terrorist handbook containing instructions on how to manufacture and use explosives and chemicals as weapons." [24]

After four of the eleven defendants pleaded guilty, the remaining seven, including Royer, were accused in a new, 32-count indictment of yet more serious charges: conspiring to help Al-Qaeda and the Taliban battle American troops in Afghanistan. [25]

Royer admitted in his grand jury testimony that he had already waged jihad in Bosnia under a commander acting on orders from Osama bin Laden. Prosecutors also presented evidence that his father, Ramon Royer, had rented a room in his St. Louis-area home in 2000 to Ziyad Khaleel, the student who purchased the satellite phone used by Al-Qaeda in planning the two U.S. embassy bombings in East Africa in August 1998. [26] Royer eventually pleaded guilty to lesser firearms-related charges, and the former CAIR staffer was sentenced to twenty years in prison. [27]

A coda to the "Virginia jihad network" came in 2005 when a Federal court convicted another Virginia man, Ahmed Omar Abu Ali, of plotting to kill President Bush. Prosecutors alleged that Abu Ali participated in the Virginia jihad network's paintball games and perhaps supplied one of his fellow jihadists with an assault rifle. [28] Royer's possible role in Abu Ali's plans are unclear.

Ghassan Elashi, the founder of CAIR's Texas chapter, has a long history of funding terrorism. First, he was convicted in July 2004, with his four brothers, of having illegally shipped computers from their Dallas-area business, InfoCom Corporation, to two designated state-sponsors of terrorism, Libya and Syria. [29] Second, he and two brothers were convicted in April 2005 of knowingly doing business with Mousa Abu Marzook, a senior Hamas leader, whom the U.S. State Department had in 1995 declared a "specially designated terrorist." Elashi was convicted of all twenty-one counts with which he was charged, including conspiracy, money laundering, and dealing in the property of a designated terrorist. [30]

Third, he was charged in July 2004 with providing more than $12.4 million to Hamas while he was running the Holy Land Foundation for Relief and Development, America's largest Islamic charity. [31] When the U.S. government shuttered Holy Land Foundation in late 2001, CAIR characterized this move as "unjust" and "disturbing." [32]

Bassem Khafagi, an Egyptian native and CAIR's onetime community relations director, pleaded guilty in September 2003 to lying on his visa application and passing bad checks for substantial amounts in early 2001, [33] for which he was deported. CAIR claimed Khafagi was hired only after he had committed his crimes and that the organization was unaware of his wrongdoing. [34] But that is unconvincing, for a cursory background check reveals that Khafagi was a founding member and president of the Islamic Assembly of North America (IANA), [35] an organization under investigation by the U.S. Department of Justice for terrorism-related activities. CAIR surely knew that IANA under Khafagi was in the business of, as prosecutors stated in Idaho court papers, disseminating "radical Islamic ideology, the purpose of which was indoctrination, recruitment of members, and the instigation of acts of violence and terrorism. [36]

For example, IANA websites promoted the views of two Saudi preachers, Salman al-Awdah and Safar al-Hawali, well-known in Islamist circles for having been spiritual advisors to Osama bin Laden. [37] Under Khafagi's leadership, Matthew Epstein has testified, IANA hosted a conference at which a senior Al-Qaeda recruiter, Abdelrahman al-Dosari, was a speaker. [38] IANA disseminated publications advocating suicide attacks against the United States, according to federal investigators. [39]

Also, Khafagi was co-owner of a Sir Speedy printing franchise until 1998 with Rafil Dhafir, who was a former vice president of IANA and a Syracuse-area oncologist convicted in February 2005 of illegally sending money to Iraq during the Saddam Hussein regime as well as defrauding donors by using contributions to his "Help the Needy" charitable fund to avoid taxes and to purchase personal assets for himself. Dhafir was sentenced to twenty-two years in prison. [40]

Rabih Haddad, a CAIR fundraiser, was arrested in December 2001 on terrorism-related charges and deported from the United States due to his subsequent work as executive director of the Global Relief Foundation, a charity he co-founded [41] which was designated by the U.S. Treasury Department in October 2002 for financing Al-Qaeda and other terrorist organizations. [42]

Siraj Wahhaj, a CAIR advisory board member, was named in 1995 by U.S. attorney Mary Jo White as a possible unindicted coconspirator in the plot to blow up New York City landmarks led by the blind sheikh, Omar Abdul Rahman. In defense of having Wahhaj on its advisory board, CAIR described him as "one of the most respected Muslim leaders in America." [43] In October 2004, he spoke at a CAIR dinner. This roster of employees and board members connected to terrorism makes one wonder how CAIR remains an acceptable guest at

U.S. government events—and even more so, how U.S. law enforcement agencies continue to associate with it.

Links to Hamas

First, CAIR has a number of links to the terror organization Hamas, starting with the founder of its Texas chapter, Ghassan Elashi, as noted above.

Second, Elashi and another CAIR founder, Omar Ahmad, attended a key meeting in Philadelphia in 1993. An FBI memo characterizes this meeting as a planning session for Hamas, Holy Land Foundation, and Islamic Association of Palestine to find ways to disrupt Israeli-Palestinian diplomacy and raise money for Hamas in the United States. [44] The Philadelphia meeting was deemed such strong proof of Islamic Association of Palestine's relation to Hamas that a federal judge in Chicago in December 2004 ruled the Islamic Association of Palestine partially liable for US$156 million in damages (along with the Holy Land Foundation and Mohammad Salah, a Hamas operative) [45] for having aided and abetted the Hamas murder of David Boim, an American citizen. [46]

Third, CAIR's founding personnel were closely linked to the Islamic Association of Palestine, which was founded by Ibrahim Abu Marzook, a senior Hamas operative and husband of Elashi's cousin; according to Epstein, the Islamic Association of Palestine functions as Hamas's public relations and recruitment arm in the United States. [47]

The two individuals who established CAIR, Ahmad and Nihad Awad, had been, respectively, the president and public relations director of the Islamic Association of Palestine. Ibrahim Hooper, CAIR's director of communications, had been an employee of the Islamic Association of Palestine. [48] Rafeeq Jabar, president of the Islamic Association of Palestine, was a founding director of CAIR.

Fourth, the Holy Land Foundation, which the U.S. government has charged with funneling funds to Hamas, provided CAIR with some of its start-up funding in 1994. ($5,000 money transfer) In the other direction, according to Joe Kaufman, CAIR sent potential donors to the Holy Land Foundation's website when they clicked on their post-September 11 weblink, "Donate to the NY/DC Disaster Relief Fund."
[49]

Fifth, Awad publicly declared his enthusiasm for Hamas at Barry University in Florida in 1994: "I'm in support of Hamas movement more than the PLO." As an attorney pointed out in the course of deposing Awad for the Boim case, Awad both supported Hamas and acknowledged an awareness of its involvement in violence. [50]

Impeding Counterterrorism

A class-action lawsuit brought by the estate of John P. O'Neill, Sr. charges CAIR and its Canadian branch of being, since their inception, "part of the criminal conspiracy of radical Islamic terrorism" with a unique role in the terrorist network: both organizations have actively sought to hamper governmental anti-terrorism efforts by direct propaganda activities aimed at police, first-responders, and intelligence agencies through so-called sensitivity training. Their goal is to create as much self-doubt, hesitation, fear of name-calling, and litigation within police departments and intelligence agencies as possible so as to render such authorities ineffective in pursuing international and domestic terrorist entities. [51]   It would be hard to improve on this characterization; under the guise of participating in counterterrorism, CAIR does its best to impede these efforts. This approach can be seen from its statements.

CAIR encourages law enforcement in its work—so long as it does not involve counterterrorism. Wissam Nasr, the head of CAIR's New York office, explains: "The Muslim community in New York wants to play a positive role in protecting our nation's security, but that role is made more difficult if the FBI is perceived as pursuing suspects much more actively than it is searching for community partners." [52] Nasr would have the FBI get out of the unpleasant business of "pursuing suspects" and instead devote itself to building social good will—through CAIR, naturally.

Likewise, on the eve of the U.S. war with Iraq in March 2003, CAIR distributed a "Muslim Community Safety Kit", that advised Muslims to "Know your rights if contacted by the FBI." It tells them specifically, "You have no obligation to talk to the FBI, even if you are not a citizen. ... You do not have to permit them to enter your home. ... ALWAYS have an attorney present when answering questions." On the other hand, when it comes to protecting Muslims, CAIR wants an active FBI.

The same "Muslim community safety kit" advised: "If you believe you have been the victim of an anti-Muslim hate crime or discrimination, you should: 1. Report the incident to your local police station and FBI office IMMEDIATELY." [53]   In January 2006, CAIR joined a lawsuit against the National Security Agency demanding that the U.S. intelligence agency cease monitoring communications with suspected Islamist terrorists. Part of its complaints concerned a belief that the U.S. government monitored its communications with Rabih Haddad, the suspected Al-Qaeda financier who has since moved to Lebanon. [54]   Upon learning that CAIR was a fellow plaintiff in the suit, political writer Christopher Hitchens said, "I was revolted to see who I was in company with. CAIR is a lot to swallow." [55]

Sixth, CAIR discourages Americans from improving their counterterrorism skills. Deedra Abboud, CAIR's Arizona director, approves of police learning the Arabic language if that lowers the chances of cultural and linguistic misunderstandings. "However, if they're learning it in order to better fight terrorism, that concerns me. Only because that assumes that the only fighting we have to do is among Arabic speakers. That's not a long-term strategy." [56]

Apologizing for Islamist Terrorism

CAIR has consistently shown itself to be on the wrong side of the war on terrorism, protecting, defending, and supporting both accused and even convicted radical Islamic terrorists.

In October 1998—months after Osama bin Laden had issued his first declaration of war against the United States and had been named as the chief suspect in the bombings of two U.S. embassies in Africa—CAIR demanded the removal of a Los Angeles billboard describing Osama bin Laden as "the sworn enemy," finding this depiction offensive to Muslims. CAIR also leapt to bin Laden's defense, denying his responsibility for the twin East African embassy bombings. CAIR's Hooper saw these explosions resulting from "misunderstandings of both sides." [57]   Even after the September 11 atrocity, CAIR continued to protect bin Laden, stating only that "if [note the "if"] Osama bin Laden was behind it, we condemn him by name." [58]   Not until December 2001, when bin Laden on videotape boasted of his involvement in the attack, did CAIR finally acknowledge his role.

CAIR has also consistently defended other radical Islamic terrorists. Rather than praise the conviction of the perpetrators of the 1993 World Trade Center bombing, it deemed this "a travesty of justice." [59] It labeled the extradition order for suspected Hamas terrorist Mousa Abu Marzook "anti-Islamic" and "anti-American." [60] CAIR has co-sponsored Yvonne Ridley, the British convert to Islam who became a Taliban enthusiast and a denier that Al-Qaeda was involved in 9-11. [61] When four U.S. civilian contractors in Falluja were (in CAIR's words) "ambushed in their SUV's, burned, mutilated, dragged through the streets, and then hung from a bridge spanning the Euphrates River," CAIR issued a press release that condemned the mutilation of the corpses but stayed conspicuously silent on the actual killings. [62]

During the 2005 trial of Sami Al-Arian, accused of heading Palestinian Islamic Jihad in the United States, Ahmed Bedier of CAIR's Florida branch emerged as Al-Arian's effective spokesman, providing sound bytes to the media, trying to get his trial moved out of Tampa, commenting on the jury selection, and so on. [63]

More broadly, TheReligionofPeace.com website pointed out that "of the more than 3100 fatal Islamic terror attacks committed in the last four years, we have only seen CAIR specifically condemn 18." [64]

Ties to Extremists, Left and Right

The Council on American-Islamic Relations has affinities to extremists of both the left and right, sharing features with both. Its extensive ties to far-left groups include funding from the Tides Foundation for its "Interfaith Coalition against Hate Crimes"; [65] endorsing a statement issued by Refuse & Resist [66] and a "National Day of Protest ... to Stop Police Brutality, Repression and the Criminalization of a Generation." [67] CAIR supported the "Civil Liberties Restoration Act," legislation drafted by Open Society Policy Center, an organization founded by George Soros that would obstruct U.S. law enforcement from prosecuting the "War on Extremism." Far-left members of Congress such as Dennis Kucinich (Democrat, Ohio) and Jim McDermott (Democrat, Washington) have turned up as featured speakers at CAIR fundraising events.

Its neo-Nazi side came out most clearly in CAIR's early years. In 1996, according to testimony by Steven Emerson, Yusuf Islam—the

Muslim convert formerly known as the singer Cat Stevens—gave a keynote speech at a CAIR event. The contents of the speech itself are not known but Islam wrote a pamphlet published by the Islamic Association of Palestine, CAIR's stepparent, which included these sentences:

The Jews seem neither to respect God nor his Creation. Their own holy books contain the curse of God brought upon them by their prophets on account of their disobedience to Him and mischief in the earth. We have seen the disrespect for religion displayed by those who consider themselves to be "God's Chosen People." [68]

In 1998, CAIR co-hosted an event at which an Egyptian Islamist leader, Wagdi Ghunaym, declared Jews to be the "descendants of the apes." [69]

CAIR continues to expose its fascistic side by its repeated activities with William W. Baker, exposed as a neo-Nazi in March 2002. [70] Even after that date, CAIR invited Baker to speak at several events, for example in Florida on August 12, 2003 [71] and New Jersey on October 18, 2003. [72] CAIR liked Baker's work so much, it used the title of his book, *More in Common Than You Think*, in one of its ad campaigns in March 2004 and as the title of an Elderhostel lecture. [73]

Foreign Funding

According to filed copies of its annual Internal Revenue Service Form 990, CAIR's U.S. chapters have more than doubled their combined revenues from the $2.5 million they recorded in 2000 to $5.6 million in 2002, though the number dipped slightly to $5.3 million in 2003, the most recent year for which figures are available. That CAIR has recorded at least $3.1 million on its year-end combined balance sheets since 2001, combined with its minimal grant-making ($27,525 was the total that all CAIR chapters granted in 2003), suggests that CAIR is building an endowment and planning for the long term.

The Internal Revenue Service filings claim that the bulk of its funds come from "direct public support" [74] and its website explicitly denies that CAIR receives support from foreign sources: "We do not support directly or indirectly, or receive support from, any overseas group or government." [75]

However, this denial is flatly untrue, for CAIR has accepted foreign funding, and from many sources.   [76]

A press release from the Saudi Arabian embassy in Washington indicates that in August 1999, the Islamic Development Bank—a bank headquartered in Jeddah, Saudi Arabia—gave CAIR $250,000 to purchase land for its Washington, D.C. headquarters.   [77]   CAIR's decision to accept Islamic Development Bank funding is unfortunate, given the bank's role as fund manager of the Al-Quds and the Al-Aqsa Funds, established by twelve Arab countries in order to fund the Palestinian intifada and provide financial support to the families of Palestinian "martyrs."   [78]

According to records made public by Paul Sperry, CAIR purchased its national headquarters in 1999 through an unusual lease-purchase transaction with the United Bank of Kuwait.   [79]   The bank was the deed holder and leased the building to CAIR; yet despite not owning the building, CAIR recorded the property on its balance sheet as a property asset valued at $2.6 million.   [80]   This arrangement changed in September 2002 when CAIR bought out the Kuwaiti bank with funds provided, at least in part, by Al-Maktoum Foundation, based in Dubai and headed by Dubai's crown prince and defense minister, Sheikh Mohammed bin Rashid al-Maktoum. The markings on the deed indicate that the foundation provided "purchase money to the extent of $978,031.34" to CAIR, or roughly one-third the value of the property. [81] One only wonders what a more complete investigation of its real estate transactions would turn up.

In December 1999, the World Assembly of Muslim Youth (WAMY), an organization benefiting from Saudi patronage, [82] announced at a press conference in Saudi Arabia that it "was extending both moral and financial support to CAIR"   [83]   to help it construct its $3.5 million headquarters in Washington, D.C. WAMY also agreed to "introduce CAIR to Saudi philanthropists and recommend their financial support for the headquarters project."   [84]   In 2002, CAIR and WAMY announced, again from Saudi Arabia, their cooperation on a $1 million public relations campaign. The Saudi Gazette, which reported the story, said that CAIR's leader, Nihad Awad, "had already met leading Saudi businessmen" in order to "brief them about the projects and raise funds."   [85]

Later that week on the same fundraising trip through the Middle East, CAIR reportedly received $500,000 from Saudi prince Al-Waleed bin Talal, reputed to be one of the world's richest men. [86] Waleed also, in May 2005, stated that he is "more than prepared" to work with organizations such as CAIR, "and to provide needed support" to them. [87]

CAIR has received at least $12,000 from the International Relief Organization (also called the International Islamic Relief Organization, or IIRO), which itself was the recipient of some $10 million from its parent organization in Saudi Arabia. (1994 check from the IIRO for $5,000)

The International Institute of Islamic Thought (IIIT) gave CAIR's Washington office $14,000 in 2003. According to a court-filed affidavit, David Kane of the U.S. Customs Service determined that the IIIT receives donations from overseas via its related entities. [88]

Law enforcement is looking at the IIIT connection with Operation Green Quest, the major investigation into the activities of individuals and organizations believed to be "ardent supporters" of the Palestinian Islamic Jihad, Hamas, and Al-Qaeda. [89] CAIR, not surprisingly, criticized the probe of its donor, telling the Financial Times of London that the investigation is an attack on "respected Islamic institutions." [90] Despite these many foreign sources, CAIR still claims to receive no funds from outside the United States.

An Integral Part of the Wahhabi Lobby

CAIR has a key role in the "Wahhabi lobby"—the network of organizations, usually supported by donations from Saudi Arabia, whose aim is to propagate the especially extreme version of Islam practiced in Saudi Arabia. For one, it sends money to other parts of the lobby. According to CAIR's Form 990 filings for 2003, its California offices invested $325,000 with the North American Islamic Trust (NAIT). [91] the NAIT was established in 1971 by the Muslim Student Association of the U.S. and Canada, which bills itself as the precursor to the Islamic Society of North America. [92] now the largest member of the Wahhabi lobby.

According to Newsweek, authorities say that over the years "NAIT money has helped the Saudi Arabian sect of Wahhabism—or Salafism, as the broader, pan-Islamic movement is called—to seize control of hundreds of mosques in U.S. Muslim communities." [93] J. Michael Waller, a terrorism expert, testified before the Senate Judiciary Committee that NAIT is believed to own 50 to 79 percent of the mosques in North America. According to Waller, NAIT was raided as part of Operation Green Quest in 2002, on suspicions of involvement in terrorist financing. [94]

CAIR affiliates regularly speak at events sponsored by the Islamic Society of North America (ISNA), an umbrella organization of the Wahhabi lobby. Nabil Sadoun, a director of CAIR-DC, spoke at the ISNA's regional conference in 2003. Hussam Ayloush, executive director of CAIR's Southern California chapter, and Fouad Khatib, the CAIR-California chairman, spoke at an ISNA-sponsored event. [95] Safaa Zarzour, president of CAIR-Chicago, was also an ISNA speaker, as was Azhar Azeez, a board member of CAIR-Dallas, who has spoken at several ISNA conferences. [96]

In January 2003, the Saudi newspaper Ar-Riyadh reported that Nihad Awad appeared on a panel along with 'Aqil ibn 'Abd al-'Aziz al-'Aqil, secretary-general of the Saudi charity Al-Haramain Foundation [97] — despite that organization's well-known ties to terrorism and the fact that already in March 2002, long before Awad's visit with Al-Haramain, the U.S. and Saudi governments had jointly designated eleven of its branches "financial supporter[s] of terrorism." [98] The U.S.-based branch of the organization was also subsequently designated in September 2004. [99]

To fully appreciate what it means that more than half of U.S. mosques are promoting Saudi Islam, we refer to the Freedom House report, "Saudi Publications on Hate Ideology Invade American Mosques." It explains that Saudi documents disseminated at U.S. mosques are telling America's Muslims that it is a religious obligation for them to hate Christians and Jews and warning that Muslims should not have Christians and Jews as friends, nor should they help them. [100]

The Freedom House report indicates that Saudi publications disseminated by U.S. mosques: say it is lawful for Muslims to physically harm and steal from adulterers and homosexuals; condemn interpretations of Islam other than the strict "Wahhabi" version preached in Saudi Arabia; advocate the killing of those who convert out of Islam; assert that it is a Muslim's duty to eliminate the State of Israel; and promote the idea that women should be segregated and veiled and, of course, barred from some employment and activities. [101] But not to worry; CAIR's spokesman, Ibrahim Hooper, tells us, "The majority of the stuff they picked is in Arabic, a language that most people in mosques don't read." [102]

Muslim Supremacism

CAIR's personnel are normally tight-lipped about the organization's agenda but sometimes let their ambitions slip out. CAIR's long-serving chairman, Omar Ahmad, reportedly told a crowd of California Muslims in July 1998, "Islam isn't in America to be equal to any other faith, but to become dominant. The Koran ... should be the highest authority in America, and Islam the only accepted religion on earth." [103] Five years later, Ahmad denied having said this and issued a press release saying he was seeking a retraction. [104] But the reporter stood behind her story, and the newspaper that reported Ahmad's remarks told WorldNetDaily it had "not been contacted by CAIR." [105]

In 1993, before CAIR existed, Ibrahim Hooper told a reporter: "I wouldn't want to create the impression that I wouldn't like the government of the United States to be Islamic sometime in the future." [106] On the Michael Medved radio show in 2003, Hooper made the same point more positively: if Muslims ever become a majority in the United States, it would be safe to assume that they would want to replace the U.S. Constitution with Islamic law, as most Muslims believe that God's law is superior to man-made law. [107]

Other CAIR personnel also express their contempt for the United States. Ihsan Bagby of CAIR's Washington office has said that Muslims "can never be full citizens of this country," referring to the United States, "because there is no way we can be fully committed to the institutions and ideologies of this country." [108] Ayloush said that the war on terror has become a "war on Muslims" with the U.S. government the "new Saddam." He concluded: "So let's end this hypocrisy, this hypocrisy that we are better than the other dictator." [109]

In a bizarre coda, Parvez Ahmed, the current CAIR chairman, touted the virtues of Islamic democracy in 2004 by portraying the Afghan constitutional process as superior to the U.S. one:

The new Afghan constitution shows that the constitution of a Muslim nation can be democratic and yet not contradict the essence of Islam. During my meeting with a high-ranking Afghan delegation during their recent visit to the United States, I was told that the Afghan constitutional convention included Hindu delegates despite Hindus accounting for only 1 percent of the population. Contrast this with our own constitutional convention that excluded women and blacks. [110]

Intimidation

CAIR attempts to close down public debate about itself and Islam in several ways, starting with a string of lawsuits against public and private individuals and several publications. [111] CAIR's Rabiah Ahmed has openly acknowledged that lawsuits are increasingly an "instrument" for it to use. [112]

In addition, CAIR has resorted to financial pressure in an effort to silence critics. One such case concerns ABC radio personality Paul Harvey, who on December 4, 2003, described the vicious nature of cock fighting in Iraq, then commented: "Add to the [Iraqi] thirst for blood, a religion which encourages killing, and it is entirely understandable if Americans came to this bloody party unprepared." [113] CAIR responded a day later with a demand for "an on-air apology." CAIR then issued a call to its supporters to contact Harvey's advertising sponsors to press them to pull their ads "until Harvey responds to Muslim concerns." [114] Although Harvey quickly and publicly retracted his remarks, CAIR continued its campaign against him.

Another case of financial intimidation took place in March 2005, when CAIR campaigned to have *National Review* remove two books --- Serge Trifkovic's *The Sword of the Prophet* [115] and J. L. Menezes' *The Life and Religion of Mohammad* [116] --- as well as the positive reviews of those books, from its on-line bookstore. CAIR claimed the books defamed Islam and the Prophet Muhammad. When it did not get immediate satisfaction from *National Review*, CAIR instructed its partisans to pressure the Boeing Corporation to withdraw its advertising from the magazine. National review briefly took down both books but then quickly reposted the one by Trifkovic. Trifkovic himself argued that CAIR's success here "will only whet Islamist appetites and encourage their hope that the end-result will be a crescent on the Capitol a generation or two from now." [117]

CAIR resorted to another form of intimidation versus Florida radio show host and Baptist pastor Mike Frazier. Frazier had criticized local and state officials in September 2004 for attending a CAIR awards dinner because, as he put it, "If these people would have bothered to check CAIR out beforehand, they would have seen that it is a radical group." He termed what followed "absolutely undeliverable." Within a month, he says he received six death threats and forty-seven threatening phone calls; he was labeled an "extremist" and a "fundamentalist zealot"; and he was accused of "propagating fear, terror and disunity" by the *St. Petersburg Times.* Several members of his church fled his congregation because, according to Frazier, "they were afraid." [118]

Other CAIR targets of intimidation have included the Simon Wiesenthal Center for juxtaposing a picture of the Ayatollah Khomeini next to Adolf Hitler. [119] and the Reader's Digest for an article, "The Global War on Christians," [120] which CAIR found "smears Islam" by citing well-documented cases of Christian persecution. CAIR's Nihad Awad faulted the Reader's Digest for leaving the impression that "Islam somehow encourages or permits rape, kidnapping, torture, and forced conversion." [121]

In December 2003, CAIR ruined the career of an army officer and nurse, Captain Edwina McCall, who had treated American soldiers wounded in Iraq and Afghanistan but ended up resigning under a cloud of suspicion. Her crime? Using her military e-mail address on an Internet discussion board concerning the Islamist agenda. CAIR sent the comments to the secretary of defense, calling attention to her allegedly "bigoted, anti-Muslim comments" and demanding that her "extremist and Islamophobic views" be investigated and then followed by "appropriate action." The Army immediately cast the officer under suspicion, leading her to resign from a career she had loved. [122]

At times, CAIR inspires its attack dogs to make threats and sits back when they follow through. After Daniel Pipes published an article in July 1999 explaining the difference between moderate and radical Islam. [123] CAIR launched fifteen separate attacks on him in the space of two months, attacks widely reprinted in Muslim publications. Dozens of letters followed to the newspapers that carried Pipes' articles, some calling him harsh names ("bigot and racist"), others comparing him to the Ku Klux Klan and the neo-Nazis, or characterizing his writings as an "atrocity" filled with "pure poison" and "outright lies." More alarmingly, the letter-writers accused the author of perpetrating a hate crime against Muslims or of promoting and abetting such crimes. One threatened: "Is Pipes ready to answer the Creator for his hatred or is he a secular humanist ...? He will soon find out." [124]

CAIR metes out even worse treatment to Muslim opponents, as the case of Khalid Duran shows. Duran taught at leading universities and wrote about Islam for think tanks; he was commissioned by the American Jewish Committee to write *Children of Abraham: An Introduction to Islam for Jews*. Fourteen scholars of Islam endorsed the manuscript prior to publication; it won glowing reviews from such authoritative figures as Cardinal William Keeler of Baltimore, the eminent church historian Martin Marty, and Prince Hassan of Jordan. Then, before the book was even released, CAIR issued two press releases insulting Duran personally and demanding that the Children of Abraham be withheld until a group of CAIR-approved academics could review the book to correct what it assumed (without having read the manuscript) would be its "stereotypical or inaccurate content." Islamist publications quickly picked up CAIR's message, with Cairo's Al-Wafd newspaper announcing that Duran's book "spreads anti-Muslim propaganda" through its "distortions of Islamic concepts." A weekly in Jordan reported that 'Abd al-Mun'im Abu Zant --- one of the country's most powerful Islamist leaders --- had declared That Duran "should be regarded as an apostate," and on this basis called for an Islamic ruling to condone Duran's death. Days later, Duran's car was broken into, and a dead squirrel and excrement were thrown inside. CAIR, far from apologizing for the evil results of its handiwork, accused the American Jewish Committee of fabricating the death edict as a "cheap publishing stunt, to boost book sales. [125]

Deceit

CAIR has a long record of unreliability and deceit even in relatively minor matters. To begin with, it has the audacity to claim to be "America's largest civil rights group," [126] ignoring much larger groups by far, such as the National Association for the Advancement of Colored People and the Anti-Defamation League.

In May 2005, CAIR published its annual report on the violations of Muslim civil rights in America which purported to document a significant rise in the number of hate crimes directed at Muslims. According to the report, "anti-Muslim hate crimes in the United States" have gone up dramatically: from 42 cases in 2002, to 93 cases in 2003, to 141 in 2004. [127] The mainstream media dutifully recycled CAIR's press release, effectively endorsing this study by reporting it as a serious piece of research. [128] But closer inspection shows that of twenty "anti-Muslim hate crimes" for which CAIR gives information, at least six are invalid. [129]

David Skinner points out a further problem with the 2004 report: its credulity in reporting any incident, no matter how trivial, subjective or unsubstantiated. One anecdote concerns a Muslim college student who encountered "flyers and posters with false and degrading statements about the Qur'an and the prophet Muhammad"; another concerns a student at Roger Williams in Rhode Island who wrote that "a true Muslim is taught to slay infidels." Also, any reluctance to accommodate Muslim women wearing a headscarf or veil was tallied as a bias incident, even in the case of genuine quandaries (such as veiled athletes or drivers applying for their licenses). [130]

Nor is this the first unreliable CAIR study. Referring to the 1996 version, Steven Emerson noted in congressional testimony that "a large proportion of the complaints have been found to be fabricated, manufactured, distorted, or outside standard definitions of hate crimes." [131] Jorge Martinez of the U.S. Department of Justice dismissed CAIR's 2003 report, Guilt by Association, as "unfair criticism based on a lot of misinformation and propaganda." [132]

CAIR's manipulative habits assert themselves even in petty ways. For example, CAIR is not above conducting straw polls in an effort to forward its political agenda and may even be willing to exaggerate its own outreach efforts. This seems to be the case in CAIR's library project, where it claims to have sent thousands of packages of books and tapes to American libraries. An inquiry turned up the curious fact that while CAIR claimed the District of Columbia had received thirty-seven such packages, records showed only one such copy being recorded. [133] Maybe the mailmen lost the remaining thirty-six?

In September 2005, CAIR indulged in some Stalinist revisionism: as Robert Spencer revealed, CAIR doctored a photo on 1st website to make it more "Islamically correct" by manually adding a hijab onto a Muslim woman. [134] Despite all this, CAIR's statements continue to gain the respectful attention of uncritical media outlets. The few hard-hitting media analyses of CAIR generally turn up in the conservative press. [135] Otherwise, CAIR generally wins a pass from news organizations, as Erick Stakelbeck has documented. The mainstream media treat BAIR respectfully, as a legitimate [136] organization, avoiding the less salutary topics explored here, even the multiple connections to terrorism.

One telling example of the media's negligence in investigating CAIR occurred when Ghassam Elashi --- a founding board member of CAIR's Texas chapter --- was indicted and convicted of supporting terrorism by sending money to Hamas and Mousa Abu Marzook. Reporting on this, not one single mainstream media source mentioned Elashi's CAIR connection. Worse, the media went to CAIR and quoted it on Elashi's arrest, without noting their close connection. [137]

The Washington Post seems particularly loath to expose CAIR's unsavory aspects. For example, on January 20, 2005, it ran a story about the opening of CAIR's new Virginia office on Grove Street in Herndon. The article not only passed up the opportunity to consider CAIR's presence in a town notorious for Islamist organizational connections to Al-Qaeda and to Wahhabi network, [138] but it was also remarkably similar in tone and style to CAIR's own press release on the same subject. [139] (A later Washington Post article did mention that the new CAIR offices are located on the very street where federal agents had conducted a major raid in March 2002.) [140]

There is much else for the press to look into. One example: CAIR-DC lists the Zahara Investment Corporation as a "related organization" on its FORM 990. Curiously, Zahara Investment Corporation was listed as a tax-exempt entity 2002; in 2003, it became a non-tax-exempt entity. [141] This prompts several questions: how is a tax-exempt like CAIR related to an investment company, much less a company? How does an investment corporation become tax-exempt? And how does it change itself into a non-exempt? And why did CAIR-DC invest $40,000 of the public's money in 1998 in securities that it would have to write off less than three years later? Whose securities were these? The usual databases have nothing on Zahara Investment Corporation; all this took place under the radar screen.

That the U.S government, the mainstream media, educational institutions, and others have given CAIR a free pass amounts to a dereliction of duty. Yet, there appear to be no signs of change. How long will it be until the establishment finally recognizes CAIR for what it is and denies it mainstream legitimacy?

REFERENCES CITED FOR APPENDIX D

1 Columbus Dispatch (Ohio); January 1, 2002.
2 "What's CAIR's Vision and Mission," CAIR website, accessed January 13, 2006.
3 FDCH Political Transcript, September 10, 2003.
4 "Bad CAIR Day: Ex-staffer pleads guilty to terror charges, Senate asks questions on 9/11 anniversary," accessed January 9, 2006.
5 Joseph Farah, "Between the Lines, The Real CAIR," *WorldNetDaily*, April 23, 2003; Steve Pomerantz, "Counterterrorism in a Free Society," the *Journal of Counterterrorism and Security International,* Spring 1998.
6 *Estate of John P. O'Neil, Sr. et al. vs. Al Baraka Investment and Development Corporation*, DanielPipes.org, accessed January 9, 2006.
7 "Steven Emerson, "Re: Terrorism and the Middle East Peace Process," prepared testimony before the U.S. Senate Foreign Relations Committee, Subcommittee on Near East and South Asia, Mar. 19, 1996.
8 The Jerusalem Post, Mar. 5, 1999.
9 Personal communication from Jamal Hasan to Daniel Pipes, July 25, 2003.
10 The Washington Times, Oct. 1, 2004.
11 Melissa Radler, "A Different Face of Islam," Jerusalem Post International Edition; July 18, 2003.
12 "An Activist's Guide to Arab and Muslim Campus and Community Organizations in North America," Stephen Schwartz, FrontPageMagazine.com, May 26, 2003.- 126 -
13 Free Muslims Coalition, July 5, 2004.
14 Colin Powell, remarks at Iftaar dinner, Benjamin Franklin Room, Washington, D.C., Nov. 18, 2002.
15 "CAIR-St. Louis Meets with Palestinian Journalists," CAIR, July 27, 2004; Nihad Awad biography, CAIR website, accessed Jan. 12, 2006.
16 "CAIR Conducts Diversity Training for NASA," CAIR, July 7, 2004.
17 "Partial List of CAIR's Work with Local State and Federal Law Enforcement Authorities," CAIR website, accessed Jan. 9, 2006.
18 The Connection Newspapers, July 8, 2004.
19 "Muslim-American Activism: CAIR Marks Decade of Dedication," The Washington Report on Middle East Affairs, Oct. 2004, p. 76.
20 "CAIR-Chicago Extends Lecture Series on Islam, 'Building Bridges to Islam' Events Co-hosted by Edlerhostel," CAIR, Feb. 1, 2005.
21 United States of America v. Randall Todd Royer, et al, United States District Court for the Eastern District of Virginia, Alexandria Division, June 2003.
22 BBC News, June 28, 2003.
23 CNN, June 27, 2003.
24 FDCH Political Transcripts, June 27, 2003.
25 Associated Press, Sept. 25, 2003.

26 Reasononline, July 2, 2003.
27 U.S. Department of Justice, news release, Apr. 9, 2004.
28 All Things Considered, National Public Radio, Nov. 22, 2005.
29 U.S. Department of Justice, news release, July 8, 2004.
30 Associated Press, Apr. 13, 2005.
31 U.S. Department of Justice, news release, July 27, 2004.
32 "Freeze on Group's Assets Questioned by U.S. Muslims," CAIR, Dec. 4, 2001.
33 Associated Press, Sept. 10, 2003.
34 Parvez Ahmed, "Accusations of Terrorist Support Are Wrong, Divisive,"St. Petersburg Times, Sept. 27, 2004.
35 "Articles of Incorporation of a Colorado Nonprofit Corporation, 931135840," Dec. 8, 1993.
36 The Washington Post, Oct. 2, 2003.
37 Associated Press, Sept. 10, 2003.
38 Matthew Epstein, "Saudi Support for Islamic Extremism in the United States," testimony before the U.S. Senate Judiciary Committee, Subcommittee on Terrorism, Technology, and Homeland Security, Sept. 10, 2003.
39 Associated Press, Sept. 10, 2003.
40 The Post-Standard (Syracuse), Jan. 23, 2004.
41 CAIR et al v. Ashcroft and Mueller complaint, p. 13.
42 U.S. Department of the Treasury, news release, Oct. 18, 2002.
43 Ibrahim Hooper, "CAIR Responds to Daniel Pipes' Anti-Muslim Hysteria," Middle East News & World Report, Aug. 25, 2000.
44 Estein, "Saudi Support for Islamic Extremism."
45 Mohammad Salah also appears to be the uncle of Abdullah Salah, vice president of CAIR's Chicago chapter.
46 USA Today, Dec. 9, 2004.
47 Epstein, "Saudi Support for Islamic Extremism."
48 "Text from Lawsuit Response," Council on American-Islamic Relations, Inc. vol. Andrew Whitehead, law no. CL04-926, Virginia: In the Circuit Court for the City of Virginia Beach, Apr. 30, 2004.
49 Joe Kaufman, "The CAIR-Terror Connection," FrontPageMagazine.com, Apr. 29, 2004.
50 Steven Emerson, American Jihad: The Terrorists Living Among Us (New York: Free Press, 2003); Deposition of Nihad Awad, Oct. 22, 2003, In the Matter of: Stanley Boim, et al. v. Quranic Literacy Institute, et. al, p. 58.
51 John P. O'Neill vs. Al Baraka.
52 "Muslims Meet with FBI in AZ, NY," CAIR, July 14, 2004.
53 "CAIR Muslim Community Safety Kit," CAIR, Mar. 17, 2003.
54 ACLU et al. vs. National Security Agency, U.S. District Court, Eastern District of Michigan, Southern Division, Jan. 17, 2006, pp. 30-1.
55 The New York Sun, Jan. 18, 2006.
56 The Arizona Republic (Phoenix), Mar. 25, 2004.
57 Chip Joyce, "Council on American-Islamic Relations Attacks Daniel Pipes— An In-Depth Analysis of Their Charges," AboutTheWar.com, Jan. 7, 2003.

58 Steven Emerson, statement to the National Commission on Terrorist Attacks upon the United States, July 9, 2003.

59 Jake Tapper, "Islam's Flawed Spokesmen," Salon, Sept. 26, 2001.

60 Newsletter of the Marzuk Legal Fund, June 1996.

61 The Oracle (University of South Florida), Mar. 31, 2004.

62 "CAIR Condemns Mutilation of Bodies in Iraq," CAIR, Mar. 31, 2004.

63 Joe Kaufman, "CAIRing for Sami Al-Arian," FrontPageMagazine.com, June 22, 2005.

64 "This Week in Islam," TheReligionofPeace.com, Oct. 31, 2005.

65 "The Tides Community Responds to 9/11/01," Groundsprings.org, accessed Jan. 10, 2006.

66 "February 20, 2002—National Day of Solidarity with Muslim, Arab and South Asian Immigrants," Refuse and Resist, New York, N.Y., accessed Jan. 10, 2006.

67 "The Call for a National Day of Protest on October 22nd, 2002, to Stop Police Brutality, Repression and the Criminalization of a Generation," October 22 Coalition, accessed Jan. 10, 2006.

68 "Foreign Terrorists in America: Five Years after the World Trade Center Bombing," Steven Emerson statement before the U.S. Senate Judiciary Committee; Subcomm on Terrorism, Technology and Government Information, Feb. 24, 1998.

69 Pomerantz, "Counterterrorism in a Free Society"; Schwartz, "An Activist's Guide."

70 Orange County Weekly (Costa Mesa, Calif.), Mar. 7, 2002.

71 The Palestine Chronicle (Mountlake Terrace, Wash.), Aug. 4, 2003.

72 "CAIR Promotes and Hosts William W. Baker, Neo-Nazi," DanielPipes.org, Mar. 9, 2004.

73 "A Day of Discovery: Building Bridges to Islam in Arizona," program guide, Islamic Community Center, Tempe, Ariz., May 31, 2005 and June 14, 2005.

74 The IRS offers several choices under the item "Revenues," including direct public support, indirect public support, government contributions (grants), membership dues and assessments, and net income or (loss) from special events or rental properties—the categories in which CAIR has classified its revenues.

75 "Islamophobic Smear Campaign Goes Public," CAIR, Nov. 8, 2001.

76 Epstein, "Saudi Support for Islamic Extremism."

77 "IDB Approves New Projects Worldwide," Royal Embassy of Saudi Arabia, news release, Aug. 15, 1999.

78 Arab News (Jeddah), Aug. 26, 2001.

79 Paul Sperry, "Chapter 13: The 9/11 Imam," SperryFiles, accessed Jan. 10, 2006.

80 SperryFiles, accessed Jan. 10, 2006.

81 Deed of Trust, Doc. # 2002105143, Commercial Settlements, Inc., Washington, D.C., Aug. 7, 2002, SperryFiles, accessed Jan. 10, 2006.

82 WAMY's relationship to Saudi Arabia was described this way by its secretary general: "The Kingdom provides us with a supportive environment that allows us to work openly within the society to collect funds and spread

activities. It also provides us with protection abroad through Saudi embassies and consulates, in addition to financial support." "WAMY Team in Afghanistan Risks Life to Deliver Aid," Middle East Newsfile, Nov. 20, 2001.

83 "WAMY Spends SR12m on New Mosques," Middle East Newsfile, Dec. 23, 1999.

84 Arab News, Dec. 23, 1999.

85 Epstein, "Saudi Support for Islamic Extremism."

86 ArabicNews.com, Nov. 19, 2002.

87 Kingdom Holding Company, news release, May 20, 2005.

88 David Kane, "(Proposed Redacted) Affidavit in Support of Application for Search Warrant (October 2003)," United States District Court, Eastern District of Virginia.

89 "Operation Green Quest," brochure, U.S. Customs Service, Office of Investigations, Washington, D.C.

90 Financial Times (London), Mar. 28, 2002.

91 Form 990 filings for CAIR, 2003.

92 "A Little Taste of History," Muslim Student Association of the United States and Canada website, accessed Jan. 11, 2006.

93 Newsweek, Sept. 25, 2002.

94 J. Michael Waller, statement before the Senate Committee on the Judiciary, U.S. Subcommittee on Terrorism, Technology and Homeland Security, Oct. 14, 2003.

95 "Muslims and the Information Superhighway (MSIC 2000)," Hilton Long Beach, Long Beach, Calif., July 14 -16, 2000.

96 "Upcoming conferences," ISNA website, accessed Jan. 17, 2006.

97 Ar-Riyadh, Jan. 15, 2003.

98 "U.S.-Saudi Arabia Terrorist Financing Designations," U.S. Department of the Treasury, news release, Mar. 11, 2002.

99 Office of Foreign Assets Control, U.S. Department of the Treasury, news release, Sept. 9, 2004.

100 "New Report on Saudi Government Publications," Center for Religious Freedom, Freedom House, accessed Jan. 11, 2006.

101 Ibid.

102 Dallas Morning News, Feb. 5, 2005.

103 San Ramon Valley (Calif.) Herald, July 4, 1998.

104 National Review, Apr. 8, 2003.

105 WorldNetDaily, May 1, 2003.

106 Star Tribune (Minneapolis), Apr. 4, 1993.

107 Personal communication from Michael Medved, Oct. 21, 2004.

108 Quoted in Steve A. Johnson, "Political Activities of Muslims in America," in Yvonne Yazbeck Haddad, ed., The Muslims of America (New York: Oxford University Press, 1991), p. 115.

109 Associated Press, May 8, 2004.

110 Orlando Sentinel, Feb. 23, 2004.

111 "CAIR's Growing Litigiousness," DanielPipes.org, Sept. 13, 2004.

112 The New York Sun, Dec. 9, 2005.

113 WorldNetDaily, Dec. 6, 2003.

114 CAIR Action Alert #408, Dec. 8, 2003.

115 Regina Orthodox Press, 2002.

116 Sands Publishers, 1912.

117 Srdja Trifkovic, "Caving in to Jihad: National Review, CAIR, and My Book," Chronicles Magazine, Apr. 6, 2005.

118 Erick Stakelbeck, "Jihad at the St. Petersburg Times," FrontPageMagazine.com, Nov. 3, 2004.

119 "Muslims Exchange Letters with Wiesenthal Center about Possible Changes to Museum of Tolerance," CAIR, Jan. 6, 1998.

120 Ralph Kinney Bennett, "The Global War on Christians," Reader's Digest, August. 1997.

121 "'Global War on Christians' Smears Islam," CAIR, July 24, 1997.

122 Andrew Whitehead and Lee Kaplan, "CAIR's War from Within," FrontPageMagazine.com, Mar. 9, 2004.

123 Daniel Pipes, "It Matters What Kind of Islam Prevails," Los Angeles Times, July 22, 1999.

124 Daniel Pipes, "How Dare You Defame Islam," Commentary, Nov. 1999.

125 Daniel Pipes, "An American Rushdie?" The Jerusalem Post, July 4, 2001.

126 Interview with Ahmed Bedier, Fox Hannity & Co., Fox News Network, Feb. 15, 2005.

127 The Status of Muslim Civil Rights in the United States, 2005: Unequal Protection, CAIR, 2005.

128 See, for example, The New York Times, May 12, 2005; The Washington Post, May 12, 2005; and Los Angeles Times, May 12, 2005.

129 Daniel Pipes and Sharon Chadha, "CAIR's Hate Crime Nonsense," FrontPageMagazine.com, May 18, 2005.

130 David Skinner, "Behind CAIR's Hate Crimes Report," The Daily Standard (Washington, D.C,), May 6, 2004.

131 Emerson, "Foreign Terrorists in America."

132 CBS News, July 16, 2003.

133 The Washington Times, Oct. 20, 2003.

134 Robert Spencer, "Stalinism at CAIR: Photo Doctored for Islamic Correctness," Jihad Watch, Sept. 15, 2005.

135 Zev Chafets, "Beware the Wolves Among Us," The New York Daily News, Sept. 28, 2001; editorial, "CAIR and Terrorism," The Washington Times, July 24, 2004; David Frum, "The Question of CAIR," The National Post, Nov. 23, 2004Eli Lake, "Me Rethinks a CAIR Event," The New York Sun, Nov. 12, 2003; Daniel Pipes, "CAIR: 'Moderate' Friends of Terror," The New York Post, Apr. 22, 2002; Michael Putney, "Pressure May Smother Dialogue," The Miami Herald, Sept. 10, 2003; Stephen Schwartz, "Not So Holy after All; The Bush Administration Takes on a Hamas Front Group," The Weekly Standard, Dec. 17, 2001; and Glenn Sheller, "Muslim Group's Conflict with Discrimination Is Uphill Fight," The Columbus Dispatch, Aug. 31, 2004.

136 Erick Stakelbeck, "NY Times' Wahhabi Apologists," FrontPageMagazine.com, Mar. 7, 2005.

137 "4 Indicted in Texas Terror Probe," The Boston Globe, Dec. 19, 2002; "5 Brothers Charged with Aiding Hamas," The New York Times, Dec. 19, 2002; "Hamas Arrests Called Unfair," Fort Worth Star-Telegram, Dec. 20, 2002; "Aid Sought for 5 Suspected of Terror Ties," Associated Press, Feb. 15, 2003; "Muslim Leader Criticizes Prosecution," United Press International, July 9, 2004; "Muslim Leaders Blast Brothers' Convictions," The Dallas Morning News, July 10, 2004.
138 The Washington Post, Jan. 20, 2005.
139 "CAIR Opens New Office in Virginia," CAIR, Dec. 14, 2004.
140 The Washington Post, Jan. 27, 2005.
141 CAIR's DC office is required to make its Form 990 available to the public upon request

Appendix E

US GOVERNMENT PERSONNEL AND THE MUSLIM BROTHERHOOD

Sources: Wikipedia & References Cited by Wikipedia

BILL CLINTON ADMINISTRATION

PERSONNEL SYMPATHETIC TO ISLAMIC SUPREMACY
(PARTIAL LIST)

Huma Abedin,

Abedin has had an ongoing, employment relationship with Secretary Hillary Clinton from 1996 through 2017. She served as Hillary's longtime Deputy Chief of Staff and has worked with her for more than 20 years.

She was born in 1976 to Syed Zainul Abedin & Sahela Mahhood Abedin (Kalamazoo, MI). At age two she and her parents moved to Saudi Arabia.

Huma grew up in a family where her father, Sayed Z. Abedin, served on the Board of Directors of The Muslim Brotherhood. Her mother, Shelab Abedin, was a founding director of The Muslim Sisterhood and continues to be active in the organization. Her brother, on faculty at Oxford University, is an active member of The Muslim Brotherhood. She had to have been significantly influenced by the beliefs and philosophies of the Brotherhood.

Abedin, her father, her mother and her brother each have ties to The Muslim Brotherhood and to other Islamic Supremacist organizations, including al-Qaeda, bent on the destruction of western civilization and the United States. *WorldNetDaily* has reported extensively on these relationships and on the positions of authority which each has held in these organizations.

Huma also was a member of the Executive Board of the Muslim Student Association, which was identified as a Muslim Brotherhood front group in a 1991 document introduced into evidence during the terror-financing trial of the Texas-based Holy Land Foundation.

She was assistant editor for a dozen years of the *Journal of Muslim Minority Affairs* for the Institute of Muslim Minority Affairs. The Institute, founded by her late father and currently directed by her mother, is backed by the

Muslim World League, an Islamic organization headquartered in the Saudi holy city of Mecca. It was founded by Muslim Brotherhood leaders.

The 2002 Saudi Manifesto, commissioned by the ruling Saudi Arabian monarchy, places the work of the Institute which employed Abedin at the forefront of "A Grand Plan" to mobilize U.S. Muslim minorities to transform America into a Saudi-style Islamic state, according to Arabic-language researcher Walid Shoebat.

The *Journal of Muslim Minority Affairs* was to encourage Muslims to spread Islam instead of assimilating into the population. This is a key strategy in the ongoing effort to establish Islamic rule in the United States and a global Sharia or "Islamic law", the 3rd Caliphate of modern times.

At her father's Saudi financed Islamic think tank, Huma worked alongside Abdullah Omar Naseef, who is accused of financing al-Qaeda fronts. Naseef is deeply associated with the Abedin family. Saleha Abedin, Huma's mother, was the official representative of Naseef's terror-stained Muslim World League in the 1990's. The London office of the Muslim World League & Abedin family business have the same address.

Abdurahman Alamoudi

Abdurahman served in the Clinton Administration as:

Goodwill Ambassador
Advisor to Israel-Palestinian Peace Talks
Advisor to Military & Prison Chaplain Oversight Committee

Summary of Muslim organizations, affiliated with Abdurahman Alamoudi's, founder of Muslim prison chaplains program:
    * the organization was raided in federal counterterrorism probes

Executive Assistant to President of SAAR Foundation*
Regional Representative for DC Chapter, Islamic Society of North America (ISNA)
Acting President, Muslim Students Association, U.S. & Canada
Founder, former executive director, American Muslim Council (AMC)
President, American Muslim Foundation (AMF)
Board Member, American Muslim Council (AMC)
Founding Trustee, Fiqh Council of North America, Inc.*
Board member, Mercy International*
Secretary, Success Foundation*
Founding Secretary, United Association for Studies and Research*
Director, Taibah International Aid Association*
Board Member, Somali Relief Fund
        (Prominent Al-Qaeda operative, Wadih El Hage, now serving life in prison for masterminding 1998 embassy bombings in Kenya and Tanzania, reportedly had Somali Relief Fund business card in his possession during a 1997 raid on his home by Kenyan officials.)
First Endorsing Agent for Muslim Chaplains, US Military
Board member, American Muslims for Jerusalem
President, Muslims for a Better America
Head, American Task Force for Bosnia (group founded by AMC and directed by Khaled Saffuri)
Board member, Interfaith Impact for Justice and Peace
Board member, the Council on National Interest Foundation (founded by Paul Findley www.cionline.org)

American Muslim Council

1990: Alamoudi founded the American Muslim Council as a tax-exempt 501(c)(4) organization, based at 1212 New York Avenue NW in Washington. The AMC has been described as a de facto front of the Muslim Brotherhood. The AMC's affiliate, the American Muslim Foundation, is a 501(c)(3) group to which contributions are tax-deductible. SAAR family assets financed the building at 1212 New York Avenue NW

Chaplain Selection & Training

1993 December: In December 1993, Alamoudi attended the swearing-in ceremony of Army Capt. Abdul Rasheed Muhammad (formerly Myron Maxwell), the first Muslim chaplain in the U.S. military, and pinned the crescent moon badge on the captain's uniform. "The American Muslim Council chose and endorsed Muhammad."

1995: Alamoudi accompanies American Muslim Armed Forces and Veterans Affairs Council chief Qaseem Uqdah on a tour of naval installations in Florida to assess the needs of Muslims in the U.S. Navy

Chaplains, The Wahhabi Lobby, and The Muslim Brotherhood

The process for becoming a Muslim chaplain for any branch of the U.S. military, currently involves two separate phases. First, individuals must complete religious education and secondly, they must receive an ecclesiastical endorsement from an approved body.

As several recent media reports have noted, federal investigators long have suspected key groups in the chaplain program - the Graduate School of Islamic and Social Sciences the American Muslim Armed Forces and Veterans Affairs Council (AMAFVAC) and the Islamic Society of North America of links to terrorist organizations.

The Graduate School of Islamic & Social Sciences (GSISS) trains Muslim chaplains for military and prison appointments. Operation Green Quest investigators raided GSISS offices in March 2002, along with 23 other organizations. According to search warrants, federal agents suspected GSISS and the others of "potential money laundering and tax evasion activities and their ties to terrorist groups such as al Qaeda as well as individual terrorists . . . [including] Osama bin Laden."

Agents also raided the homes of GSISS Dean of Students Iqbal Unus, and GSISS President Taha Al-Alwani. Press reports identify Al-Awani as Unindicted Co-Conspirator Number 5 in the Palestinian Islamic Jihad case of Sami Al-Arian in Florida.

The AMAFVAC accredits or endorses chaplains already trained under GSISS or trained at other places, like schools in Syria.

AMAFAC operates under the umbrella of the American Muslim Foundation, led by Abdurahman Alamoudi.

According to Sen. Schumer's office, the AMAFAC & AMF share the same tax identification number making them the same legal organization.

The Islamic Society of North America endorses trained chaplains for the military.

As of 8 June 2002, nine of the fourteen Islamic chaplains in the U.S. military received their religious training from the Graduate School of Islamic and Social Sciences in Leesburg, Virginia.

Following training at GSISS or another religious school, the majority of Muslim chaplains receive their endorsement from the American Muslim Armed Forces and Veterans Affairs Council.

1993 WTC Attack

1993 March: Alamoudi assailed the federal government's case against Mohammed Salameh who was arrested ten days after the first World Trade Center bombings in February: "All their [law enforcement] facts are - they are flimsy. We don't think that any of those facts that they have against him, or the fact that they searched his home and they found a few wires here or there - are not enough."

Salameh was convicted in the bombing plot and is currently serving a life sentence in prison. From about 1993 to 1998, the Pentagon retained Alamoudi on an unpaid basis to nominate and to vet Muslim chaplain candidates for the U.S. military.

1994: Alamoudi complained that the judge picked on the 1993 World Trade Center bombers because of their religion: "I believe that the judge went out of his way to punish the defendants harshly and with vengeance, and to a large extent, because they were Muslim."

1996: Alamoudi called on President Clinton to "free Sheikh Omar Abdul Rahman," the Egyptian Islamic Jihad leader serving a life sentence for his role in the early 1990s of bombings and attempted bombings in New York, and for plotting to destroy civilian airliners.

Support of Hamas

1994: Alamoudi began a public defense of Hamas: "Hamas is not a terrorist group ... I have followed the good work of Hamas...they have a wing that is a violent wing. They had to resort to some kind of violence."

1995: He continued his Hamas defense, arguing that "Hamas is not a terrorist organization. The issue for us (the American Muslim Council) is to be conscious of where to give our money, but not to be dictated to where we send our money."

1996: Alamoudi spoke out in response to the arrest at New York's JFK Airport of his admitted friend, Hamas political bureau leader Mousa Abu Marzook. Months after the arrest, Alamoudi blamed the February 25th Hamas suicide bombings of Israeli citizens on Marzook's detention: "If he was there things would not have gone in this bad way. He is known to be a moderate and there is no doubt these events would not have happened if he was still in the picture."

Khail Suffari

1987 served as Development Director of the American Arab Anti-Discrimination Committee.

1990 served as Assistant Executive Director of the National Association of Arab-Americans.

1995 served as Director of Government Affairs for the American Muslim Council, reporting directly to Abduraham Al-Amoudi.

GEORGE W. BUSH ADMINISTRATION
PERSONNEL SYMPATHETIC TO ISLAMIC SUPREMACY
(PARTIAL LIST)

Sources: Wikipedia & References Cited by Wikipedia

Abduraham Al-Amoudi

In 1998, leadership of The Muslim Brotherhood realized that they have very few contacts within the Republican party and that the 2000 US elections were up for grabs. They understand it is most likely that Al Gore will be the Democratic party nominee, but the Republican field was wide open.

The Muslim Brotherhood asked Al-Amoudi to reached out through Jack Abramoff, Grover Norquist, and Karl Rove in order to establish himself with the Republican Party. It is well known that Al-Amoudi was the founder/president of the American Muslim Council and had been an effective fund raiser for the Democrats and for Al-Qaeda.

In spite of these troublesome associations, Al-Amoudi was invited to join the G W Bush campaign team as a liaison to the Muslim committee. After President Bush won the election, Al-Amoudi was:

2001 appointed to select, train & credential Muslim military & prison chaplains

2003 tried, convicted and served time in federal prison (Al-Qaeda fund raiser).

Legal Notes on Al-Amoudi

Al-Amoudi founded the American Muslim Council (AMC) as a tax-exempt 501(c)(4) organization, based at 1212 New York Avenue NW in Washington. The AMC has been described as a de facto front of the Muslim Brotherhood. The AMC's affiliate, the American Muslim Foundation (AMF), was a 501(c)(3) group to which contributions were tax-deductible. SAAR family assets financed the building at 1212 New York Avenue NW.

AMC advisory board member Soloman Biheiri, whom federal prosecutors say was "the financial toehold of The Muslim Brotherhood in the United States," was convicted of violating U.S. immigration law.

Al-Amoudi was arrested in late September 2003 at Dulles International Airport after British law-enforcement authorities stopped him with $340,000 in cash that he was trying to take to Syria.

U.S. officials alleged that the money may have been destined for Syrian-based terrorist groups to attack Americans in Iraq. Charges include illegally receiving money from the Libyan government, passport and immigration fraud, and other allegations of supporting terrorists abroad and here in the United States. He is presently in jail on federal terrorism-related charges.

Kaled Suffuri

1987 served as Development Director of the American Arab Anti-Discrimination Committee.

1993 served as Assistant Executive Director of the National Association of Arab-Americans.

1995 served as Director of Government Affairs for the American Muslim Council, reporting to Abduraham Al-Amoudi.

Ali Tulbah

Associate Director, White House Office of Cabinet Affairs;

Pres. Bush Liaison to Arab/Muslim American communities;

Pres. Bush Liaison to Arab/Muslim Int'l organizations.

Sami Al-Arian

Enlisted Norquist to lobby Pres. Bush to abolish Secret Evidence law.

Professor at the University of South Florida;

Founded National Coalition to Protect Political Freedom (renamed Defending Dissents Foundation);

Al-Arian was tried and convicted of raising money for the Holy Land Foundation. He was deported.

Huzammil Siddiqui

Selected by President Bush in 2001 to represent Muslim faith in the Ecumenical Memorial Service at the National Cathedral.

Presented copy of the Koran to President Bush, who responded, "the teachings of Islam are the teachings of peace and good."

BARRACK HUSSEIN OBAMA ADMINISTRATION
PERSONNEL SYMPATHETIC TO ISLAMIC SUPREMACY
(PARTIAL LIST)

Sources: Wikipedia & References Cited by Wikipedia

Huma Abedin was born in 1976 to Syed Zainul Abedin & Sahela Mahhood Abedin (Kalamazoo, MI). Her father was a Board Member of The Muslim Brotherhood and her mother was a Founder of The Muslim Sisterhood. At age two she and her parents moved to Saudi Arabia, where her mother still resides.

Her brother is on the faculty of Oxford University and is a member of The Muslim Brotherhood.

Abedin has had a long ongoing, employment relationship with Secretary Hillary Clinton from 1996 through 2017.

1996 Before graduating from Georgetown University in 1996, Huma began a White House internship, assigned to the First Lady.

2000 Abedin became fulltime aide and personal advisor to Ms. Clinton during her successful 2000 Senate campaign.

1996 Abedin served as Assistant Editor of *Journal of Muslim* to *Minority Affairs* the quarterly journal published by the Institute of Muslim Minority Affairs since 1979. The Institute, founded by her father, is devoted to the study of the Muslim communities in non-Muslim countries.

2007 Abedin was traveling chief-of-staff for Ms. Clinton during her to 2008 presidential campaign.

2009 She was Deputy Chief-of-Staff to Secretary Clinton, US Department to 2013 of State.

2009 Under a "special government employment agreement," created by the State Department and signed off by Secretary Clinton, Abedin was allowed to perform outside consulting activities (during 2016) for Teneo, whose clients include Coca Cola and MF Global.

Teneo was founded by Douglas Band, an aide to President Bill Clinton and an official of the Clinton Foundation. According to her testimony before US Senate committee, Abedin sent & received more than 7,300 e-mails with Douglas Band, while serving as Deputy Chief-of-Staff to Secretary Clinton.

2009 Under the same "employment agreement," Abedin also served to 2017 as a paid consultant for the Clinton Foundation.

2013 Abedin served as Director of the Transition Team, which coordinated Secretary Clinton's return to private life in 2014.

2015 Abedin served as Vice Chairwoman of the 2016 Hillary Clinton Presidential Campaign.

Oborn'go Malik Obama

Half Brother of President Obama

2017 President of the Barack Hussain Obama Foundation.

Treasurer in the Sudan of the Missionary work of The Muslim Brotherhood.

Member of The Muslim Brotherhood.

Valerie Jarrett

1956 Jarrett was born in Shiraz, Iran to American parents, Dr. John E. Bowman and Barbara Taylor Bowman, both African-American of the Muslim faith. Dr. Bowman was a geneticist who ran the hospital for children in Shiraz, Iran.

1978 She earned a BA in psychology from Stanford University and to JD from the University of Michigan School of Law. **In the 1977 Stanford year book, Jarrett stated, "I am an Iranian by birth and of my Islamic Faith. I am also an American citizen and I seek to help change America to become a more Islamic country. My faith guides me and I feel like it is going well in the transition of using freedom of religion in America against itself."**

Jarrett has frequently reaffirmed her strong Muslim faith.

1983   Jarrett married Dr. William Jarrett, son of Chicago Sun-Times reporter Vernon Jarrett. They divorced in 1988. He died in 1993 at the age of 40.

1987   Her political career began in Chicago, where she worked in the Office of the Mayor, Harold Washington. She later served as Dep. Chief of Staff for Mayor Richard Daley.

In 1991 she hired Michelle Robinson (then engaged to Barack Obama) away from a private law firm. From 1996 - 2005, she was Chairwoman of the Chicago Transit Board.

2009   She served as Senior Advisor to President Obama and Assistant to the President for Public Engagement and International Affairs.

2017   She held many other powerful positions of responsibility at the White House. Many recognize her as being the "most influential advisor" to the President.

Currently, it appears that she is involved in "the Deep State" & "Shadow Government" being run by the Democrats against the Trump Administration.

Rashad Hussain

Hussain was born in Wyoming, the son of Indian born US citizens, Mohammad Akbar Hussain and Ruqaiya Hussain.

Hussain earned a BA with double majors in philosophy and political science from University of NC Chapel Hill. He also holds MPA (JFK School of Government) and MA in Arabic and Islamic Studies both from Harvard.

Hussain earned a J.D. from Yale Law School.

2009   He was appointed Deputy Associate Counsel to President Obama and named Special Envoy to the Organization of the Islamic Conference (OIC), the second largest inter-governmental organization after the United Nations, charged with safe-guarding & protecting "the interests of the Muslim world."

Member of The Muslim Brotherhood.

President Obama proudly announced that Hussain is a "Hafiz," someone who has completely memorized the Qur'an, but he did not spell out what qualifies Hussain to meet with foreign leaders at a diplomatic level in a role that approximates that of an ambassador.

Mehdi K. Alhassini

2005   President Muslim Student Association, Georgetown University. Muslim Student Association official anthem is restatement of The Muslim Brotherhood Credo.

2009   Appointed by President Obama, Special Assistant, Chief-of-Staff, National Security Council.

Member of The Muslim Brotherhood.

Arif Alikhan

1968   Born to emigrant Muslim parents (mother Pakistani and father Indian).

1990   Earned BA from University of California in Social Ecology.

1992   Graduate Loyola Law School of Los Angeles.

1993   Admitted to California Bar Association.

2011   Assistant Secretary for Policy Development for the U.S. Department of Homeland Security

Member of The Muslim Brotherhood.

Mohamed Elibiary -

Born Alexandria, Egypt

Graduate of University of Medina, known as the center of The Muslim Brotherhood in Saudi Arabia. Also, Member of the Assembly of American Muslim Jurists.

2010   Appointed by President Obama to Department of Homeland Security

Security Advisory Council.

Member of The Muslim Brotherhood.

Kareem Shora

Born in Damascus, Syria

Earned JD from University of West Virginia School of Law.

1999   National Executive Director of American-Arab Anti-Discrimination Committee (ADC). ADC has history of defending Hamas and Hezbollah, as non-terrorist organizations.

2005   Lobbied against Bush Administration anti-terrorist initiatives.

2009   Appointed by President Obama to Department of Homeland Security Advisory Council

Iman Mohamed Magid

1965   Born northern Sudan.

His father was the Grand Mufti of Sudan

1987   Migrated to United States.

Obama's Sharia Czar.

President, the Islamic Society of North America.

Executive Director of ADAMS Center Mosque, Sterling, VA.

Member of The Muslim Brotherhood.

Salam al-Marayati

1960   Born in Baghdad, Iraq

2009   Obama Adviser to President Obama

2010   Represented USA at annual Organization for Security and Cooperation in Europe human-rights meeting. US Embassies in Poland and Belgium condemned his participation.

1988   Founder and current Executive Director of the Muslim Public Affairs Council.

Member of The Muslim Brotherhood.

Nawar Shora

1977   Born Damascus, Syria.

1987   Immigrated to United States.

1997   Earned BA in Broadcasting from Marshall University.

2001   Graduated University of West Virginia School of Law.

2009   Senior Advisor to Civil Rights and Liberties Office, Transportation Security Administration.

Luoay Safi

Born Damascus, Syria.

Earned Ph.D. Wayne State University in political science.

1993   President, Association of Muslim Social Scientists.

2003   Editor, Journal of Islamic Social Sciences.

Executive Director, International Institute of Islamic Thought

Executive Director, Islamic Society of North America.

Former Advisor to US Department of Defense.

Member of The Muslim Brotherhood.

Appendix F

WHAT MUSLIMS IN AMERICA BELIEVE 2007 ᴴᴴ 2015

(Pew Research Survey; The Polling Company and Wenzel Strategies)

19% of Muslim-Americans say that violence is justified in order to make Sharia the law in the United States (66% disagree);

SOURCE: The Polling Company 2015

25% of Muslim-Americans say that violence against Americans in the United States is justified as part of the "Global Jihad" (64% disagree);

SOURCE: The Polling Company 2015

26% of younger Muslims in America believe suicide bombings are justified to advance Jihad.

SOURCE: Pew Research Survey 2007

8% of all Muslims in America believe suicide bombings are often or sometimes justified (81% never)

SOURCE: Pew Research Survey 2011

Muslims in America, who identify more strongly with their religion, are 3x more likely to feel that suicide bombings are justified to advance Jihad.

SOURCE: Pew Research Survey 2007

5% of American Muslims have a favorable view of al-Qaeda (27% can't make up their mind). Only 58% reject al-Qaeda outright. In a more recent poll, 5% of American Muslims have a favorable view of al-Qaeda (14% can't make up their mind)

SOURCE: Pew Research Survey 2011

33% of Muslim-Americans say al-Qaeda beliefs are Islamic or correct (49% disagree).

SOURCE: The Polling Company 2015

8% of Muslim-Americans say Islamic State (ISIS) beliefs are Islamic or correct. (43% disagree).

SOURCE: The Polling Company 2015

24% of Muslim-Americans say violence is justified against those who "offend Islam" (60% disagree, the rest not sure).

29% of Muslim-Americans agree that violence against those who insult Muhammad or the Koran is acceptable (61% disagree, the rest are not sure).

SOURCE: The Polling Company 2015

33% of Muslim-Americans say that Islamic Sharia should be supreme to the US Constitution (43% disagree; the rest are not sure).

SOURCE: The Polling Company 2015

58% of Muslim-Americans believe criticism of Islam or Muhammad is not protected free speech under the First Amendment.

SOURCE: Wenzel Strategies 2012

45% of Muslim-Americans believe mockers of Islam should face criminal charges (38% say they should not).

SOURCE: Wenzel Strategies 2012

12% of Muslim-Americans believe blaspheming Islam should be punishable by death.

SOURCE: Wenzel Strategies 2012

43% of Muslim-Americans believe people of other faiths have no right to evangelize Muslims.

SOURCE: Wenzel Strategies 2012

32% of Muslims in American believe that Sharia should be the supreme law of the land.

SOURCE: Wenzel Strategies 2012

The Truth About Islam

Traditional Values Coalition 2016

Appendix G

SURVEYS OF WORLD-WIDE MUSLIM OPINIONS

(World Public Opinions - 2015)

62% of Jordanians approve of some or most groups that attack Americans (21% oppose).
61% of Egyptians approve of attacks on Americans
42% of Turks approve some or most groups that attack Americans
41% of Pakistanis approve of attacks on Americans
38% of Moroccans approve of attacks on Americans
32% of Indonesians approve of attacks on American

(Pew Research Foundation - 2007)

84% Egyptian Muslims; 86% of Jordanian Muslims; 51% Nigerian Muslims support the death penalty for leaving Islam
82% of Egyptian Muslims favor stoning adulterers to death
41% of Indonesians supported Osama bin Laden in 2007
34% of Nigerian Muslims believe suicide bombings are often/sometimes justified.
15% of Indonesians believe suicide bombings are often/ sometimes justified
1 in 4 Muslims worldwide do not object to violence against civilians.
Only 57% of Muslims worldwide disapprove of al-

Appendix H

ISLAMIC ORGANIZATIONS TO BE REPRESENTED AT

CANCELLED 9-11-01 WHITE HOUSE MEETING

Representatives of US based, Islamic organizations which met at the offices of Grover Norquist (Americans for Tax Reform) when their September 11, 2001 meeting at the White House was cancelled.

MB   The Muslim Brotherhood
IAP   Islamic Association for Palestine **
ISNA   Islamic Society of North America
AMC   American Muslim Council
FID   Foundation for International Development
MSA   Muslim Student Association
MCA   The Muslim Communities Association
NAIT   North American Islamic trust

PARTIAL LIST OF OTHER US BASED, ISLAMIC ENTITIES CREATED BY THE MUSLIM BROTHERHOOD SINCE 1991

AMSS The Association of Muslim Social Scientists
AMSE The Association of Muslim Scientists & Engineers
ATP   American Trust Publications
IBS   Islamic Book Services
ICD   Islamic Center Diversities
IED   Islamic Education Department
IFC   ISNA FIQH Committee
ITC   Islamic Teaching Center
IMA   Islamic Medical Association
IHC   Islamic Housing Cooperative
IPAC   ISNA Political Awareness Committee

LASR   Limited Association for Studies and Research
MAYA Muslim Arab Youth Association
MBA   Muslim Business Association
MYNA   Muslim Youth of North America
CAIR   Council on American-Islamic Relations **
              (not listed in aforementioned 29 organizations)
              CAIR founded 1994 as the successor to The Islamic
              Association of Palestine)

OTHER INTERNATIONAL ORGANIZATIONS FOUNDED BY THE MUSLIM BROTHERHOOD

	Al Qaeda
	Hamas
	Hezbollah
AVC	Audio-Visual Center
BMI	Baitul Mal Inc.
ICNA	Islamic Circle of North America
IIC	International Information Center
IIIT	International Institute of Islamic Thought
MIA	Mercy International Association
MISG	Malaysian Islamic Study Group
OLF	Occupied Land Fund

Source: Center for Security Policy

Appendix I

OBAMA EXECUTIVE ORDERS & EXECUTIVE MEMORANDUM

FAVORING ISLAMIC SUPREMACISTS
(partial list)

$770 million to Save Mosques Overseas

A CBS news investigation found that the Obama State Department spent millions of dollars to save mosques overseas and other Islamic sites. **The State Department displayed before and after pictures of mosques refurbished with U.S. tax dollars.**

The State Department declined a CBS Atlanta News request for an interview. Anchor Justin Farmer wanted to ask, "Why are we using tax dollars to refurbish religious buildings overseas?" The State Department did send CBS Atlanta News an e-mail saying that they are "fighting Islamic extremism by building relationships with Islamic leaders".

Egyptian-American human rights activist Nonie Darwish told Farmer that trying to buy respect in the Middle East only shows our weakness.

"This part of the world has a lot of respect for power and America is not showing its power, it's showing its appeasement. They are laughing all the way to the bank," said Darwish. Darwish was born in Egypt and is now a former Muslim. Darwish told Farmer that she moved to America and has written several books critical of radical Islam. Darwish said that most of the mosques in Egypt are run by extremists who have ordered former Muslims like herself to be killed.

Your tax dollars also funded computers and mosques in places like Tajikistan and Mali. At an ancient mud brick mosque in Mali, the State Department has provided Internet service and computer equipment to local imams. http://toprightnews.com/?p=1929

Muslim Federal Holidays

"President Obama, through executive orders, declared both Eid al-Fitr and Eid al-Adha federal holidays until Congress was able to make them permanently recognized holidays. The White House felt strongly that since the Christian holiday of Christmas is a federally recognized holiday, Muslim holidays should also be recognized." said Jay Carney. This policy decision should not be a shock, as President Obama had previously shown strong support of the Muslim community, including personally funding a Muslim museum during the government shutdown.

Additionally, American cities have been inundated with requests to abide by Muslim laws, including one instance in which Muslim residents voted to implement Sharia Law. http://nationalreport.net/inspired-whitehouse-gov-petition-obama-will-issue-executive-order-federally-recognize-muslim-holidays/#sthash.2NOP2xzD.dpuf

Embedding The Enemy in Our Military

In 2010, Obama issued an executive order to expedite immigrant visa requests from Islamic countries. A person from a Muslim country could become a U.S. citizen in as little as ten weeks, with no I.D. and no declaration of allegiance to the U.S. Constitution:

"Under the program, illegal aliens with "special skills," such as speaking Arabic, Dari, Pushti and other languages are now allowed to enlist in the U.S military. There is NO requirement that they be in the United States legally. No background check! A Muslim Pushti speaker could sneak across the Rio Grande today and be getting "3 hots and a cot" (meals and a place to sleep) in the U.S. Military tomorrow! Even worse, he would be on a path to get citizenship in less time than any other naturalized citizen in history! Special "citizenship expediters" at military bases across the country rush their citizenship papers through in as little as 10 weeks.

The program is also open to Muslims with other special, non-language skills. For example, Muslim physicians [remember terrorist murderer Major Nidal Malik Hasan or MD Rabbi Alam] are especially recruited for this new "10-weeks to Citizenship" program…

The Obama administration claimed we need these people's skills, but the less than 100-day rush to citizenship has some outraged. The ten weeks is supposedly used to process their paperwork and ensure they have no ties to radical Islam. There is no possible way these checks could be done in 10 weeks. These are people who have arrived in the US illegally, with no ID, and no proof of anything they say.

The military has been a path to citizenship before. After WWII,German soldiers were quietly allowed to enter the US Amry. After 5 years, they got their US citizenship. In the 1960's, there was more Greman spoken after hours in a 10th Special Forces barracks than English. The program worked, because the former Wermacht soldiers were screened and had to improve themselves over 5 years. Even so, two were weeded out and jailed as Stassi sleepers.

Under Obama, Muslims with no background checks were allowed to serve in the US military, simply by promising to serve in the military. Many of these Muslims became full US citizens even though they had already proven their willingness to flout our laws by sneaking into the country."

To be fair, the Bush and the Obama Administrations, both facilitated the access to visas for Saudi nationals. "Bush administration officials claimed that the students wouldn't become security risks, thanks to the Student and Exchange Visitor Information System [SEVIS}, instituted in 2002. In addition, to background checks, SEVIS was supposed to monitor details about foreign students, where they lived and whether they continued to pursue legitimate student programs.

Nevertheless, Saudi Arabian, Hani Hasan Hanjour, who got a visa to study English at ELS Language Centers (a Berlitz-owned school in Oakland, CA), never completed the course. Instead, he was one of the terrorists on the plane that crashed into the Pentagon on 9/11.

RightSideNews by Eliana Benador

http://thehuffingtonriposte.blogspot.com/2011/02/obama-continues-to-flood-america-with.html#ixzz35kpKwewC

Appendix J

BENGHAZI ... THE REST OF THE STORY

The material presented in Appendix J includes some information from *"The Real Benghazi Story"* by Aaron Klein, WND Books, 2014

THE NEW OBAMA ADMINISTRATION DOCTRINE TOWARDS ISLAM

Background

While President Bush has a strong heritage and sense of patriotism, President Obama did not grow up in America and does not recognize American uniqueness nor its exceptionalism. President Obama does not regard the founding of America as having been divinely directed nor divinely protected.

On numerous occasions, President Obama supported the ouster of a US ally in the Middle East and North Africa. His support of replacement leaders, radical Islamic Supremacists, had been a great detriment to US foreign policy and reduced our effectiveness in containing and defeating radical Islam. These Western friendly leaders had been supported by previous US administrations (G. W. Bush; Clinton; G. H. W. Bush; Reagan; Ford; Nixon; Johnson and Kennedy) for many decades.

Change in Direction

In a completely opposite approach, President Obama sought:

1) to work with Islamist Supremacists in Afghanistan, Iraq, Iran and the Middle East;

2) to negotiate with the Islamist Supremacists to find "common ground;"

3) to trust the Islamist Supremacists; and

4) to compromise with the Islamist Supremacists.

If you try to meet an ENEMY half way, your opponent has you on a one-way bridge … a bridge to nowhere. The only exit is for you to acquiesce to their demands.

THE NEW COURSE OF ACTION

President Barack Obama reset the "inconsistent" foreign policy of the George W. Bush administration towards Islam and Islamic Supremacy, from one of:

"Strength through controlled force, with some appeasement;"

to a policy of:

"Weakness by inconsistent accommodation, with insufficient force."

The Result of President Obama's New Approach was:

1) to play down the real threat of Islamic Supremacists;

2) to offer support to the Muslim Brotherhood and its affiliates;

3) to embolden our foes;

4) to snub our allies; and

5) to weaken the United States at home and abroad.

"Fast and Furious …. Middle East Style"

"Prior to the establishment of the 'special mission' in Libya, United States agents provided aid to the Libyan rebels, who eventually toppled Muammar Gaddafi. That aid included weapons which were carefully purchased through extremist middlemen. They used financing in Saudi Arabia, Qatar and Turkey, so as to avoid US government accountability … to US citizens and to US allies around the world." [1]

Ambassador Stevens' original role in Libya was to serve as the main "interlocutor" between the Obama administration and the rebels based in Benghazi. During late 2010 and early 2011, Stevens made numerous trips in and out of Benghazi, identifying a strategic plan by which the United States could support the over throw of the Gaddafi government. "At that time the news media had churned out reports of U.S coordinated arms being funneled to the anti-Gaddafi rebels." [2]

Subsequently, "the U.S. 'special mission' and the CIA annex in Benghazi served as intelligence and planning centers, for sending U.S. aid to rebels in the Middle East, with particular emphasis on shipping weapons to Jihadists fighting in Libya and later in Syria. [3]

"Chris Stevens himself played a central role in recruiting and vetting Jihadists and in coordinating arms shipments into and out of Libya, before he became the ambassador." [4]

In March 2011, *Reuters* exclusively reported, "that President Obama had signed a secret executive order, authorizing covert U.S. government support for the rebel forces in Libya seeking to oust Gaddafi." [5]

Also in March 2011, the UK-based *Independent* reported, "that the Americas have asked Saudi Arabia if it can supply weapons to the rebels through U.S. contacts in Benghazi." [6]

In April 2011, Stevens returned to Libya aboard a Greek cargo ship, carrying "a dozen American diplomats, guards and enough equipment, including vehicles, to set up a diplomatic beachhead in the middle of an armed rebellion." [7]

In December 2012, the *New York Times* reported that the Obama administration "secretly gave its blessing [in 2011] to arms shipments to Libyan rebels from Qatar, but American officials later grew alarmed as evidence surfaced that Qatar was turning some of the weapons over to Islamic militants." [8]

It was not until after the successful overthrow of the Gaddafi regime, that the United States government applied to the new Libyan government for permission to "establish" a mission in Benghazi. No such notice was ever given to the new government for the existence of the CIA annex. [9]

Security for Benghazi Mission: May -- September 2012

In March 2012, the US State Department, with the approval of Sec. Clinton, awarded a one-year contract to Blue Mountain Group, a small British firm located in Wales, to protect the US mission in Benghazi, despite the fact that the company had only limited experience in Libya. The amount of the contract was $387,000.00. [10]

Sources told the *Daily Telegraph* that the protection consisted of just five unarmed, locally hired Libyans, placed on duty at the compound on eight-hour shifts, under the supervision of one armed, British employee. Even though this staffing was irresponsibly <u>inadequate, and</u> fell outside the State Department's global security contracting guidelines, the contract was nevertheless awarded. [11]

The New York Times reported that major security firms, each with track records of guarding US premises elsewhere had submitted proposals to the US State Department to undertake work in Libya, including supplying protection for the US mission in Benghazi, but they were rebuffed. [12]

In June, Jairo Saravia, the State Departments acting Security Regional Officer in Tripoli, sent an email to David Oliveira, Regional Security Officer, in Benghazi, alerting him that the company was having problems in Libya. "Just a quick note, in regards to Blue Mountain. The company has lost several security contracts here in Tripoli, including The Corinthian Hotel and Palm City complex," Saravia said in a June 7th email. "The latest information is Blue Mountain is not licensed by the government of Libya (GOL) to provide security services in Libya. I would advise not to use their services to provide security for any of our annexes and/or offices due to the sensitivity this issue has with the current GOL." [13]

Also in June, the British consulate in Benghazi was closed because of danger from radical Islamic Jihadists. The US mission was the only western government facility left in Benghazi.

Just days before the September 11, 2012 attack in Benghazi, Torres Advanced Enterprise Solutions was asked to assess the problem, to clean up the mess, and to implement appropriate security/protection for the mission. The attacks came before any changes could be made. [14]

BENGHAZI: SEPTEMBER 11, 2012

Ambassador Stevens' contact person with the Turkish government was the Turkish consul general stationed in Benghazi. September 11, 2012, Stevens had dinner with the consul general. They parted company about 9:00 pm. [15]

Background

Recall that the United States established the "special mission" and the CIA annex in secret and without giving formal notice to the Gaddafi government. Under these circumstances, these facilities were not provided with required fortification and perimeter security as set forth by the US State Department protocols. "As far as security was concerned, the U.S. facility in Benghazi was one of a kind." According to the State Department's Libya desk officer, Brian Papanu, "Benghazi was definitely unique in almost every [way] --- I can't think of a mission similar to this ever, and definitely not in recent history." [16]

Only after the change of regime in Libya and the location of the "special mission" was known by the new regime, did the Clinton State Department add limited security improvements, still well below protocols. [17]

"The Clinton State Department continued to operate a temporary residential facility in a violent and unstable environment, without adequate U.S. security and only limited host nation security support. To supplement the inadequate security, the State Department made the 'mind-blowing decision' to hire armed members of the local February 17 Martyrs Brigade, an affiliate of al-Qaeda." [18]

In June and again in July 2012, the special mission had come under attack by unknown terrorists. The British closed their consulate in Benghazi in June 2012, because of rising danger to their personnel. [19]

On August 15, 2012, Ambassador Stevens requested in writing that security and fortification of the "special mission" be increased. Secretary of State Clinton denied the request. Instead, her office reduced the number of personnel in the security force at the mission on August 31st. [20]

The Attacks - First Wave & Second Wave

The *First Wave* of the attacks began at 9:41 pm (local time; 3:41 pm EDT) and lasted most of the night. The *Second Wave* began at 5:15 am (local time: 11:15 pm EST). Both waves were well planned, well-coordinated, and carried out by well-armed Jihadists. [21]

"The United States has surveillance video from the mission that showed no popular protest. Gregory Hicks, the No. 2 U.S. official in Libya at the time of the September 11, 2012 attacks, testified that he knew immediately the attacks were terror strikes, not a protest turned violent." [22]

Hicks notified the office of Secretary of State Clinton when the attacks began, that the attackers were well armed. He said it never occurred to him that the attacks were a protest gone violent. [23]

Likewise, within hours after the attack began, Secretary Clinton had spoken with the Libyan President Mohammed el-Megarif and with the Libyan Deputy Ambassador to London Ahmad Jibril, stating that a terrorist attack had occurred at the US mission in Benghazi. She also sent a personal email to her daughter, Chelsea, confirming the same attack. [24]

Unanswered Question ...

Was Stevens murdered because he knew too much about: 1) the "US gun running activities": and 2) the "U.S. involvement in the 'Arab Springs' uprisings?"

Was this attack a botched kidnapping that went wrong? Was Stevens going to be used as ransom in a trade for Jihadi prisoners?

Whatever the plot, shortly after the first wave began, Gregory Hicks informed Security Clinton's office that Ambassador Stevens was missing. [25]

As the attackers approached the residence Villa C, Ambassador Stevens, Sean Smith, information management officer (IMO) and an assistant regional security officer (ARSO) sought refuge in the "safe room". The well-informed attackers assumed that was where Ambassador Stevens had retreated and proceeded to smoke them out. [26]

The three managed to crawl to a bathroom, where upon the ARSO lead the way out the window to fresh air. However, Stevens and Smith did not escape out the window. Later Smith's body was found in the villa, but Stevens was missing. [27]

"There was no knowledge of Stevens' whereabouts until approximately 2:00am the next morning, when the Tripoli embassy received a phone call through the ARSO's cell phone. 'It was determined to have come from the Benghazi Medical Center. A male, Arabic-speaking caller said an unresponsive male, who matched the physical description of the Ambassador, was at the hospital.' The Ambassador's identity was later confirmed, but by then he was deceased. Later, Gregory Hicks would testify that the U.S. Embassy in Tripoli had been told that Stevens had been taken to a hospital controlled by Ansar al-Sharia, the group originally believed to have been behind the attack."[28]

The Cover Up

Beginning on September 12, 2012, the Obama administration attempted to mislead the American people, by not wanting to characterize the attacks in Benghazi as having any terrorist related aspects. "Not only did the White House obfuscated legislative inquiries and other investigations into the September 11, 2012 Benghazi attacks, but they completely fabricated information and events so as not to change the President's political narrative 'That al-Qaeda was on the run'." This was a major theme of his re-election campaign of 2012. [29]

On Sunday, September 16, 2012, UN Ambassador Susan Rice appeared on five morning television programs to offer the official Obama administration response to the Benghazi attacks. In nearly identical statements, she asserted that the attacks were a spontaneous protest in response to a "hateful video." Secretary of State Clinton and other administration officials made similar claims. On September 25th, in a speech at the UN, President Obama blamed the attacks on the U.S. mission as a response to a video. [30]

"The day after the attack, Libya's deputy ambassador to London, Ahmad Jibril, told the BBC that Ansar al-Sharia carried out the assault. Libyan President Mohammed el-Megarif was even more direct, saying foreign Jihadists, who infiltrated Libya, planned the attack and used some local Libyans during the event." [31]

Time Lines

For national security purposes, the physical whereabouts of the President, the Secretary of Defense, and the Secretary of State are known all the time and are permanently recorded.

The recorded "time line" of the Secretary of Defense, reveals Leon Panetta was aware of the attack and started watching it in his office at the Pentagon at approximately 3:42 pm (recall the 1st wave attack began at 3:41 pm). Sec. Panetta had a previously scheduled 5:00 pm meeting with the President in the Oval Office at the White House.

At approximately 4:30 pm, Sec. Panetta left the Pentagon; continued to watch the attack through communications equipment in his government car; and went to the White House. Upon arrival at the White House, he went to the Oval Office and there continued to watch the attack with President Obama and Vice-President Biden. They may have been the only ones in the Oval Office. [32]

Where was Secretary of State Hillary Clinton during the Benghazi attacks?

"What difference at this point does it make?!" [33]

Ms. Clinton's very public display of arrogance must now be answered, as it applies to her actions before, during, and after the attacks.

Secretary Clinton personally approved, in writing, each of the following:

A) "The stunning backwardness of the U.S. 'special missions' so-called security posture, including: denied guard towers; reduction in special reaction forces (SST - Security Support Team) in August 2012 in Libya's hot zone; and aircraft recall on September 2012." [34]

B) "Internal protection of the compound was provided by armed members of the February 17 Martyrs Brigade militia, affiliated with al-Qaeda, linked to Ansar al-Sharia terrorist organization, later linked to the Benghazi attack." [35]

C) "Special legal waivers were necessary whenever any U.S. personnel visited or occupied the 'special mission', because of the unusual 'co-location' setup in Benghazi (ie offices, residence and CIA annex at separate locations),” Secretary Clinton was required by law to sign all waivers. [36]

D) State Department ARB report conceded that there was a “flawed process by which Special Mission Benghazi’s extension [Security Protocol] until the end of December 2012 was approved and admitting that the decision did not take security considerations adequately into account.” [37]

E) Special waiver, allowing Ambassador Stevens to travel to Benghazi over the period of September 11th, was approved and signed by Sec Clinton. [38]

The June-September 2012 events leading up to the Benghazi attacks, took place with the knowledge that “al-Qaeda and other Islamic extremist groups gained major ground in Libya following U.S. intervention there, to the point that they were establishing training camps in Benghazi. These al-Qaeda linked groups, including the parent organization of February 17 Martyres Brigade, held a Sharia Islamic law confab not far from the Benghazi mission. [39]

Testimony before the House of Representatives investigative committee revealed that Sec. Clinton, Assistant Sec. Eric Boswell, Principal Deputy Assist. Sec. Scott Bultrowicz, Deputy Assist. Sec. Charlene Lamb, and Deputy Assist. Sec. Raymond Lamb were each aware of these circumstances. [40]

Arms Shipments from Benghazi to Syria

The United States continued to supply weapons to the new Libyan government. When the Libyan rebels ask for permission to ship weapons to the Jihadists fighting the Syrian army of Bashar al-Assad, President Obama issued an executive order, authorizing shipments of existing arms from stockpiles located in Libya. The Libyan rebels reduced their weapons stockpiles to a point and then they asked the United States to provide new weapons shipments from outside Libya. [41]

All of the weapons shipments from Benghazi to Syria went through Turkey and then were moved over land into Syria. These shipments were coordinated by Ambassador Stevens with full cooperation by the Turkish government.

"In October 2012, Fox News reported that the Libyan-flagged vessel *Al Entisar* had been received in the Turkish port of Iskenderun, about thirty-five miles from the Syrian border, just five days before Stevens was killed in the attack on the Benghazi mission. Weapons were hidden in 460 metric tons of humanitarian aid destined for Syrian refugees. *Reuters* noted that a UN panel found that: 1) the loading port for the shipment was Benghazi; 2) that the exporter was 'a relief organization based in Benghazi;' and 3) that the consignee was the same Islamic Foundation based in Turkey that Libyan warlord, Abdul Basit Haroun. had help *Reuters* with documentation." [42]

Haroun was a member of the February 17 Brigade until he quit to form a brigade of his own. Haroun had also helped *Reuters* with documentation for their report.

On March 24, 2013. the *New York Times* reported, that 'the CIA started in early 2012, helping Arab governments and Turkey to obtain and ship weapons to the rebels, fighting the regime of Syrian President Bashar al-Assad. These Syrian weapons shipments started on a small scale and continued intermittently through the fall of 2012. Most of the weapons shipments were by cargo vessel, hidden in humanitarian relief aid. Some weapons were also shipped by airlifts dropped to the rebels in Syria." [43]

"The *Times* reported that 'from offices at 'secret locations,' American intelligence officers 'helped the Arab governments shop for weapons ... and vetted rebel commanders and group to determine who should receive the weapons as they arrive'." [44]

The *Times* quoted a former American official as saying that "General David Petraeus, CIA director until November 2012, had been instrumental in helping set up an aviation network to fly the weapons to Syria. It further said that Petraeus 'had prodded various countries to work together' on the plan." [45]

Retrieving Weapons in Libya

After the new rebel government took power in Libya, Islamic Supremacists tried to get their hands-on weapons, which were freely flowing in Libya. Stevens was charged with the task of recovering the MANPADS (anti-aircraft missiles), which the U.S. government did not want in the hands of these extremists. Al-Qaeda and their affiliates were working hard to secure these MANPADS and to smuggle them to other parts of the Middle East.

"On the night of the attacks, Ambassador Stevens was in Benghazi to keep weapons caches from falling into terrorist hands. Benghazi was where the action was, regarding the increasing power of the Islamic Separatists."

"This weapons collection efforts may go a long way toward explaining the motive behind the Benghazi attacks. The jihadist organization, which looted Gaddafi's man-portable air-defense systems reserves and the rebel groups which received the weapons during the NATO campaign in Libya, would feel threatened by American efforts to try to retrieve those weapons." [46]

REFERENCES CITED FOR APPENDIX J

1   *"The Real Benghazi Story"*; by Aaron Klein, WND Books, 2014
2   *Reuters,* March 2001
3   ibid #1
4   ibid #1
5   ibid#2
6   *Independent,* March 2001
7   ibid #1
8   *New York Times,* December 2012
9   ibid #8
10 *Daily Telegraph,* October 2012
11 ibid #10
12 ibid #10
13 ibid #10
14 Fox News, September 2017
15 ibid #1
16 ibid #1
17 ibid #1
18 ibid #1
19 ibid #1
20 ibid #1
21 ibid #1
22 ibid #1
23 ibid #1
24 ibid #1
25 ibid #1
26 ibid #1
27 ibid #1
28 ibid #1
29 ibid #1
30 ibid #1
31 ibid #1
32 ibid #1
33 ibid #1
34 ibid #1
35 ibid #1
36 ibid #1
37 ibid #1
38 ibid #1
39 ibid #1
40 ibid #1
41 Fox News, December 2015
42 *New York Times,* March 24, 2013
43 *New York Times*, November 2012
44 ibid #44
45 ibid #1
46 ibid #1

Appendix K

"IRAN NUCLEAR ACCORD"

BACKGROUND: IRANIAN HOSTAGE CRISIS

The Iran hostage crisis was a diplomatic crisis between Iran and the United States. Fifty-two American diplomats and citizens were held hostage for 444 days (November 4, 1979, to January 20, 1981). A group of Iranian students, belonging to the Muslim Student Followers of the Imam's Line, who were supporting the Iranian Revolution, took over the U.S. Embassy in Tehran. President Jimmy Carter called the hostages "victims of terrorism and anarchy," adding that "the United States will not yield to blackmail."

The crisis was described by the western media as an "entanglement" of "vengeance and mutual incomprehension." In Iran, the hostage taking was widely seen as a blow against the United States and its influence in Iran, its perceived attempts to undermine the Iranian Revolution, and its longstanding support of the recently overthrown Shah of Iran, Mohammad Reza Pahlavi, who had led a totalitarian regime with American support.

Following his overthrow in 1979, the Shah was admitted to the U.S. for medical treatment of cancer. The Iranians demanded that the Shah be returned to Iran for trial and execution for crimes he was accused of committing during his reign. They accused the Shah of crimes against Iranian citizens with the help of his secret police, the SAVAK. Iranians saw the asylum granted by the U.S. as American complicity in the atrocities the Shah had committed. In the United States, the hostage-taking was seen as an egregious violation of the principles of international law which granted diplomats immunity from arrest and diplomatic compounds' inviolability.

NUCLEAR PROGRAM

The nuclear program of Iran has been a matter of contention with the international community since 2002, when an Iranian dissident group revealed the existence of two undeclared nuclear facilities.

The International Atomic Energy Agency, charged with monitoring and ensuring peaceful nuclear activities, referred the matter of Iran's nuclear program to the UN Security Council in February 2006, after finding that Iran had not been in compliance with its duties as a signatory of the Nuclear Non-Proliferation Treaty (NPT). For what the IAEA judged to be continued non-compliance, the UN Security Council has voted four times since 2006 to impose limited economic sanctions against Iran. In its resolutions, the Council required Iran to fully cooperate with the IAEA and to suspend all uranium enrichment-related activities. Dore Gold, Israel's former ambassador to the United Nations, has emphasized that the resolutions were adopted under Chapter VII of the United Nations Charter and "are legally binding under international law, adding further legal force to the argument that Iran has no legal right whatsoever to enrich uranium".

CHRONOLOGICAL HISTORY OF IRANIAN-AMERICAN RELATIONS.

January 12, 1979

Gen. Robert Husyer was sent to Iran with the mission to convince the Iran's army chief commanders to obey Bahkitar - the Shah's prime minister - and prepare for the Shah's departure. He also met with pro-Khomeini religious leaders, according to some reports including Ayatollah Beheshti who later became the key leader of Islamic Republic.

February 11, 1979

The Shah regime collapsed after an armed uprising that included parts of the military and various rebel groups. The US recognized the new government that was headed by Mehdi Bazargan, a representative of liberal democratic Islamic thought who was appointed by Khomeini.

October 22, 1979

The Shah, who at this point had terminal stage cancer, was finally allowed to enter the US and was hospitalized in New York.

November 4, 1979

A group of pro-regime students led by Mohammad Mousavi Khoeiniha attacked the US Embassy.

January 30, 1980

Six US embassy employees who escaped from Iran with Canadian passports arrived in the US.

April 7, 1980

The US government ended diplomatic relations with Iran and ordered remaining Iranian diplomats to leave the US.

August 25, 1980

Operation Eagle Claw - an attempted to rescue the hostages with some help from the Iranian army insiders - failed and 8 US soldiers were killed in northern Iran.

January 21, 1981

Less than an hour after Ronald Reagan's inauguration, the hostages were released, after being held for 444 days, in an accord brokered by the Algerian government.

1981

The Reagan administration started to support Saddam Hussein in his war against Iran.

July 3, 1988

Tensions between Iran military and the US Navy in the Persian Gulf increased dramatically, culminating when the USS Vincennes shoots down an Iran Air civilian flight bound for Dubai killing 290 passengers including 66 children. Tehran called the act intentional and interpreted it as signal from the Reagan administration that the covert war between the two countries in the Persian Gulf would continue. While the US did not admit any wrongdoing, nor submitted any apology, in 1996 the US did agree to pay $ 131.8 million to Iran and the victim's families in compensation for the incident.

1996

President Clinton increased trade sanction against Iran, accusing the Islamic Republic of terrorism and nuclear weapons projects.

March 2000

Madeleine Albright, US Secretary of State, called for a new start in Iranian-US relations and apologized for The US role in the coup d'etat against the Mosadegh government in 1953. She announced the lifting of some sanctions, a move which Kharrazi, the Iran Foreign Minister welcomed.

August 2000

Albright and Kharrazi met in New York during the UN general Assembly, the first time such a meeting took place in post-1979.

US accused Iran for bombing a US base in Saudi Arabia, the same year as CIA reported that Iran was about to reach nuclear weapons capabilities.

January 29, 2002

President George W. Bush called Iran, Iraq and North Korea the Axis of Evil.

December 2003

The US sent humanitarian aid to 60,000 Iran earthquake victims.

March 2006

Condelessa Rice, US Secretary of State, announced that Iran's nuclear program is the greatest challenge to the US.

2011

President Obama extends Iranian sanctions.

September 2012

Secret diplomatic meetings between the two countries are reported by the NY Times.

October 27, 2012

Mansour Arabasitor, an Iranian-American, charged in a plot to kill the Saudi ambassador to the United States, plead guilty.

INTERIM AGREEMENT

For almost two decades, Iran has skillfully dodged and delayed the efforts of the western nations to curtail and/or to eliminate its nuclear program. These western nations have known all along that Iran's objectives were not to develop nuclear capabilities for peaceful, commercial applications.

Iran is the number one international sponsor of terrorism world-wide. They certainly plan to use any financial advantage or violent tactical weapon available to them, as they pursue and support terrorist activities throughout the Middle East, Central Asia, north Africa and around the world.

On 24 November 2013, the **Geneva interim agreement**, officially titled the **Joint Plan of Action**, was a pact signed between Iran and the P5+1 countries (US, UK, France, Russia and China plus Germany) in Geneva, Switzerland. It consists of a short-term freeze of portions of Iran's nuclear program in exchange for decreased economic sanctions on Iran, as the countries work towards a long-term agreement. It represented the first formal agreement between the United States and Iran in 34 years. Implementation of the agreement began 20 January 2014.

The Joint Plan of Action and the negotiations under it which followed eventually led to an April 2015 framework agreement and then a July 2015 final agreement, the Joint Comprehensive Plan of Action.

FINAL NUCLEAR ACCORD

After more than two weeks of wrangling and missed deadlines in Vienna, Iran and its international interlocutors have finally clinched a historic accord over Tehran's nuclear program. The diplomacy with Iran, an endeavor that faced vociferous opposition throughout, was aimed at curbing the Islamic republic's ability to produce a nuclear weapon. A tentative framework was inked in April between Iran and its negotiating partners, which include the United States, Russia, Britain, France, China and Germany.

MAIN CONDITIONS OF THE NUCLEAR ACCORD

Six world powers, led by the United States, announced a framework deal with Iran limiting its nuclear program. The agreement outlines major points to be fleshed out in a final deal, the details of which have to be completed by the end of June 2015. Negotiators in Lausanne, Switzerland, twice extended the talks past Tuesday's deadline for a framework because of deep differences between the parties. So what exactly did they finally agree to? Here are 8 key points, as conveyed by U.S. officials.

1. Centrifuges

Iran would have to reduce its total of about 19,000 centrifuges -- 10,000 of which are still spinning today -- down to 6,104 under the deal, with only 5,060 allowed to enrich uranium over the next 10 years. Centrifuges are tube-shaped machines used to enrich uranium, the material necessary for nuclear power -- and nuclear bombs.

2. Uranium Enrichment

Iran's centrifuges will only enrich uranium to 3.67% -- enough for civil use to power parts of the country, but not enough to build a nuclear bomb. That agreement lasts 15 years. And Tehran has agreed not to build any new uranium enrichment facilities over that period as well. The 3.67% is a major decline, and it follows Iran's move to water down its stockpile of 20% enriched uranium last year. In addition, Iran will reduce its current stockpile of 10,000 kilograms of low-enriched uranium to 300 kilograms for 15 years.

3. Breakout Time

The period of time that it would take for Iran to acquire the material it needs to make one nuclear weapon, currently assessed at two to three months, would be extended to about one year under the deal. That year-long breakout period would be in place for at least 10 years.

4. Fordow Facility

Iran's Fordow nuclear reactor would stop enriching uranium for at least 15 years. It will not have fissile material at the facility, but it will be able to keep 1,000 centrifuges there. Fordow, one of the country's biggest reactors, is buried more than 200 feet under the side of a mountain and was hidden from the international community until the U.S. revealed it in 2009.

5. Research and Development

Iran can continue its research and development on enrichment, but that work will be limited to keep the country to its breakout time frame of one year. Though Iran will be required to make changes at a number of its facilities -- including reducing centrifuges and rebuilding a heavy water reactor in Arak -- the country will get to maintain its current facilities.

6. Inspections

Iran will be required to provide inspectors from the International Atomic Energy Agency, the U.N.'s nuclear watchdog, access to all of its declared facilities so that the agency can ensure there is no potential for military-related developments. That includes access to Parchin, an Iranian military facility related to its nuclear program. Western countries have been seeking unfettered access throughout Iran, not just declared facilities, as Iran has previously conducted nuclear work in secret.

7. Sanctions Lifted

The United States and the European Union would lift their nuclear-related sanctions on the Iranian economy -- a priority for Iran -- after a U.N. watchdog verifies it has taken key steps. If there are violations, the sanctions will snap back into place. U.N. sanctions will also be lifted when Iran completes its nuclear-related steps, though some peripheral restrictions will be contained in a new Security Council resolution. International reductions in purchases of Iranian oil and increased isolation of the Middle Eastern country had squeezed its economy in recent years, and the lifting of those sanctions could bring the country major financial rewards.

8. Cash Payment to Iran by US

The United States agreed to pay the government of Iran $150 Billion up front. Sharia Law, through the process of zakat, requires that Iran use 12% of this amount to support the spread of Islam. 3% of the moneys (25% of the 12%), handled through banking system must be used for violent jihad! This qualifies the US as the largest funder of violent Muslim terrorist in the world.

While the JCPoA was signed by five countries (UK, France, Germany, Russia and China); The US and Iran never signed the Accord.

PROS AND CONS OF THE DEAL

1. Deal Opponents

What's wrong with the deal?

"Critics contend that the agreement doesn't go far enough to make it worth halting the sanctions regime. If Iran wants a reprieve, it should halt all uranium enrichment; make clear that Iran has no right to enrich uranium; tell the world what nuclear activities it is conducting at the Parchin military base; freeze all centrifuge production; and start dismantling its nuclear facilities," says Danielle Pletka at the American Enterprise Institute's *AEIdeas*.

And what Iran gets for merely pushing the pause button is "the beginning of the end of international cooperation on sanctions," says Pletka. "The reversal in momentum for sanctions and the loss of the psychology of impenetrable sanctions is of immeasurable value to Tehran."

Yes, "this interim agreement is badly skewed from America's perspective," says John Bolton at *The Weekly Standard*. Allowing Iran to continue enriching uranium, especially, amounts to "abject surrender by the United States." Along with buying time and sapping the sanctions of potency, the deal is rotten because "Iran has gained legitimacy," Bolton adds. "This central banker of international terrorism and flagrant nuclear proliferator is once again part of the international club."

The lead dissenting voice isn't a pundit or member of the U.S. Congress, though; it's Israeli Prime Minister Benjamin Netanyahu. "What was reached last night in Geneva is not a historic agreement, it is a historic mistake," he said as soon as the news broke. "Today the world became a much more dangerous place because the most dangerous regime in the world made a significant step in obtaining the most dangerous weapons in the world."

What comes next?

Just like a similar, phased-nukes deal with North Korea, this agreement will lead nowhere, says AEI's Pletka. Six months will pass, and Iran will continue its drive for a nuclear missile. "There will be no phase two."

With the U.S. and Europe committed to appeasement, says Bolton at *The Weekly Standard*, "in truth, an Israeli military strike is the only way to avoid Tehran's otherwise inevitable march to nuclear weapons, and the proliferation that will surely follow."

2. Deal Supporters
What's good about the deal?

The six-month deal "does not achieve permanent and total dismantlement of Iran's nuclear program," but "no one can seriously argue that it doesn't make the world safer," says *The New York Times* in an editorial. Obama and Rouhani deserve credit for "resisting fierce domestic opposition and a 30-year history of animosity between the two countries" to take this "important step toward resolving the increasingly dangerous dispute over Iran's progress on production of a nuclear weapon."

The Iranian deal is nothing less than a "triumph," and it "goes way beyond what anybody could reasonably have hoped for" even a few weeks ago, says Fred Kaplan at *Slate*. It should build trust between the U.S. and Iran, giving negotiators time to do the much harder work of reaching a comprehensive agreement. If they fail, Iran will get hit by tougher sanctions and the U.S. can say it gave diplomacy a real shot. "Had George W. Bush negotiated this deal, Republicans would be hailing his diplomatic prowess, and rightly so."

Yeah, let's be real, says Martin Longman at *Washington Monthly*.

Any agreement with Iran was going to have to allow the Iranian government to argue that they'd gotten a good deal. Likewise, any agreement was going to be opposed by Israel and Saudi Arabia, and Saudi Arabia's satellites in the Gulf region. [*Washington Monthly*]

The hard work is ahead, but after a decade of no diplomatic progress and steady Iranian nuclear advancement, Rouhani's election gave us all a window to reach a breakthrough, says Amy Davidson at *The New Yorker*. "It would be self-destructive on America's part not to seize this moment." And Secretary of State John Kerry "is certainly trying."

IRAN NUCLEAR ACCORD NOT ENFORCEABLE

Legally Not Enforceable

The Iranian nuclear agreement announced on July 14 is unconstitutional, violates international law and features commitments that President Obama could not lawfully make. However, because of the way the deal was pushed through, the states may be able to derail it by enacting their own Iran sanctions legislation.

President Obama executed the nuclear deal as an executive agreement, not as a treaty. While presidents, in the past, have used executive agreements to arrange less important or temporary matters, significant international obligations have always been established through treaties, which require Senate consent by a two-thirds majority.

The Obama administration won't submit any deal limiting Iran's nuclear ambitions to Congress for approval because it won't be legally binding, Secretary of State John Kerry said Wednesday. "We've been clear from the beginning we're not negotiating a legally binding plan. We're negotiating a plan that will have a capacity for enforcement," he told the Senate Foreign Relations Committee. "We don't even have diplomatic relations with Iran right now."

244 | P a g e   Trojan Horses of Islamic Supremacy

ECONOMICS MAKE IRAN NUCLEAR DEAL UNENFORCEABLE

The nuclear deal with Iran will prove unenforceable. Ultimately, Tehran will become the dominant economic and military power in the Middle East and if it chooses, build nuclear weapons.

The United States was successful in assembling an international coalition to impose tough economic sanctions. Restrictions on access to technology, international banks and their electronic payments systems imposed double digit unemployment and inflation and brought Iran to the negotiating table.

Simply, finding buyers for oil shipped via three million-barrel supertankers was one thing, but the inability to transfer funds through western banks made securing $150 million payments quite another.

The Obama administration sought to dismantle Tehran's nuclear infrastructure, including its underground centrifuge machines, which enrich uranium into fissionable material. However, Tehran balked. Other events in the region made Obama desperate for a deal: 1) the rise of the Islamic State in Iraq and Syria; 2) its spinoff in Libya; and 3) the deteriorating relations with Israel; and with Saudi Arabia on issues transcending the Iranian nuclear challenge.

The agreement significantly reduces the number of Iranian centrifuges and other nuclear infrastructure, but only limits Tehran's ability to quickly "break out" from these restrictions and accumulate enough fissionable material to create a nuclear weapon in less than one year. Theoretically, we are told that is enough time for the West to detect Iranian violations and respond --- **But it's Not !!!**

The lifting of economic sanctions has the potential to create an economic superpower with malevolent, anti-western aspirations.

Iran has the oil reserves of Saudi Arabia, the natural gas reserves of Russia, the mineral resources of Australia-including iron ore, bauxite, cooper, and the world's largest supply of zinc, a sophisticated manufacturing sector, a stock market with strong corporate reporting requirements, a well-educated population of 80 million, and a large middle class.

In 2006, Iran produced 1.6 million automobiles, through indigenous manufacturers and joint ventures with western firms. Although sanctions pushed that number down to 1 million in 2014, it bears noting that autos are among the most difficult and complex mass production items to make, and Iran's technological potential could quickly put it in the same category as South Korea or even France.

Iran provides Western Europe and China with an alternative to Russian natural gas.

The surge of European, Chinese and American investment into Iran will be a reminder of the Gold Rush that gave rise to modern California. And once those euros, yuan and dollars are in, political pressures will make it very tough to re-impose western economic sanctions.

Were Iran to start making weapons-grade material, any western actions would be preceded by talks. But as with Russia in the Ukraine, Europe's largest economy, Germany, would be cautious about losing access to Iranian natural gas and its other commercial interests, and similar distractions would impede other European and Asian cooperation.

The U.S. trump card has been its unique grip on the global banking and payments system, but China's success in recruiting European allies to join its Asian Infrastructure Bank demonstrates that Asian alternatives to U.S. dominated western financial institutions will soon emerge.

Even as sanctions handicapped Iran, it has projected power directly and through surrogates in Lebanon, Iraq, Yemen and elsewhere. Once the Iranian industrial juggernaut gets rolling, a society with an anti-western theocratic bent, sophisticated technology and manufacturing industries, and the resource wealth of Saudi Arabia, Russia and Australia combined will emerge as an economic and military power on a par with our European allies.

Ultimately, Iranian nuclear aspirations will prove awfully difficult to contain. U.S. threats to assemble an international coalition to impose sanctions will be futile.

UNITED NATIONS SIDE AGREEMENT WITH IRAN

Unbeknownst (?) to the United States, the IAEA (International Atomic Energy Agency) of the United Nations, has been negotiating a "Special Nuclear Agreement" with Iran, to address some of the same problems and concerns of the Iranian nuclear program.

President Obama and Secretary of State John Kerry have stated that they were unaware of the IAEA agreement with Iran. and the requirements/conditions of this agreement.

The IAEA- Iran Nuclear Agreement allows for Iran to self-select and to self-inspect their own facilities for violations to the "Special Nuclear Agreement". Iran can self-select the site(s) for 24-day notice and report to the IAEA by written report and video pictures/files.

Appendix L

ISLAMIST INFILTRATION OF AMERICAN UNIVERSITIES

by Ryan Mauro;
Shillman Fellow for the Clarion Project:
March 19, 2018, pp. 3-20

In 1988, an FBI source inside the Muslim Brotherhood revealed that the Islamist group's proxies in America had a six-phase plan to "institute the Islamic Revolution in the United States."[1] Among these front groups was The International Institute of Islamic Thought (IIIT), a think tank committed to the "Islamization of knowledge."[2] This ideology, as Professor Vali Nasr writes, entails the subordination of scientific inquiry to "the mere implementation of the assorted teachings of the Shariʿa."[3]

Over the last three decades, IIIT's part in the Brotherhood's plan has met remarkable success. The institute has made itself an indispensable resource for Islamic studies scholars: It has provided funding for over 70 active researchers based at institutions across America (see appendix); it has spent millions of dollars on endowing chairs in Islamic studies;[4] and it has publicized the research of hundreds of like-minded academics at its Summer Institute for Scholars.[5]

IIIT's activities are integral to the Brotherhood's broader strategy of inciting an international Islamic revolution. As an official IIIT handbook notes:

At a time when we are forced to fight and defend ourselves on political, economic and military fronts ... (these efforts) can be accomplished by developing (the Ummah's, that is, the Muslim community's) ideological power and the power of the "islamization of knowledge (sic)" to effectively harness its full potential.[6]

In other words, the long-term success of the Islamists' revolution is dependent not only on success on the battlefield and at the ballot, but also on the cooptation of education in order to foment popular sympathy for the Brotherhood's objectives.

While IIIT's actions are ostensibly nonviolent, it has not hesitated to cultivate ties to international terrorists. In 2002, an anti-terrorism taskforce raided the IIIT's office. Based on the evidence obtained in this investigation, U.S. Customs Service Special Agent David Kane said in a sworn affidavit that IIIT co-founder and former vice president for research, Jamal Barzinji, was "not only closely affiliated with PIJ [Palestinian Islamic Jihad] . . . but also with Hamas."[7]

Furthermore, IIIT provided donations to the front organization of convicted Palestinian Islamic Jihad leader Sami al-Arian, formerly a professor at the University of South Florida. Al-Arian subsequently wrote a thank you note to IIIT, in which he emphasized that his organization and IIIT are essentially a single institution rooted in "an ideological and cultural concordance with mutual objectives."[8]

While IIIT is unapologetic about its links to violent Islamism, it is less forthright about the sources of its generous revenue. It is clear that the Brotherhood provided the start-up money for IIIT in 1988, when the aforementioned FBI memo notes that the organization had almost "unlimited funds" at its disposal.[9] That was 30 years ago. Nevertheless, today, IIIT's assets appear undiminished. Yet IIIT's website does not solicit donations; indeed, a search for "donate" on the site returns no relevant information.

This raises the question: Who is supporting IIIT today?

We cannot know for sure. However, we do know that IIIT has never shirked its loyalty to its parent organization, the Muslim Brotherhood. IIIT's website boasted—in a post that has now been removed—that two of its officials, Hisham Altalib and Abubaker Al-Shingieti, met with the leader of the Brotherhood and then-president of Egypt, Mohammed Morsi, in New York on September 24, 2012. Morsi "welcomed the participation of IIIT in the reform of higher education in Egypt."[10]

Furthermore, IIIT has cultivated relations with the wealthy Qatar Foundation, an arm of the Qatari government.[11] Qatar is one of the world's foremost state sponsors of international terrorism. Moreover, the state enforces its conception of the Shari'a at home. Its laws prescribe death for apostates and Muslims who commit adultery with non-Muslims; uphold the incarceration of men found guilty of homosexual relations; and sanction one of the world's most extensive and brutal human-trafficking systems.[12]

Qatar has sought to sanitize its illiberal reputation by constructing an "Education City" in the nation's capital, Doha. Education City is a network of campuses including Islamic colleges and proxy estates for six major U.S. universities: Texas A&M, Virginia Commonwealth, Cornell, Carnegie Mellon, Northwestern and Georgetown. The Qatar Foundation covers the expenses for these institutions to maintain their campuses in the country. It has invested over $400 million in Education City.[13]

Qatar has portrayed Education City as a repression-free zone that respects Western norms in a kingdom that otherwise upholds the rule of Islamic law.[14] Yet Islamists with terrorist affiliations, including IIIT's former director, Dr. Louay Safi, teach there.[15] Furthermore Professor Jasser Auda—an active associate of IIIT with extensive ties to the Muslim Brotherhood—is also based there.[16]

Yet the six U.S. universities listed above have shown no inclination to repudiate their Qatari sponsors. These institutions legitimize the Qatari regime, sanctioning the presence of violent Islamists in Education City. Their actions are reminiscent of IIIT-funded scholars' complicity with their own sponsors' illiberal, "revolutionary" agenda.

For too long, American universities have allowed IIIT to shape the development of Islamic Studies in this country. They have ignored IIIT's anti-intellectualism expressed in its commitment to the "Islamization of knowledge," meaning the suppression of scholarship not sympathetic to Islamists. Left-wing activists who censor campus discussions about radical Islamism provide cover for IIIT's regressive ideology. They further its agenda to suffocate any scrutiny of Islamism and the broader Islamic tradition.

It is time to bring IIIT's action to light. It is time for parents, students and policy makers to demand that IIIT ends its role in the radicalization of Islamic Studies—a discipline that has long showed itself predisposed to anti-Western agendas.

Selective List of Professors with Ties to IIIT

(The following list, while not exhaustive, demonstrates the extent of IIIT's infiltration into American universities.)

George Mason University

Abdulaziz Sachedina:: IIIT Chair in Islamic Studies. IIIT funded the position with a gift of $1.5 million.

- Cemil Aydin: member of IIIT's Council of Scholars (now at UNC-Chapel Hill).

- Sumayya Al Shingieti: IIIT recognized Sumayya Al Shingieti for completing her Bachelors' degree in film and video studies at George Mason University and receiving an award for the film she produced.

Shenandoah University

- Calvin Allen Jr.: "Dr. Allen signed last year an agreement with IIIT to cooperate in 'course development, educational programs, and research with a goal of promoting an understanding of Islam and Muslims in America, and Islamic civilization and culture,' based on 'the principles of equality and reciprocal benefit.'"

Hartford Seminary

- Heidi Hadsell: "Professor Hadsell praised the special relationship between the Harford Seminary and IIIT and the continued support that the seminary receives from IIIT, particularly in the area of ImamTraining and education, and the study of Christian-Muslim relations in general."

- Mahmoud Ayoub: member of IIIT's Council of Scholars whose teaching of courses about Shia Islam was sponsored by $35,000 from the Alavi Foundation in September 2012.

Huron University College

- Ingrid Mattson: member of the IIIT's Council of Scholars

United States Naval Academy (Formerly)

- Ermin Sinanovic: IIIT's Director of Research and Academic Programs.

Binghamton University

Seifudein Adem is there, as was the late Ali Mazrui, a very radical preacher.

Howard University

- Sulayman Nyang (retired from Howard): member of IIIT's Council of Scholars.

- Altaf Husain: IIIT recognized the academic achievements of Altaf Husain for receiving tenure at Howard University.

University of Notre Dame

- Asma Afsaruddin: member of IIIT's Council of Scholars

University of Delaware

- Muqtedar Khan: member of IIIT's Council of Scholars

American University

- Mohammed Nimer: visited IIIT with American University students in 2013 to discuss the "Islamic revival and role of Islam in politics of the Muslim world."

Univ. of Southern California College of Letters, Arts & Sciences

- Mazen Hashem: member of IIIT's Council of Scholars

University of Maryland

- Ahmad Kazemi Moussavi: former Iranian diplomat, has spoken several times for IIIT about Iran. He is no longer listed in the faculty directory on the University of Maryland's website (here).

- Fatima Mirza: IIIT recognized the academic achievements of her for completing her Ph.D. in social work at the University of Maryland.

- Charles Butterworth: participated in IIIT's 2012 Summer Institute for Scholars and the 2011 Friends of IIIT/Iftar Dinner.

Manhattanville College

- James Jones – has lectured at IIIT on the challenges of Islam to and in the U.S.

Georgetown University

- Jonathan Brown – has lectured at IIIT multiple times and participated in many of its programs.

- John Esposito – has lectured at IIIT multiple times and participated in many of its programs.

- John Voll – has lectured at IIIT multiple times and participated in many of its programs.

University of Virginia

- Rachel Mann – has lectured at IIIT about non-violent activism.

- Firas Barzinji – IIIT has recognized his achievements for completing his Masters' Degree in Business Administration, University of Virginia.

Middle Tennessee State University

- Ron Messier – has lectured at IIIT about his book, *Jesus, One man, Two Faiths; A Dialogue between Christians and Muslims.*

Santa Clara University

- Farid Senzai – IIIT recognized the academic achievements of Farid Senzai for receiving tenure at Santa Clara University

Union Theological Seminary

- Serene Jones – has attended events with IIIT and has shared her thoughts about her relationship with IIIT (https://utsnyc.edu/academics/faculty/serene-jones/)

George Washington University

- Mohamad Faghfoory – has attended events with IIIT and has shared his thoughts about his relationship with IIIT (http://religion.columbian.gwu.edu/mohammad-faghfoory)

IIIT Research Grant Recipients

Florian Pohl is an associate professor of religion at Emory University's Oxford College and received a research grant from IIIT.

Madiha Tahseen recently completed the requirements for her doctorate in Applied Developmental Psychology at the University of Maryland, Baltimore County (UMBC), and she received a research grant from IIIT.

Nazila Isgandarova is the spiritual and religious care coordinator at Ontario Multifaith Council and the spiritual care provider at the Centre for Addiction and Mental Health, and received a research grant from IIIT.

Nermeen Mouftah is a lecturer in the Departments of Anthropology and Religious Studies at the University of Illinois at Chicago, and received a research grant from IIIT.

Oliver Leaman is a professor of philosophy at the University of Kentucky, and received a research grant from IIIT.

Samy Ayoub is a postdoctoral faculty fellow at the University of California, Santa Barbara, and received a research grant from IIIT.

Aasim Padela is the director of the Initiative on Islam and Medicine and an assistant professor of medicine at the University of Chicago, and received a research grant from IIIT.

Emad Hamdeh earned his Ph.D. in Islamic and Arabic studies from the University of Exeter and is adjunct professor of Arabic and Islamic Studies at Montclair State University in Montclair, NJ; he received a research grant from IIIT.

Sameera Ahmed is director of the Family & Youth Institute (www.thefyi.org), a clinical assistant professor at Wayne State University, a scholar at the Institute for Social Policy and Understanding

(ISPU), an associate editor for the *Journal of Muslim Mental Health* (JMMH), and a board-licensed psychologist in Ohio and Michigan. She received a research grant from IIIT.

IIIT Resident Scholars

Asaad Al-Saleh is an assistant professor of Arabic Literature, Comparative Literature and Cultural Studies in the Department of Near Eastern Languages and Cultures at Indiana University.

SherAli Tareen is an assistant professor of religious studies at Franklin and Marshall College in Lancaster, PA.

Mustafa Gökçek is an associate professor of history at Niagara University in Niagara Falls, NY.

Abdulaziz Sachedina is a professor and IIIT chair in Islamic Studies at George Mason University in Fairfax, Virginia.

Nathan J. Brown, is a professor of political science and international affairs at George Washington University, former president of the Middle East Studies Association (MESA), and a scholar and author of six books on Arab politics.

Yahya M. Michot (Belgium, 1952) joined Hartford Seminary in 2008 as a professor of Islamic Studies and Christian-Muslim Relations and is editor of the journal *Muslim World*.

Najib George Awad is a Syrian-Arab Christian theologian and poet. He is an associate Ppofessor of Christian theology and the director of the international PhD program in Hartford Seminary, CT.

Syed Muhd Khairudin Aljunied is an assistant professor in the Faculty of Arts and Social Sciences, National University of Singapore.

Mohamed Mosaad Abdelaziz Mohamed is an assistant professor of religious studies at Northern Arizona University.

Imad-ad-Dean Ahmad, Ph.D., is an internationally known interdisciplinary scientist of Palestinian descent, born at sea and raised in the United States.

Abadir M. Ibrahim is a J.S.D. candidate at St. Thomas University School of Law LL.M./J.S.D. program in Intercultural Human Rights and has two LL.M. degrees — one in international law and one in human rights law.

Seifudein Adem is an associate professor of political science and the associate director of the Institute of Global Cultural Studies, SUNY Binghamton.

Emin Poljarevic is a visiting scholar at the Islamic and Middle Eastern Studies Department at the University of Edinburgh.

Ahmad Najib Burhani is a PhD candidate in religious studies at University of California-Santa Barbara.

Ahmad Kazemi Moussavi is a professor of Islamic law and modern Islamic developments who currently teaches at George Washington University.

Mojtaba Mahdavi is an associate professor of political science and Middle East studies at the University of Alberta, Canada.

Peter Mandaville is the director of the Ali Vural Ak Center for Global Islamic Studies and a professor of government at George Mason University.

John O. Voll is a professor of Islamic history and past associate director of the Prince Alwaleed Bin Talal Center for Muslim-Christian Understanding at Georgetown University in Washington, DC.

Abdullah Al-Arian is an assistant professor of history at Georgetown University's School of Foreign Service in Qatar.

Jonathan Brown is the Alwaleed bin Talal chair of Islamic Civilization and director of the Prince Alwaleed bin Talal Center for Muslim-Christian Understanding at Georgetown University.

Louay M. Safi is a professor at the Qatar Faculty of Islamic Studies.

Ali A. Mazrui, who died in 2015, was the Albert Schweitzer Professor in the Humanities and director of the Institute of Global Cultural Studies at Binghamton University, State University of New York.

Kamal Abu-Shamsieh was born in Ramallah and is currently a PhD student at the Graduate Theological Union in Berkeley, CA in the area of the cultural and historical study of religion.

Jasser Auda is a professor teaching at the Qatar Faculty of Islamic Studies in Doha, a founding member and a member of the executive board of the International Union of Muslim Scholars, a member of the academic committee of the IIIT and a fellow of the International Institute of Advanced Systems in Canada.

Mahmoud M. Ayoub was born in South Lebanon. He received his education at the American University of Beirut (BA, Philosophy, 1964), the University of Pennsylvania (M.A., Religious Thought, 1966) and Harvard University (Ph.D., History of Religion, 1975).

Usaama al-Azami is a PhD candidate at Princeton University's Department of Near Eastern Studies.

Jacquelene Brinton received her MA. and PhD. from the University of Virginia in August of 2009 in the Department of Religious Studies with a specialty in Islamic Studies.

Carl W. Ernst is the William R. Kenan, Jr. Distinguished Professor and co-director of the Carolina Center for the Study of the Middle East and Muslim Civilizations at the University of North Carolina – Chapel Hill.

Katrin Jomaa is an assistant professor at the University of Rhode Island with a joint appointment in the Departments of Political Science and Philosophy.

Mouez Khalfaoui is a junior professor of Islamic Jurisprudence at the University of Tuebingen, Germany (since 2012).

Shahirah Mahmood is a PhD candidate in the Department of Political Science at the University of Wisconsin Madison.

Hamid Mavani obtained his MA and PhD from McGill University at the Institute of Islamic Studies.

Ebrahim Moosa is a professor of Islamic Studies at the University of Notre Dame.

Asaad Al-Saleh is an assistant professor of Arabic, comparative literature and cultural studies in the Department of Languages and Literature and the Middle East Center at the University of Utah.

Christopher B. Taylor was a visiting researcher at Georgetown University in the Berkley Center for Religion, Peace and World Affairs in 2014. He is currently at George Mason University.

Sarra Tlili is an assistant professor at the University of Florida in the Department of Languages, Literatures and Cultures.

David Vishanoff is an associate professor in the Religious Studies Program at the University of Oklahoma, where he teaches courses on the Qur'an, Islamic law, Islamic theology and comparative religion.

Jamal Barzinji is the president of IIIT, USA. He was a founder and has served as president of the Muslim Students Association and is a founder of Islamic Society of North America.

Yaqub Mirza is the president and CEO of Sterling Management Group. He is also an advisor to the board of trustees of the Amana Mutual Funds, a member of the board of directors of the University Islamic Financial Corporation and a member of the Board of Trustees of George Mason University Foundation, Inc. He holds a MSc from University of Karachi, a PhD in physics and an MA in teaching science from the University of Texas at Dallas.

Abubaker Al Shingieti is the executive director of the IIIT, USA.

Ermin Sinanovic is the director of research and academic programs at IIIT.

Iqbal Unus is a former director of The Fairfax Institute (TFI), the instructional division of IIIT, where he has also served as director of human development and director of administration since 1989.

Asifa Quraishi-Landes is an associate professor of law at the University of Wisconsin-Madison.

Mohammad Fadel is an associate professor in the faculty of law at the University of Toronto.

Asma Afsaruddin is a professor of Near-Eastern languages and culture at Indiana University.

Andrew March is an associate professor of political science at Yale University.

Muqtedar Khan is a professor of political science and the director of Islamic studies at the University of Delaware.

Kenneth Honerkamp is a professor of religion at the University of Georgia.

Imad-ad-Dean Ahmed is a professor of religion and science at American University and Wesley Theological Seminary.

David Warren is a post-doctoral research fellow at the University of Edinburgh.

Abdallah El Sheikh Sidahmed is a professor of economics at El Neelain University in Khartoum, Sudan.

Charles Butterworth is a professor of government at the University of Maryland.

Abdallah Al Arian is an assistant professor of history at Georgetown University's School of Foreign Service in Qatar.

Muhammad Faghfoory is a professor of religion at George Washington University.

Douglas Johnston is the president and founder of the International Center for Religion and Diplomacy.

Ahmed Kazemi Mousavi is an adjunct professor in the School of Languages, Literature and Cultures at the University of Maryland, Baltimore.

Norton Mezvinsky is the Distinguished University Professor, Emeritus, at Central Connecticut State University and president of the International Council for Middle East Studies.

Ali Mazrui who died in 2015, was Albert Schweitzer Professor in the Humanities and director of the Institute of Global Cultural Studies at Binghamton University, State University of New York.

Seifudein Adem is the associate director of the Institute for Global Studies at SUNY Binghamton.

Muhammad Nimer is a professor of International Relations at American University.

Marybeth Acac is a PhD candidate in the Department of Religion at Temple University.

Sherman A. Jackson is the King Faisal Chair of Islamic Thought and Culture at the University of Southern California.

Khaleel Mohammed is a professor of religious studies at San Diego State University.

Aisha Musa is an assistant professor of religion and Middle Eastern and Islamic civilization studies at Colgate University.

Imtiyaz Yusuf is the director of the Center for Buddhist-Muslim Understanding in the College of Religious Studies at Mahidol University in Thailand and a senior fellow at the Prince Alwaleed Bin Talal Center for Muslim-Christian Understanding at Georgetown University.

REFERENCES CITED FOR APPENDIX L

1   The website http://www.iiit.org/ provides The International Institute for Islamic Thought's description of its own activities. For IIIT's association with the Muslim Brotherhood, see FBI Memo, "An Analysis of Religious Divisions in the Muslim Community of Toronto," 1988. The document was obtained through FIOA by The Investigative Project on Terrorism (www.investigativeproject.org).

2   The International Institute of Islamic Thought, "Islamization of Knowledge: General Principles and Work Plan," No.1 (1988).

3   Seyyed Vali Reza Nasr, "Islamization of Knowledge: A Critical Review," Islamic Studies, 30.3 (1991), 387-400.

4   IIIT has established at least three chairs over the last six years at the cost of over 3.5 million dollars. These include The IIIT Chair in Islamic Studies at the Ali Vural Ak Center for Global Islamic Studies at George Mason University (GMU), which was endowed in 2012; The Faculty Chair in Islamic Chaplaincy at Hartford Seminary currently—endowed in 2013; and The IIIT Chair in Interfaith Studies at Nazareth College in Rochester, NY— endowed in 2012.

5   See the list of scholars who have presented at IIIT conferences since 2009 at The Summer Institute of Scholars webpage on IIIT's website.

6   AbuSulayman ed., "Islamization of Knowledge," International Institute of Islamic Thought, 1989, 3rd edition, 84-85; see Kyle Shideler and David Daoud, "International Institute of Islamic Thought (IIIT): The Muslim Brotherhood's Think Tank," Center for Security Policy Occasional Paper Series (July 28, 2014).

7   "Proposed Redacted Affidavit in Support of Application for Search Warrant (October 2003)," United States District Court for the Eastern District of Virginia, published at The Investigative Project on Terrorism (www.investigativeproject.org). For more on Barzinji, who passed away in 2015, see The Investigative Project on Terrorism's biography.

8   For the letter, see "Exhibit 325," at the Investigative Project on Terrorism; on the indictment, see The US Department of Justice, "Sami Al-Arian Pleads Guilty To Conspiracy To Provide Services To Palestinian Islamic Jihad," Press Release (April 17, 2006).

9   See above, n. 1.

10 Meira Svirsky, "Brotherhood Influence OP Inside US Academia Success," Clarion Project (May 5, 2014).

11 The direct relationship between the government of Qatar and the Qatar Foundation is noted at the Foundation's official website.

12 See the official report of Human Rights Watch, an organization that usually reserves such criticism for Israel and the West.

13 Washington Post, "Texas university gets $76 million each year to operate in Qatar, contract says"(March 8, 2016). The money is paid to the Qatar Foundation, which then gives it to the school of the student.

14 The Washington Post, "In Qatar's Education City, U.S. colleges are building an academic oasis"(December 6, 2015)

15 On Qatar's Education City, see The Washington Post, "In Qatar's Education City, U.S. colleges are building an academic oasis" (December 6, 2015); on Louay Safi's position, see his faculty biography at the website of Qatar's Hamad bin Khalifah University.

16 On Auda's role in institutions in Education City, specifically the new research Center for Islamic Legislation and Ethics (CILE), see the Qatar Foundation announcement concerning "Creating CILE"; on Auda's ties to the brotherhood, see Ryan Mauro, "US Professors Participate in Brotherhood-Linked Program," Clarion Project (October 10, 2013); for IIIT's role in publishing Auda, see here.

Additional Readings

Shari'ah: The Threat to America:
  Report by Team B II

It IS About Islam
  Glenn Beck, Threshold Editions, Mercury Radio Arts

Refugee Resettlement and the Hirja to America
  Ann Corcoran, Center for Security Policy Press

American Jihad: Terrorists Among Us
  Steve Emerson, The Investigative Project

Funding Evil: How Terrorism Is Financed -- and How to Stop It:
  The Book the Saudis Don't Want You to Read
  Rachel Ehrenfeld

Muslim Mafia -- Inside the Secret Underworld That's Conspiring to
Islamize America:
  P. David Gaubatz & Paul Sperry

Defeating Jihad: The Winnable War
  Sebastian Gorka, Ph.D.

See Something; Say Nothing: HS Officer Exposes the Governments
Submission to Jihad
  Phillip Haney

Invasion 2020: What if There Is a Plan to Turn America into an
Islamic Country by 2020
  Jeanne Harrington

Stealth Invasion: Muslim Conquest Through Immigration and
Resettlement Jihad
  Leo Hohmann

Enhanced Interrogation: Inside the minds and Motives of Islamic Terrorist
James E. Mitchell, Ph.D.

The Strange Death of Europe: Immigration, Identity and Islam
Douglas Murray

The Lost Spring: US Policy in the Middle East - Catastrophes Avoid
Walid Phares

Future Jihad: Terrorist Strategies Against the West
Walid Phares

Modern Islamic Warfare: An Ancient Doctrine Marches On
Harold Rhodes

Arab Winter Comes to America: The Truth About the War We're In
Robert Spencer

FILMS (DVD'S)

The Enemy Within: Trevor Loudon

Homegrown Jihad: "The Terrorist Camps Around the US";
Christian Action Network

The Third Jihad -- "Radical Islam's Vision for America"

INTERNET WEB SITES

The Investigative Project   www.investigativeproject.org

The Clarion Project   www.clarionproject.org

The Center for Security Policy   www.centerforsecuritypolicy.org

26189261R00146

Made in the USA
San Bernardino, CA
16 February 2019